Praise for *One Nation, Uninsured*

"A strongly argued account that provides useful ammunition for anyone seeking to effect change in a medical system that willfully excludes
so many who need it."

—*Kirkus Reviews*

"Briskly written . . . an excellent primer for anybody interested in pick-
ing up the reform banner today. . . . Fresh, engaging."

—Jonathan Cohn, Washington Post Book World

"An important book. Jill Quadagno provides an impressive array of
historical evidence to advance original arguments for why the United
States lacks a comprehensive health care system and why health insurance should be viewed as a social right. This book is must reading for
those concerned about health care reform in the United States."

—William Julius Wilson, author of *When Work Disappears*

"A solid and not-too-wonkish guide to health-care reform today."

—*Booklist*

"Jill Quadagno has produced the most comprehensive and up-to-date
account of the power and effectiveness of interest groups in defeating a
century of national health insurance reform campaigns. An impressive
combination of theory and historical research, *One Nation, Uninsured*
sets the parameters for the next round of debate over why the U.S. re-
mains the only country without universal health insurance and how it
might still expand access while reigning in costs."

—Lawrence R. Jacobs, University of Minnesota

"Readable and engaging. . . . Some of the most interesting portions come
from Quadagno's own archival searches and her interviews with people
who lived the history that she describes. . . . Quadagno's sustained focus on interest-group politics seems right on target."

—*New England Journal of Medicine*

"A chilling historical account of how powerful groups with self-serving
financial interests have successfully blocked attempts to enact national
health insurance for seven decades, leaving tens of millions of our citizens without adequate health care coverage and often without even

minimal care. Anyone eager to seek reform of our badly fragmented health care system must study its lessons and its blueprint for action; a task that will require nearly unprecedented political skills and monumental organizational prowess."

—Jerome P. Kassirer, M.D., author of *On The Take: How Medicine's Complicity With Big Business Can Endanger Your Health*

"Quadagno, a distinguished sociologist with a long-standing interest in policy, explores a century of government attempts to create universal health care and the powerful forces that have defeated those attempts. ... Her sociological insights illuminate a path to reform."

—Judy Goldstein Botello, *The San Diego Union-Tribune*

ONE NATION

UNINSURED

Why the U.S. Has
No National Health Insurance

JILL QUADAGNO

OXFORD
UNIVERSITY PRESS

OXFORD

UNIVERSITY PRESS

Oxford University Press, Inc., publishes works that
further Oxford University's objective of excellence
in research, scholarship, and education.

Oxford   New York
Auckland   Cape Town   Dar es Salaam   Hong Kong   Karachi
Kuala Lumpur   Madrid   Melbourne   Mexico City   Nairobi
New Delhi   Shanghai   Taipei   Toronto

With offices in
Argentina   Austria   Brazil   Chile   Czech Republic   France   Greece
Guatemala   Hungary   Italy   Japan   Poland   Portugal   Singapore
South Korea   Switzerland   Thailand   Turkey   Ukraine   Vietnam

Copyright ©2005 by Oxford University Press

First published by Oxford University Press, Inc., 2005
198 Madison Avenue, New York, NY 10016
www.oup.com

First issued as an Oxford University Press paperback, 2006
ISBN-13: 978-0-19-531203-4

Oxford is a registered trademark of Oxford University Press

The Library of Congress has cataloged the hardcover edition as follows:
Quadagno, Jill S.
One nation, uninsured : why the U.S. has no national health insurance /
by Jill Quadagno.
p. ; cm.
Includes bibliographical references.
ISBN-13: 978-0-19-516039-0
1. National health insurance—United States—History—20th century.
2. Medically uninsured persons—United States—History—20th century.
3. Insurance, health—Government policy—United States—History—20th century.
4. Right to health care—United States—History—20th century.
5. Health services accessibility—United States—History—20th century.
6. Health care reform—United States—History—20th century.
7. Medical policy—United States—History—20th century.
[DNLM: 1. National Health Insurance, United States
2. Universal Coverage
3. Health Policy
4. Medically Uninsured
5. Politics
6. United States
W 275 AA1 Q14 2005]
I. Title
RA412.2.Q33 2005   362.1'0425—dc22   2004022644

9 8 7 6 5 4 3 2

Printed in the United States of America
on acid-free paper

For Laura

Contents

Preface

In 1994 I had the most interesting experience of my career. A Guggenheim Fellowship would pay my salary during my sabbatical from teaching while I worked in the Capitol on a committee of my choosing. Eventually I would write a book. I had taught about policy for fourteen years. Now it was my chance to observe the policy-making process up close. By sheer luck, a new government commission, the President's Bipartisan Commission on Entitlement and Tax Reform, which would be chaired by Senator Bob Kerrey, was just in the process of selecting staff. A call to a friend and I had an interview with the staff director. During the interview I learned that the commissioners' task would be to evaluate options for cutting Social Security, Medicare, Medicaid, and the hundreds of other smaller federal entitlement programs. Despite my ambivalence about the mission, I knew that I would learn a lot. Two months later I was headed to Washington to begin my job.

As the Entitlement Commission proceeded with its hatchet work, President Clinton was pursuing his own ambitious plan for a new (and most certainly costly) program for universal health care. How, I wondered, could President Clinton possibly succeed when Congress seemed determined to cut social spending? By the time the Entitlement Commission folded in December, the Democrats had lost control of Congress, the congressional staffers in the House who had been too swamped to respond to my queries in the summer were calling to ask if my university had any job openings, and health care reform was dead. As I pondered that heady but disheartening experience, I decided I needed to learn more about why a proposal that had seemed sure to succeed just a few months earlier had suffered so ignominious a fate. And so my journey began. For the next four years, I shuffled through reams of documents in the National Archives, the Library of Congress, and various presidential libraries, read many oral histories, and interviewed some of the warriors who had been involved in the struggle. Along the way I discovered that health care policy was not the arcane topic it might seem but rather was a prism that reflected the grand historical events of the twentieth century—the Red scare of the 1910s, the trade union movement in the 1930s, McCarthyism in the 1940s, the civil rights movement in the 1950s, Lyndon Johnson's Great Society in the 1960s, the impeachment of President Nixon in the 1970s, the mobilization of senior citizens in the 1980s, and the downing of the Black Hawks in Somalia in the 1990s.

My task was greatly facilitated by many colleagues who have provided helpful comments on various chapters and papers derived from the project. Thanks go to Ted Marmor, Jim Morone, Larry Jacobs, Debra Street, Larry Isaac, Pat Martin, Joane Nagel, Taeku Lee, Julian Zelizer, John Myles, Mary Ruggie, Donald Light, Edward Berkowitz, Jacob Hacker, John Manley, Karen Kruse Thomas, and David Mechanic. I benefited greatly from the insights of the group of scholars who collaborated on a retrospective assessment of Paul Starr's book *The Social Transformation of American Medicine*. Among those whose suggestions were particularly helpful were Judy Feder, Larry Casolino, Bernice Pescosolido, Sydney Halpern, Jennifer Klein, and the project editors, Mark Schlesinger, Keith Wailoo, and especially Tim Jost, who was on call at all hours of the day or night with a speedy response to my many questions regarding legal issues. Others whom I consulted on specific policy issues include Marilyn Moon and Josh Weiner.

As always, I am in the debt of archivists. I appreciate the help I received from Kristen Wilhelm, Patricia Anderson, and Marjorie Charlianti at the National Archives; John Nemmers, project librarian at the Claude Pepper Library; and Albert Nason at the Jimmy Carter Library. Over the course of the project, my graduate research assistants, Michael Stewart, Lori Parham, Steve MacDonald, Jennifer Reid Keene, and Brandy Harris, did Internet searches for historical records, helped me track obscure sources, and performed various and sundry tasks that made my job easier. I was also fortunate to receive an Investigator Award in Health Policy Research from the Robert Wood Johnson Foundation, which provided the funding for me to pursue my research and travel to collections. David Colby and Jim Knickman at the foundation encouraged me to pursue the project, and I greatly appreciate their support. I should add, however, that the views expressed in this book are my own and do not imply endorsement by the Robert Wood Johnson Foundation.

I would especially like to thank Rashi Fein, who invited me for a pleasant dinner at his home, spent hours allowing me to interview him, then mailed me his extensive files covering two decades of his work as technical director of the Committee for National Health Insurance. Others who merit special mention are Mort Lebow, the former public information officer for the Office of Equal Heath Opportunity; Mal Schechter, the former Washington editor of the journal *Hospital Practice*; Robert Ball, former commissioner of the Social Security Administration; and Carlton Spitzer, who served as director of the Office of Public Information in the Department of Health, Education, and Welfare from 1965 to 1968. The fine editorial skills of Alison Anderson, managing editor of the University of Pennsylvania Press, greatly improved the manuscript.

At Oxford University Press I was blessed with a wonderful editor, Dedi Felman, whose enthusiasm for my book kept me on track for the past four years. I eagerly looked forward to her "yay" when she was satisfied with a chapter, and knew I wasn't finished when she said "needs work." She read every chapter at least twice and some chapters three or four times. My husband patiently tolerated my late nights on the computer, and as always I am grateful to share my career with someone who understands the academic life. What would I have done these past four years without Pat, Luann, Sheryl, Lerena, and Peg? They shared their own health care struggles with me and lured me out to the tennis courts when I needed a break. But that's what friends are for. I'm fortunate to have the best.

One Nation, Uninsured

Introduction

One rainy Sunday afternoon a few years ago, I went to see *The Rainmaker*, the film based on John Grisham's legal thriller about a young lawyer who sues a large insurance company, Great Benefit, on behalf of his client, Donny Ray Black. Donny Ray dies of leukemia because Great Benefit refuses to pay for a bone marrow transplant that might save his life. When the jury awards Donny Ray's parents $50 million in punitive damages as retribution for Great Benefit's greed and arrogance, the audience in the theater cheered wildly. The film's story of an insurance company refusing to pay for necessary medical treatment clearly resonated with the experiences of many in attendance.

Perhaps some of the people in the audience had read about David Goodrich, the 41-year-old district attorney who died of stomach cancer after Aetna, his insurance company, refused to approve the cancer treatment recommended by his doctor.[1] Or perhaps they had had an experience like that of my sister, Linda, who lost her job as vice president for marketing when First Interstate Bank merged with Wells Fargo. Although her family could purchase the health insurance that First Interstate had provided, the cost would be nearly $12,000 a year. Linda decided to shop around for a less expensive policy and quickly discovered the hard truth of the health insurance marketplace. Several insurers could provide cheaper coverage for my sister and her two children, but no one wanted to insure her husband. Stan had—in insurance industry jargon—the dreaded "preexisting condition" that made him uninsurable.

When I spoke with others about my sister's dilemma, nearly everyone had similar stories to recount. My friend Connie Laughlin's husband, Michael, died suddenly of a heart attack at the age of 56. After

Michael's death, Connie found herself struggling not only with the grief of widowhood but also with the frustration of trying to find an affordable health insurance policy. As she told me one day:

> Well, I had had abnormal pap smears for about three years. Because that was on my record, the insurance that would be in my range, everything came back denied. You know, I said, I am the same person that I was six months ago before Michael died. I kept calling other insurance companies, and I went to a lot of them. They would write me insurance but they were always going to exclude these gynecological things. Well, that's a woman's entire health.[2]

Connie finally purchased a major medical policy costing $7,000 a year. Her policy would cover any large health expenses she might incur—after she had paid the $3,000 deductible. But if her abnormal pap smear turned into cervical cancer, her health insurance would pay none of the costs. How was it, I wondered, that people with seemingly secure lives could so rapidly reverse course through no fault of their own? Why should people who experience normal life events—a layoff, the death of a spouse, a serious illness—face the prospect of losing their insurance, being denied care, or having their insurer refuse to pay for the health problems they are most likely to have?

The right to health care is recognized in international law and guaranteed in the constitutions of many nations.[3] With the exception of the United States, all Western industrialized countries, regardless of how they raise funds, organize care, and determine eligibility, guarantee every citizen comprehensive coverage for essential health care services. To the extent that care is rationed, it is done on the basis of clinical need, not ability to pay.[4] Most countries allow, and some encourage, private insurance as a supplement or a means of upgrading to a higher class of service and/or a fuller array of services. In Canada private insurance covers items not included in the government program, such as prescription drugs or amenities including private hospital rooms.[5] In Great Britain private insurance is also used for extra services or quicker access for operations that have long waiting lists, such as cataract removals, hernias, and hip replacements.[6] In Denmark, too, private insurance covers various supplementary services.[7] In every case, however, the practices of insurance companies are heavily regulated to prevent them from engaging in the more pernicious forms of medical underwriting that are commonly employed in the United States.

Medical underwriting is the practice health plans use to segment people and employee groups into different risk pools according to their health profile. It is governed by what Donald Light calls the law of inverse coverage: the more coverage you need, the less you will receive and the more you will pay.[8] Thus people who have allergies, high blood pressure, depression, or arthritis will be charged higher premiums than healthy people; people with "preexisting conditions" such as cataracts, asthma, or migraine headaches may be offered a policy with an exclusion clause that does not cover those conditions; and people with serious illnesses such as AIDS, leukemia, or emphysema will likely be denied coverage altogether. Insurers may also avoid entire occupations or industries considered high risks, including beauty shops, bars, law practices, roofing companies, and restaurants.

The complexity of the health insurance marketplace, the high cost of coverage, and medical underwriting leave many people at risk of being uninsured. In 2003 45 million Americans, more than one out of every six people, had no health insurance.[9] That number, as large as it is, tells an incomplete and potentially misleading story, because many more people are uninsured for some period over any two-year time span. In 2002 and 2003 nearly 82 million people—one out of every three Americans—went without health insurance for all or part of the two years.[10] Most were average people in working families. Nearly eight out of ten were working, and another 6 percent were looking for work. Only 15 percent were not in the labor force, in most cases because they were disabled, chronically ill, or family caregivers.[11]

Many uninsured people are in the same boat as Diane MacPherson. Diane lost her job at a relocation management company and with it her health coverage for herself, her four-year-old daughter, and her husband, Bob, a construction worker whose job doesn't offer health benefits. Even though Bob made $75,000 that year, with Diane out of work, the family could not afford the $931 monthly premiums it would have cost to cover their family. Instead Bob and Diane decided to insure only their daughter at $271 a month. When Diane's unemployment benefits ran out, they had to drop even their daughter's health insurance.[12]

Some uninsured people work at jobs where health benefits are not offered. Such jobs are more likely to be with small companies rather than large firms. (You are certain to have excellent health benefits if you work for a Fortune 500 firm but likely have poorer coverage or none at all if you work for Mom and Pop's Pizza.) In other instances, uninsured people are offered health benefits from their employers but decline the offer because they can't afford to pay their share of the premiums. That is the case with Diane Schroeder, a 51-year-old woman from Coralville, Iowa, who cleans buses for a living. Because of her poor health—she suffers from migraines, arthritis, and an anxiety disorder—Diane only works part time. She takes home $400 a month.[13] Although the transit company where she works would pay half of her health insurance premium, she cannot afford her share, $122 a month. In 2003 employers contributed 73 percent of the cost of family health benefits with employees paying the remainder, at an average cost of $2,412. While $2,412 sounds like a good deal (and indeed it is), it represents 25 percent of the income for someone working full time at minimum wage ($5.15 an hour in 2004).[14] Few low-wage workers can afford to spend one-quarter of their income on health benefits when they have rent to pay, groceries to buy, and car payments to make.

Being uninsured reduces access to medical care and imperils health and well-being. Take Jesus Vivas. A native of Mexico, Jesus moved to Texas in 1994 and found a job earning $55 a day painting houses. His life was going well until he fell off a ladder. Although he was bent over in pain, his arm swollen, his boss sent him home, not wanting to pay his medical expenses. Jesus' family drove him to the emergency room of the local hospital, where doctors put a splint on his wrist, gave him pain medication, and referred him to a physician's office. When he arrived, the doctor refused to see him because he had no insurance.[15] Three weeks later he showed up at a public clinic, where doctors found that his left wrist was fractured, an injury that the emergency room doctors had missed.

The uninsured, such as Jesus, are often denied care that is available to people with insurance. Many uninsured people do not have a regular family doctor and thus do not receive preventive health services such as cholesterol-lowing drugs or screening for potentially fatal diseases such as cancer, diabetes, or heart disease. As a result, their health problems are often diagnosed at more advanced stages, resulting in higher mortality rates.[16] Frequently the care they do receive is in an emergency room where there is no primary care and no follow-up care.

Uninsured children are less likely to have a pediatrician who provides regular care or to receive basic immunizations, and they are more likely to be hospitalized for an illness that could have been treated without a hospitalization.[17]

Being uninsured can place severe financial strains on families. Nearly half of all individual bankruptcy filings are due to medical bills.[18] DeFannie Davis, an uninsured mother who is the sole caregiver for her disabled husband, describes the pall being uninsured casts over her life: "Being uninsured means living with fear every day. I fear getting sick and not being able to work, I fear an injury that will leave me with bills I am unable to pay, and I fear getting a regular check-up that results in finding something that needs further treatment."[19]

The uninsured raise the costs of health care for everyone. The expense of their care is borne by taxpayers through various government programs or through cost shifting by physicians and hospitals to privately insured patients.[20] Cost shifting, in turn, forces insurance companies to either reduce covered services or raise premiums, co-payments, and deductibles for people with insurance. As premiums rise, fewer employers offer coverage, so more people wind up being uninsured.[21] Thus a never-ending cycle is perpetuated.

In other countries, national health insurance has proved to be a major tool for restraining costs and controlling inflation, while in the United States planning the rational distribution of health care resources has been impossible. The result is duplication of services; unnecessary procedures, tests, and drugs; inefficient use of technologies; and rampant inflation that motivates employers to outsource jobs overseas.[22] Why is the United States the only nation that fails to guarantee coverage of medical services, that rations care by income, race, and health, and that allows for-profit private insurance companies to serve as gatekeepers to the health care system? As the prominent historian David Rothman remarks:

> Americans do not think of themselves as callous and cruel, yet, in their readiness to forgo and withhold this most elemental social service, they have been so. This question arises: How did the middle class, its elected representatives, and its doctors accommodate themselves to such neglect?[23]

How indeed? I believe I have an answer to Rothman's question. Current arrangements for financing care have been hammered out through contentious struggles between social reformers, physicians, employers, insurance companies, and trade unions over the proper relationship between government and the private sector. Across an entire century, each attempt to enact national health insurance has been met with a fierce attack by powerful stakeholders who have mobilized their considerable resources to keep the financing of health care a private affair. Whenever government action has seemed imminent, they have lobbied legislators, influenced elections by giving huge campaign contributions to sympathetic candidates, and organized "grassroots" protests, conspiring with other like-minded groups to defeat reform efforts. The only instance where this was not the case was with Medicare and Medicaid, programs that fund care for the residual population groups—the aged and the very poor—that private insurers have no desire to cover.[24]

This book offers an account of how those stakeholders have kept universal health insurance in the United States at bay, allowing for reforms only when it served their self-interest. It looks at how physicians and then insurers and employers were able to mobilize powerful allies to defeat national health insurance and institutionalize market-based alternatives. I argue that until we view health insurance as a social right, not a consumer product, we will never receive the coverage we need.

The Politics of Health Policy

From the Progressive Era to the 1960s, physicians were the most vocal opponents of government-financed health care. Their goal was to erect a barrier against any third-party payer, especially the government, that might intrude in the sacred doctor-patient relationship.[25] Doctors understood that if third parties assumed responsibility for financing care, these parties would need to establish some way to control their financial liability, which would invariably mean regulating physicians' fees. In the practice of medicine, physicians had the authority not only to name diseases and offer prognoses but also to make judgments that extended beyond determinations of illness. They were asked to decide whether people were disabled or fit enough to work, to pronounce death, and even to judge whether the deceased had been mentally competent when they wrote their wills.[26] Why shouldn't they also decide who would pay for medical care and how those payments would be organized?

Physicians pursued their political endeavors through the American Medical Association (AMA), a powerful professional association with an organizational structure perfectly suited to political action. At the bottom of the AMA hierarchy were the county medical societies. Membership in a county society automatically conferred membership in the state medical society, which, in turn, was part of a confederation governed at the national level by the House of Delegates.[27] This federated structure made it possible for the AMA to be converted from a professional association into a hard-driving political machine at the local, state, and national levels in each skirmish against government-financed care.

In the 1910s state medical societies worked to defeat a plan for compulsory health insurance.[28] Dr. James Rooney, president of the Medical Society of New York, rallied physicians against the proposal, declaring: "If the profession is to save itself [from health insurance] it must organize as it has never organized before."[29] During the Great Depression, the AMA waged a ferocious campaign to prevent federal officials from including national health insurance in the Social Security Act of 1935.[30] The AMA president, Dr. Morris Fishbein, condemned even a modest proposal for "voluntary" private insurance, claiming it smacked of socialism and communism and might incite revolution.[31] When a plan for national health insurance was revived in the late 1930s, the AMA reluctantly endorsed Blue Cross/Blue Shield plans that the hospitals and doctors had created themselves as a way to head off a government program. Physicians' worst fears were realized in 1946 when President Harry Truman made national health insurance the key domestic issue of his Fair Deal. The *Journal of the American Medical Association* lambasted this threat to liberty: "[If this] Old World scourge is allowed to spread to our New World, [it will] jeopardize the health of our people and gravely endanger our freedom."[32] Following a bitter campaign, Truman was forced to concede defeat.

How did physicians, merely a professional group, defeat the will of social reformers, powerful politicians, and even presidents for more than half a century? Sociologist Paul Starr argues that the key to physicians' political influence was "the absence of [any] countervailing power," but the historical evidence suggests that the opposite is the case.[33] It was not the absence of a countervailing power that allowed physicians to assert their parochial concerns into the policy making process but rather the fact that their objectives coincided with those of other groups with greater clout and deeper pockets. Once these interests diverged, the fragility of physicians' power base was revealed.

In the Progressive Era, physicians won their campaign against compulsory health insurance because they colluded with employer groups, insurance companies, and trade unions.[34] Their allies included the Insurance Economics Society, an organization of large insurance companies, which financed their campaign; the National Civic Federation, a group of employers dedicated to civic improvement; and the American Federation of Labor (AFL), whose president, Samuel Gompers, denounced compulsory health insurance as "a menace to the rights, welfare and liberty of American workers."[35] When President Truman launched his plan in the 1940s, physicians appealed to the business community, winning over organizations such as the National Association of Manufacturers and the U.S. Chamber of Commerce. The Chamber charged that Truman's plan would lead to the "widespread destruction of our voluntary institutions," create a new army of government employees who would wield "dangerous political power," and "jeopardize our traditional liberties."[36] In Congress physicians also had the support of conservative Republicans such as Ohio senator Robert Taft, a presidential hopeful who had campaigned on a promise to roll back the New Deal, and of southern Democrats such as South Carolina senator Strom Thurmond, who feared any program that might give federal officials the right to intervene in local racial practices. From 1938 until 1964 this conservative coalition endured, thwarting all efforts to enact national health insurance.

Physicians' power base first began to erode in the 1950s, when the trade unions abandoned their preference for collectively bargained benefits and won a campaign for disability benefits in 1956, negotiating behind the scenes with members of Congress who depended on trade union support for reelection. The labor victory demonstrated organized medicine's vulnerability when faced with an opponent with equal resources and organizational strength and greater political savvy. The trade unions next turned to health insurance for the aged. The AMA was as vehemently opposed to Medicare as it had been to national health insurance and disability insurance. When Medicare was under consideration in the 1960s, a Virginia physician sent a letter to Representative

Aime Forand (D-RI), the sponsor of the legislation, declaring that he "should be castrated and his progeny die in embryo."[37] Although it took more than a decade, Medicare was finally enacted in 1965, following a Democratic sweep of the House and Senate and an AFL-CIO campaign that mobilized trade union members and retirees in every key congressional district.

Although Medicare was a victory for reformers, it was also a victory for providers. Medicare would not intervene in the health care system but merely serve as a neutral conduit through which all federal funds would pass.[38] Hospitals would be reimbursed on a cost-plus-2-percent basis, physicians would be paid their "usual and customary" fees with no upper limit, and the provider-friendly private insurance industry would monitor charges and pay claims. Given these arrangements, health care inflation was inevitable. Before Medicare, hospital daily charges had increased between 6 and 9 percent per year. In 1965 they jumped nearly 17 percent. The fees of general practitioners rose 25 percent, those of internists 40 percent. By 1966 there were predictions that overall health care inflation might top 25 percent.[39] According to one critic, Connecticut senator Abraham Ribicoff, public funds and third-party payments had spawned "the civilian equivalent of the defense establishment.... Both [had] an apparently insatiable appetite for money and an enormously well developed talent for avoiding public accountability and controls."[40]

As health care costs skyrocketed, the major purchasers of care—the federal government and employers—began asking what they were receiving for their money and whether medical services were worth the costs. Answering these questions required close scrutiny of core aspects of medical practice, jeopardizing physicians' essential prerogatives: the ability to restrict competition, limit regulation, and define standards.[41] The first challenge to physicians' professional sovereignty came from the federal government. Before Medicare made a single payment, federal officials forced hospitals to create utilization review boards, set quality standards for hospitals and nursing homes, and dealt a death blow to racial segregation by withholding funds from hospitals that refused to integrate.

These initial forays into the providers' domain were followed by attempts, first by President Richard Nixon and then by President Jimmy

Carter, to control hospital costs. Carter's first plan, to set a yearly cap on hospital cost increases, sparked a flurry of lobbying activity by the American Hospital Association and the Federation of American Hospitals. Conceding defeat, the following year Carter tried to enact a weaker measure but failed to win congressional support. Carter's beleaguered secretary of health and human services, Joseph Califano, wearily concluded that health care reform was impossible with "a Congress whose members depend on private contributions for election campaigns . . . and who will always worry about offending hospital trustees and influential state and local medical societies."[42] Despite Carter's failure, in 1983 Medicare's open-ended method of reimbursing hospitals was replaced with a prospective payment system that set a fixed amount for each hospital stay, depending on the patient's diagnosis and regardless of the cost of treatment. The prospective system was tacked onto a Social Security reform bill at the last minute and generated little attention at the time. It was followed a few years later by a fee schedule for physicians' services.

The second challenge to physicians' autonomy came from large corporations such as Chrysler and Bethlehem Steel and business associations such as the Chamber of Commerce and the National Association of Manufacturers. With their powerful lobbyists, ample economic resources, connections with insurance companies, and captive patient-employees, these organizations seemed well positioned to confront the medical profession.[43] Leading corporate employers lobbied for greater regulation of providers and a larger voice for business in health policy decisions and helped win the prospective payment system and physician fee schedules for Medicare, which they hoped would exert a constraining influence on private sector payments. But when they tried to exert their clout as large purchasers to negotiate lower fees and premium charges in their company health plans, the providers refused to cooperate.[44] Then corporations turned to managed care, unleashing a powerful adversary whose sole objective was to tame the health care system. Managed care firms delved deeply into the most minute details of physicians' practices. They reviewed tests and procedures, evaluated charges, analyzed patient records to see if unnecessary procedures were being performed, and then held physicians financially accountable for the costs of their medical decisions.[45] Thus, ironically, the private health insurance system that physicians had helped to construct became a mechanism for undermining their sovereign rule.

As physicians' antipathy to national health insurance dwindled, tempered by the benefits of guaranteed payment and splits among various specialty groups, health insurers moved to the forefront of public debates. In the 1980s the Health Insurance Association of America, an organization that represented most of the small and medium-sized insurance companies in the country, joined with the National Federation of Independent Business to crush a proposal for home care benefits for the disabled. Insurers saw home care as a threat to the fledgling private long-term care insurance market, while small-business owners feared the tax hike that would be needed to pay for the benefit. When President Bill Clinton proposed a plan to guarantee universal health care coverage in 1993, the same coalition of insurers, corporations, and small-business groups mobilized against him. The coalition funded a public relations campaign against the Clinton plan, hired lobbying firms, and stepped up their campaign contributions, with the largest contributions going to members of the committees that had jurisdiction over health reform.[46] Besieged by the opposition, the Clinton plan met the same fate as had its predecessors.

The defeat of national health insurance in the United States can only be understood in the context of the shifting power structure within the health care system, signified by the erosion of physicians' cultural authority, the corporate purchasers' revolt, and the ascendance of managed care. The changing composition of the antireform coalition, dominated first by physicians and then by insurers and business groups, has obscured the persistence of stakeholder mobilization as the primary obstacle to national health insurance. Given the ever-shifting scope of these debates, it is not surprising that many Americans find the health care issue too confusing to understand or resolve.

Other social scientists attribute the lack of national health insurance to such factors as enduring antigovernment sentiment, a weak labor movement, the racial politics of the South, the distinctive character of American political institutions, or the way early policy choices crowded out subsequent policy options. I would argue not that these explanations are incorrect but rather that they are incomplete in a crucial way. They take as the object of analysis the programs and policies surrounding the health care system and largely ignore medical care and the political battles fought over its control as the object of study and primary forces in their own right.

Political Theories of the Welfare State

Antistatist Values

According to one common argument, the chief impediment to national health insurance has been an antistatist political culture. Because Americans honor private property, hold individual rights sacred, and distrust state authority, reformers have found it difficult to make a convincing case for government financing of health care.[47] Americans' ambivalence toward government and their bias toward private solutions to public problems stands in the way. We can no more trust the state to make decisions about our health care than we can about what make of car to drive, what color shirt to wear, or which brand of dental floss to use, or so the thinking of many goes.[48]

Antistatism has been described as the underlying force in the various failed attempts to guarantee universal coverage across the entire twentieth century. In the Progressive Era, the compulsory state health insurance plan was supposedly defeated by the public's antipathy toward a larger government role in health care.[49] Medicare's peculiar public-private formula, with its numerous concessions to providers and insurers, was a way to assuage public concern about government intervention.[50] Distrust of government undermined public confidence in Clinton's health plan, allowing his opponents to claim that federal bureaucrats would destroy the doctor-patient relationship and take away people's right to choose their own doctors.[51]

Certainly, antistatist themes have been used in political debates to undermine public confidence in national health insurance. Less certain is whether values were a principal causal force. If antistatism has been an enduring feature of American politics, then why have some programs been enacted that contradict this core value? After all, Medicare involved as significant a federal presence in the health care system as national health insurance would. What is also uncertain is how antistatist values get translated into policy decisions. In most accounts, values are simply presumed to have some kind of unexplained effect on the policy-making process. How do antistatist values shape the decisions that elected officials make?[52]

Weak Labor

A second argument attributes the failure of national health insurance in the United States to the absence of a working-class movement and labor-based political party such as the Labour Party in Great Britain.[53] In many European countries working-class parties have organized on behalf of public pension programs such as Social Security that provide older workers with a dignified exit from the labor force and a dependable source of retirement income. They have also fought for unemployment insurance to provide workers with a buffer against downturns in the economy. In the United States, by contrast, the trade unions pursued a different path. They never formed a separate political party and in some instances actively opposed government social programs. As noted previously, early in the twentieth century the AFL denounced state health insurance proposals, claiming that they would subordinate workers to the state and undermine workers' efforts to resolve their own problems.[54] The Social Security Act of 1935, the single most important piece of social welfare legislation of the twentieth century, was enacted without strong labor backing.[55] In other instances, however, state federations and local union chapters challenged their national leaders on these issues. In the 1910s some AFL chapters endorsed the compulsory health insurance bill. In the 1920s the United Mine Workers worked for state old-age pensions, then supported a federal old-age pension plan.[56] The question, then, is why the trade unions have supported some legislative measures but not others and what allowed them, in some instances, to mobilize politically absent a labor party.

Racial Politics of the South

A third explanation attributes the failure of national health insurance to the racial politics of the South.[57] For the first two-thirds of the twentieth century, southern politicians opposed any government intrusion into the health care system because they feared federal intervention in local racial practices. They used their control of key congressional committees to bottle up legislation entirely or to demand that new social programs be locally administered. At their insistence, agricultural and domestic workers (two-thirds of all black workers) were excluded from the Social Security and unemployment insurance programs of the Social Security Act, and local welfare authorities were allowed to determine who would receive benefits from the means-tested programs for the poor (Aid to Dependent Children and old-age assistance).[58]

Health care financing would seem to be distantly removed from the racial politics of the South. Yet the southern health care system, like other southern institutions, was racially segregated. Most hospitals maintained "white" and "colored" floors, labeled equipment by race, and denied staff privileges to black physicians. National health insurance posed the threat that federal funding of health care services would lead to federal demands to integrate health care facilities and tear down racial barriers.

The racial politics of the South had a stifling effect on health policy debates from the 1930s to the 1960s. What is less clear is how racial politics influenced debates over health care reform in the post-civil-rights era, when the conservative coalition no longer exerted a negative, controlling influence on federal policy.

State Structures and Policy Legacies

According to a fourth argument, the structure of the American state has continually frustrated efforts to enact national health insurance.[59] In the United States, political power is diffused to a degree unmatched in any other country. At the national level, authority is divided among three branches of government—the executive branch, Congress, and the courts, each with its own independent authority, responsibilities, and bases of support—and among the sovereign states, which have the right to nullify federal legislation. At the legislative level, authority is further split between the House and the Senate as well as numerous committees and subcommittees.[60] This decentralized structure impedes policy innovation by increasing the number of veto points (i.e., the courts, the legislative process, the states) where even small numbers of opponents can block policy initiatives. It allows special interests to exercise a unique influence on policy outcomes through lobbying of individual legislators to support their preferred policies, opposing those that obstruct their agendas and helping to determine the issues that legislators interpret as important in the first place.[61]

This "state structure" argument is often used in comparative studies to explain cross-national variations in policy outcomes. Thus, for example, some would argue that national health insurance failed in the United States but succeeded in Canada because the Canadian parliamentary political system is more centralized and less diffuse than the American political system.[62] However, this argument falls flat when applied to variations across time in policy decisions within the United States. Why did Medicare succeed when confronted with the same institutional arrangements as national health insurance? A variable (social welfare benefits) cannot be explained by a constant (decentralized institutions). Few would disagree that the American political system with its checks and balances is designed to slow down the policy-making process and prevent decisions from being made abruptly. But that argument explains little about how the complex configuration of public and private health benefits came to be. Although a state structure argument may predict the prospects for reform, it cannot explain why one policy succeeds while another fails, nor can it account for the form of policies that are enacted.[63]

Critics of the state structure approach counter that it is more important to understand how early policy choices influence subsequent policy options by giving rise to widespread public expectations and vast networks of vested interests.[64] Initial policy decisions narrow the menu of future options by forming self-reinforcing paths that become increasingly difficult to alter. Thus Social Security succeeded while national health insurance failed. Social Security was enacted before a private pension system developed. By contrast, the private health insurance system was solidly entrenched by the time reformers began to press for a government solution, crowding out the public alternative.[65] But to say that national health insurance failed because it was crowded out by private health benefits begs the question of why national health insurance was not on the political agenda in the first place.

Each of these forces—antistatist values, weak labor, racial politics, policy legacies—may account for the defeat of national health insurance in a given instance. None provides an overarching framework that can explain the outcome of health care reform debates across the grand panorama of twentieth-century history. That is the task that I undertake in the chapters that follow. By clarifying the persistent threads in the campaign against universal health care, my hope is that the organizational steps for easing the crisis and facilitating the adoption of national health insurance may become clearer as well.

Chapter 1 describes how, from the Progressive Era to the 1950s, physicians mobilized against proposals for government health insurance. Chapter 2 investigates why the trade unions helped promote the nascent private health insurance system but also led the drive for disability insurance and Medicare. Chapter 3 shows how the racial politics of the South were played out within the health care system and how the enactment of Medicare provided federal officials with the resources to impose racial integration on southern hospitals. Chapter 4 explains how Medicare and Medicaid created uncontrollable inflation in the health care system, triggering a purchaser's revolt. Chapter 5 describes the decade-long struggle of federal officials to introduce cost containment measures and discusses the effect this struggle had on the prospect of national health insurance. Chapter 6 explains how the failure of federal cost containment aroused corporate purchasers to experiment with their own tactics for controlling costs, giving way to managed care in the 1990s and triggering internecine warfare between physicians and insurers. Chapter 7 shows how a coalition of insurance companies, small businesses, and managed-care firms crushed a proposal for home care for the disabled in the 1980s, then launched an attack on President Clinton's plan for universal health care in the 1990s. Finally, Chapter 8 evaluates alternative explanations of the American case in light of the historical evidence presented and analyzes prospects for health care reform in the twenty-first century. I argue that the reason we don't have the health care system we need is not because the solution is too difficult to grasp or because of the legacies of antistatism, racial politics, or something inherent in the American political system. The reason we don't have the system we need is because we have failed to grasp how much we have ceded our health care to private interests. Once we understand, to return to the chapter's opening, how Donny Ray's death could be in our hands, not Great Benefit's, we will be more than halfway to the health care reform that is so desperately needed.

one

Doctors' Politics and the Red Menace

In 1911 Eugene V. Debs, the presidential candidate of the Socialist Party, declared that the "class of privilege and pelf has had the world by the throat and the working class beneath its iron-shod hoofs long enough." Deep-seated discontent had "seized upon the masses"; capitalism was "rushing blindly to its impending doom."[1] In the 1912 election Debs won over 900,000 votes, 6 percent of the presidential total. Scores of Socialist Party candidates were elected as well, including 1,200 municipal officials, 79 mayors in 24 states, and 2 members of Congress.[2] As the public took note of this turn of events, alarm about the spread of socialism was heightened by the bloody Russian Revolution of 1917. Consternation increased when Russian communists made peace with Germany in the closing months of World War I.

Postwar unemployment sparked a rash of over 3,300 labor strikes that involved over 4 million workers in 1919, sending a ripple of fear across the nation. In May bombs were sent through the mail to prominent business leaders and politicians, inflaming anxieties that anarchists were bent on destroying the American way of life. When Russian communists established the Comintern to promote world revolution, Americans found a convenient scapegoat for their troubles.[3] A police strike in Boston and a steelworkers' strike in Pittsburgh were thought to be Bolshevik-inspired. Any departure from conventional thought was seen as part of a diabolical communist plot. The Red scare reached a climax in 1920 when the attorney general staged raids on pool halls, bowling alleys, and restaurants—anyplace suspected communist sympathizers might congregate. Four thousand people were jailed, and 550 of these were deported. The raids paralyzed the Socialist Party, which had split into factions with one group rejecting Soviet communism and the other breaking away to form the American Communist Party.

Despite the weakening of the radical movement, the socialist threat hovered over the political landscape for the next half century, providing a rallying cry for conservatives against any plan for government intervention in the private sector. The Red scare's lasting legacy was a suspicion of socialist sympathies attached to any group looking to alleviate social problems through government action.

The Campaign for Compulsory Health Insurance in the Progressive Era

Socialism stood in contrast to Progressivism, the spirit of reform that swept the nation between the 1890s and the end of the First World War. Progressivism was inspired by the same problems that gave rise to socialism—harsh working conditions, unemployment, urban poverty, and labor unrest—but the remedies were reformist rather than revolutionary. The vanguard of the progressive movement was the new middle class, young educated professionals who believed that they could use their expertise to improve society. These progressives, as they were called, formed hundreds of voluntary organizations such as the National Child Labor Committee, the National Consumers League, and the Women's Trade Union League to "root out corruption in government, make cities more liveable and improve industrial working conditions."[4] Whereas socialists believed that the existing government was a tool of capitalists, progressives were convinced that public power could be used to protect the common welfare. They sponsored state laws for minimum wages, an eight-hour workday, old-age pensions, insurance against industrial accidents, and limits on the working hours of women and children.

The American Association for Labor Legislation (AALL) was one of the many reform organizations created during the Progressive Era. Founded by academics and upper-middle-class social reformers, AALL members disavowed socialism and sought to use scientific methods to identify the needs of wage earners and curtail the worst abuses of the capitalist system.[5] One prominent AALL member was social worker Jane Addams, who had founded Hull House in the slums of Chicago to connect college-educated and wealthy young people with "the starvation struggle."[6] Another member was AFL president Samuel Gompers. A cigar maker by trade, Gompers was a squat but powerful man with "a huge torso, short legs, magnetic hazel eyes and a pipe organ voice."[7] He believed that the way to improve workers' condition was to use whatever means were available under the law. That meant organizing to increase wages and improve working conditions through strikes and boycotts that put direct economic pressure on employers but not through partisan politics. Gompers never attempted to deliver the labor vote to any politician and explicitly rejected the idea that workers should form a separate political party. Business leaders such as Frederick Hoffman, a Prudential insurance executive who was a renowned medical statistician and pioneer in public health research, also joined.

Beginning in 1914 the AALL took on three major campaigns aimed at improving workers' health. The first, to eliminate poisonous materials in the workplace, resulted in federal legislation banning the use of phosphorus in match factories. The second, to provide compensation for workplace injuries, succeeded in getting 33 states to adopt workmen's compensation laws. Elated by these victories, AALL leaders felt optimistic about securing support for their next goal: compulsory health insurance. The idea of providing insurance against the risk of medical expenses was largely unknown at that time. No government programs existed, and commercial insurance companies had not yet ventured into the business of insuring health, which was considered an uninsurable moral hazard.

In 1914 the AALL Social Insurance Committee began drafting a model bill that would provide workers with free medical services and hospital care, sick pay, and a modest death benefit. Hoping to win physicians' support, the AALL intentionally left out any specific provisions regarding how physicians would be paid.[8] Those details would be decided after medical opinion on the issue had been gathered.

By 1917 the AALL bill had been introduced in 14 state legislatures, but the only states in which it was seriously considered were New York and California. The battle in California was short-lived. When the California social insurance commission recommended a state health insurance plan along the lines of the AALL bill, physicians formed the League for the Conservation of Public Health to coordinate the opposition. Their ally was the Insurance Economic Society, an organization of insurance companies led by the major insurers, Prudential and Metropolitan.[9] Commercial insurers feared that a government program would undermine the private market for life insurance and funeral benefits and eventually lead to a government takeover of all industry products. The Insurance Economic Society financed the campaign against the AALL bill, and in 1918 the referendum was defeated by a large margin.[10]

When the AALL bill was first introduced in New York, reformers were optimistic about its prospects. It had the support of some socialists who believed that compulsory health insurance did not contradict their own goals. While they were waiting for the revolution, workers needed immediate reforms. Compulsory health insurance represented the first step toward socialism.[11] New York Medical Society officers also hailed the AALL bill as "the next step in social legislation" and worked with AALL leaders to draft provisions that would be acceptable to physicians. But they hadn't reckoned with physicians from upstate New York's cities and rural areas, who decried the bill as "un-American," not democratic. Their leader, Dr. James Rooney, traveled around the state, encouraging the county medical societies to denounce compulsory health insurance as striking at the "fundamental law of our land: life, liberty and the pursuit of happiness" and representing the first step toward "state socialism."[12] County doctors deposed the physician who had chaired the state committee that endorsed the AALL bill, and they elected new representatives to the national House of Delegates. Even though the AALL tried to mollify physicians by agreeing that they could set their own fees and head the health insurance commission that would be created to run the program, the doctors' wrath only increased in intensity.

Despite physicians' opposition, the New York Senate passed the AALL bill, arousing employers and insurance companies to action. Employers' organizations created a health insurance committee to gather statistics that could be used to discredit AALL estimates of illness rates among workers and began investigating the feasibility of employer-sponsored health plans as an alternative to a government program.[13] Frederick Hoffman, himself an AALL member, turned against his colleagues and became Prudential's unofficial lobbyist against compulsory health insurance. He lectured extensively around the country and took several trips to Europe, financed by Prudential, to investigate the evils of the German social insurance system. Another insurers' association, the Insurance Federation of New York, lamented that the AALL bill was just the entering wedge that "would mean the end of all Insurance Companies and Agents."[14] Some insurance companies began to reconsider the possibility of offering a health insurance product. Equitable added disability benefits to its life insurance policies in 1917, Metropolitan sold its first individual health policy in 1921, and Prudential began selling group health insurance in 1925.[15]

The labor movement was deeply divided on the issue of compulsory health insurance. On one side was the national AFL, led by Gompers, who teamed up with the National Civic Federation, an organization of business leaders, to work against the plan in the state legislature.[16] On the other side were some AFL affiliates, such as the United Mine Workers and the International Ladies' Garment Workers' Union, who broke with Gompers and championed the AALL bill. The AALL could not overcome the combined force of the opposition, and the bill died in committee in 1919, ending the Progressive Era campaign for compulsory health insurance. But the AALL plan coalesced physician opinion on government-financed health care, initiated the themes that would dominate all subsequent debates about health care reform, and gave physicians a false sense of the extent of their political power. As historian Beatrix Hoffman noted, the defeat of the AALL plan "contributed to the making of a limited welfare state, a distinctive health care system and a political culture and configuration of interest-group power that would resist universal health coverage for the rest of the century."[17]

Compulsory Health Insurance in the New Deal

Compulsory health insurance was revived in 1929 when a group of social reformers, physicians, and academics formed the Committee on the Costs of Medical Care. For five years the committee studied the problem of paying for health care and finally issued a 27-volume report, which was endorsed by the majority of its members. Among their numerous recommendations, the two that generated the most opposition among physicians were that medical care could be more effectively provided through groups rather than solo practices and that the costs of care could best be met through some sort of voluntary group prepayment arrangement. Isidore (Ig) Falk, the quiet, competent, and politically liberal professor who had served as associate director of the committee, recalled, "These . . . were the two on which the battles really centered."[18] The physician members issued a blistering minority report, condemning any departure from individual, fee-for-service medicine and denouncing voluntary insurance as communistic.[19] AMA president Dr. Morris Fishbein denounced the majority report, and shortly thereafter the House of Delegates unanimously endorsed the minority report. Given the intransigence of the AMA, Falk became convinced that voluntary insurance had no chance. For the rest of his career, he became the foremost advocate of a compulsory government program:

> I saw potentials for voluntary insurance rather optimistically at that time. I did not swing back to the compulsory insurance approach until the AMA made this colossal blunder of taking a firm position against voluntary insurance. . . . When the AMA pulled the rug from under all of us . . . I changed.[20]

The stock market crash of 1929 sent the economy into a tailspin, ushering in an economic crisis of unprecedented magnitude. As the Depression deepened, hospital occupancy rates dropped steeply, because most people had no way to pay for medical care.[21] Some hospitals, seeking a way to develop a stable source of revenue, set up prepayment "service" plans where members would pay a monthly fee and then be eligible for free hospital services if they needed care. These plans initially covered just hospital employees but were then extended to other groups such as teachers and firefighters. Although the AMA thundered against them, the American Hospital Association (AHA) helped hospitals establish these group plans and succeeded in rescuing many floundering community hospitals. Prepayment plans became the precursor to what would become Blue Cross.[22]

As the social devastation of the depression revealed the inadequacies of state relief programs for the aged, the unemployed, and the poor, it became apparent that some federal response was required. In 1934 President Roosevelt created an advisory Committee on Economic Security to determine the best way to safeguard people "against misfortunes which cannot wholly be eliminated."[23] The committee considered including national health insurance in its model bill for economic aid in a preliminary report, alarming the AMA. Fearful that a legislative proposal might follow, the AMA called a special meeting of the House of Delegates, which adopted a resolution that "all features of medical service . . . should be under the control of the profession."[24] In a small concession to moderates, the House of Delegates accepted the concept of voluntary insurance as long as it was controlled by county medical societies. Then the siege began. AMA members bombarded members of Congress with letters, postcards, and phone calls decrying compulsory health insurance. As the executive director of the Committee on Economic Security, Edwin Witte, recalled, we were "at once subjected to misrepresentation and vilification" by the AMA.[25] Even the president's personal physician, Dr. Ross McIntyre, lobbied the First Lady, Eleanor Roosevelt, warning "that national health insurance would be very bad for the country."[26] According to one federal official, national health insurance was dropped at the last minute: "It was really very much nip and tuck whether or not the recommendations for the Social Security Act would not include some provision for health insurance."[27] Perhaps President Roosevelt could have one of his "fireside chats and carry it along." But the president felt he had "bitten off about as much as he could chew."[28] Worried about jeopardizing his entire Social Security bill, Roosevelt decided to put national health insurance on hold. As a result, the Social Security Act of 1935, the largest expansion of federal authority into the social welfare system in American history, created new programs for the unemployed, the aged, widows, single mothers, and poor children but did not include national health insurance.[29]

With the threat of a public program temporarily abated, Blue Cross solidified its status as the major hospital insurance carrier. In 1938 all Blue Cross local member plans were organized into corporations. Each local plan was required to join the national Blue Cross Association and to establish an agreement with at least 75 percent of the hospitals in its area.[30] In return, member organizations had the advantages of national advertising, the exclusive right to provide benefits in a given service area, and a mechanism for transferring subscribers who moved from one area to another. The AHA then lobbied to exempt these corporations from state laws that regulated commercial insurance companies and from state taxation; by 1945 these laws were operating in 35 states.[31] The Internal Revenue Service, following the precedent accepted by the states, exempted Blue Cross plans from federal income taxes as well.

These arrangements allowed Blue Cross plans to grow unimpeded by competition from commercial insurance companies.[32] Blue Cross thus stabilized the flow of income to hospitals and gave the AHA a virtual monopoly over health care financing in most communities.

Blue Cross plans were able to achieve these tax advantages because they differed from commercial insurance in two key ways. First, they were "community-rated," meaning that everyone who belonged to the group paid the same rate and received the same benefits, regardless of age or health status. By contrast, commercial insurance plans were "experience-rated," with rates determined by the perceived risk factors of the group or individual.[33] A second difference was that Blue Cross offered service benefits that provided subscribers with free hospital care when needed, while commercial insurers offered indemnity plans that reimbursed patients a fixed amount for expenses incurred during a hospital stay. For these reasons, Blue Cross could serve the community in ways commercial insurance could not. Despite their fundamental differences, neither Blue Cross nor commercial insurers imposed any controls on hospital charges. Thus the fledgling health insurance industry evolved as a passive vehicle for the transmission of funds from patients to providers and exerted no oversight.

Blue Cross was given a boost by the trade unions. For decades some unions had maintained old-age pension and health funds for their members and retirees, but the Depression had revealed the insufficiencies of these funds. Many unions were unable to pay promised pension benefits or meet members' medical bills. Beginning in the late 1930s, some unions began negotiating their own group plans with hospitals. After Blue Cross was formed, the unions worked to formalize agreements to cover their members' health expenses. From the unions' perspective, Blue Cross was preferable to commercial insurance, because it was non-profit, it was community-rated, and it offered full benefits with no deductibles or co-payments.[34]

Even though Blue Cross was provider-controlled, the medical societies often opposed these efforts. Walter Reuther, the United Auto Workers (UAW) vice president at that time, recalled:

We then went to the medical society in Flint where we got one lone doctor to agree to participate in Blue Cross. The medical society launched a propaganda campaign that charged that this was socialism. We pointed out that the government was not involved at all—that this was a non-governmental, voluntary group through which we could share the cost through an insurance approach. Two weeks later, our one doctor asked for his contract back. He said, "My wife and I are both being ostracized socially, and they're threatening to take away my hospital privileges."[35]

Medical societies opposed Blue Cross because some plans sought to include medical care in their service benefits. Because medical care was a standard part of many commercial insurance plans, Blue Cross had a difficult time competing with these more comprehensive benefits. But the Depression had also had a negative impact on physicians' ability to practice medicine. In many communities doctors didn't know from month to month whether they could keep their practices open or how they would pay their rent, their secretaries, their nurses, or even their electric bills.[36] In 1939 California physicians developed a medical care benefit plan as part of a successful effort to derail a state health insurance program. Medical societies in other states followed suit. In 22 states medical societies lobbied for legislation to restrict the creation of competing commercial health plans, those not controlled by physicians, and ostracized physicians who joined such plans. According to one state legislator, "No measure opposed by the medical societies had a chance of passage."[37] In 1943 the AMA created a commission to coordinate these statewide physicians' plans on a national basis, giving birth to Blue Shield, a national organization of medical care plans designed and controlled by doctors.[38]

National Health Insurance in the Postwar Era

The Social Security Act had introduced new programs to ameliorate the uncertainty that accompanied old age or downswings in the economy. It also created a new federal agency, the Social Security Board, to run these programs. In 1938 the Social Security Board organized a conference on the health needs of the nation. In response, the AMA called an emergency meeting of the House of Delegates. Conceding that federal aid for the medically indigent might be necessary, AMA officers insisted that the needs of the rest of the population could best be met by the nascent private health insurance system. National health insurance was not an acceptable option. Nor was a measure proposed by Senator Robert Wagner (D-N.Y.) to provide federal funds for state health programs. President Roosevelt remained silent on the Wagner bill, and it died in committee.

In 1943 Senator Claude Pepper (D-Fla.) introduced a resolution to establish the Committee on Wartime Health and Education. Pepper, a farm boy from the red clay country of eastern Alabama who never saw a paved road until he went to college, entered public life because he believed that government could be a force to enhance the greater good. He liked to describe himself as Roosevelt's ideological soul mate, a New Dealer before there was a New Deal.[39] When Pepper's committee was convened, the AMA opened a Washington office to keep closer tabs on political events.[40] The Pepper committee surveyed the health needs of the nation and was disturbed to learn that thousands of young men and women had been rejected for military service because of poor health. The committee evaluated existing private health insurance plans and concluded that national health insurance was the only effective way to ensure access to health care. Being the first congressional committee ever to endorse national health insurance made the announcement a newsworthy event. As Senator Pepper recalled, "What we were doing more than anything else was developing, stimulating, cultivating public opinion to a degree of acceptability."[41] The release of the committee's report generated a flood of newspaper articles on national health insurance, and a poll found that 82 percent of the public agreed that something should be done to help people pay for medical care.[42] That year a national health insurance bill was introduced in Congress (Wagner-Murray-Dingell), but it suffered the same fate as the Wagner bill that preceded it. Speaking to a member of the Senate, President Roosevelt admitted, "We can't go up against the State Medical Societies; we just can't do it."[43]

The entry of the United States into World War II derailed any further plans for domestic welfare legislation. The nation could scarcely afford national health insurance in the midst of war. In the 1944 election Roosevelt won an unprecedented fourth term as president. He promised to unveil a proposal for national health insurance in the spring, but he never had a chance to fulfill that promise. On April 12, 1945, the president died of a massive stroke, and his vice president, Harry Truman, took over the reins of government.[44] Unlike the patrician Roosevelt,

Truman came from humble origins. A Missouri native, he had plowed corn, clerked in a bank, run a failed haberdashery business, and entered politics when Mike Prendergast, boss of the Democratic Party machine in Kansas City, asked him to run for county judge. Despite his start in ward politics, Truman became known for his honesty and personal integrity, a reputation that helped propel him to a Senate seat in 1934.[45] When Roosevelt decided to replace his vice president, Henry Wallace, with a more moderate running mate in 1944, he selected Truman. Truman had compiled an impressive record uncovering waste and corruption in wartime production and would solidify Roosevelt's support in the Midwest.

Now, having served as vice president for less than four months, Truman faced the daunting task of calming the fears of a bereaved nation and converting an economy mobilized for war to peacetime purposes.[46] On September 6, 1945, President Truman delivered a message to Congress outlining his Fair Deal, an ambitious plan to expand Social Security benefits, raise the minimum wage, build public housing, clear slums, and improve health care. Health care was his special concern. As a county judge, Truman had "been troubled by seeing so many sick people unable to get the care they need, turned away from hospitals because they had no money."[47] He had witnessed doctors refusing to treat his poor clients and "built up a very strong feeling about their negative attitudes at the time."[48] His Fair Deal was to fund hospital construction, provide grants to states for public health, and create a national health insurance program.[49] On the same day that Truman made his speech, bills were introduced in the Senate (S. 1606) and in the House (H.R. 4730), but no action was taken during the following year. In the 1946 congressional election, Truman's grandiose plan provided a rallying theme for Republicans, who blasted big government, big labor, big regulation, and the New Deal, which they claimed had created a welfare state inspired by communist ideals and principles.[50] Thirty-nine of the 69 most liberal Democrats in Congress lost their seats, and Republicans trumpeted their win, their largest midterm victory since 1894, as a mandate to toss out the communists and "fellow travelers."

The charge that the New Deal was communist-inspired was given credence by the ambience of the postwar era, as tensions between the United States and the Soviet Union over communist aggression in Central and Eastern Europe escalated into a protracted cold war.[51] On March

11, 1945, federal agents raided the offices of *Amerasia*, a left-wing scholarly journal, and found thousands of classified State Department documents. They arrested the journal's publisher and editor, a journalist, a naval reserve officer, and two State Department employees. An FBI investigation into the incident revealed that government employees had been passing secret documents to the Communist Party.[52] Following the release of the FBI report, Republicans charged that communists had infiltrated the State Department, and they demanded that federal employees be screened to weed out security risks. To alleviate concerns that the American Communist Party was preparing the way for a military conquest, Truman appointed a temporary loyalty board that would review federal job applicants, a measure he made permanent the following March. Congress also passed a provision permitting the secretary of state to fire without a hearing any foreign-service employee who appeared to be a security risk. The House Appropriations Committee then began examining files of State Department employees to identify suspects and uncovered several employees who were affiliated with communist organizations.[53]

Beyond Soviet espionage, public alarm over communism was heightened by revelations of the House Un-American Activities Committee, known as HUAC. HUAC was created in the 1930s to investigate American fascism and Nazism. It took on renewed energy in 1938 under the chairmanship of Representative Martin Dies (D-Tex.), one of a sizable group of conservative Democrats from the rural South and West who "resented the domination of the Democratic party by the New Deal coalition of urban liberals, organized labor, Jews, blacks, Catholics and Eastern European ethnics."[54] Dies, hoping to weaken the coalition by tainting the entire enterprise as communist, used HUAC investigations to tarnish liberal Democrats and undermine public support for New Deal legislation.

When Republicans gained control of the House in 1946, HUAC launched a widely publicized investigation of communist infiltration of the movie industry. Screenwriters, actors, and producers were called to testify about their political beliefs and organizational affiliations. Although the hearings failed to show that Hollywood communists had inserted anti-American propaganda into films, they were a huge success in inflaming public fears.[55]

Mostly the bailiwick of extremists and bigots, HUAC's newest member in the 80th Congress was freshman Republican Richard Nixon (R-Calif.), the only member to advance in politics. Nixon gained prominence for the role he played in HUAC's investigations of communists in government. The target of one investigation was Alger Hiss, a Harvard Law School graduate who had left a prestigious law firm to work for a New Deal agency, rising to become a high-ranking State Department official. HUAC charged Hiss with being a member of the Communist Party and passing secret documents to a communist agent. While Hiss was convicted only of perjury, the case convinced the public that communists had actually infiltrated the government, and Nixon was credited with nailing the most notorious spy in the State Department's history.[56] As fear of communist subversion gripped the entire country, state and local governments, the judiciary, universities, and labor unions all sought to purge themselves of real or imagined subversives.

Although Truman had no chance of gaining legislative support for any of his programs in the Republican-controlled 80th Congress, nonetheless in 1947 he reaffirmed his commitment to national health insurance.[57] To get the ball rolling, he appointed Oscar Ewing to head the Federal Security Agency (the precursor of the Department of Health, Education, and Welfare). Ewing, the son of a midwestern farmer turned businessman, had attended Indiana University, where he had served as president of both his junior and senior classes. After graduation, he went to Harvard Law School, where he was elected to the *Harvard Law Review*. He became a captain in the army during World War I, then was offered a position with the prestigious law firm of Hughes, Schurman, and Dwight when the war ended. Although Ewing had no special qualifications to head the Federal Security Agency, he had many influential connections. His law firm's senior partner, Charles Evans Hughes, had served as secretary of state from 1921 to 1925 and became chief justice of the Supreme Court in 1930. One of his fraternity brothers, Paul McNutt, had been elected governor of Indiana in 1932, and aspired to be a candidate for president in 1938.

When Ewing's nomination was submitted to the Senate for confirmation, a Dr. Robins, the Democratic national committeeman from Arkansas and a high-level AMA official, wrote asking his position on national health insurance. Robins suggested that the AMA might oppose Ewing's nomination if he gave the wrong answer. Ewing answered truthfully that he didn't know enough at that time to say where he stood, and the AMA allowed him to be confirmed.

Truman then ordered Ewing to mobilize "all the resources within the Federal Security Agency for vigorous and united action toward achieving public understanding of the need for a National Health Program."[58] Ewing's first step was to convene the National Health Assembly to help educate the country, "so that [he] would have the people of the country with [him]."[59] In February 1948 the assembly held a conference in Washington, D.C. More than 800 representatives from farm, business, labor, civic, and professional organizations participated. The assembly agreed on two objectives: that medical care should be financed by contributory health insurance and that everyone should have adequate medical care without regard to race, color, or creed. Notably, it did not endorse national health insurance as a way to achieve these objectives.[60]

The following September, Ewing released his own analysis, *The Nation's Health: A Report to the President*. Ewing noted that great disparities existed in services across the country. Sixty percent of Blue Cross enrollees lived in the six most affluent industrial states. In Rhode Island and Delaware, for example, more than 50 percent of the population was covered by Blue Cross, compared to only 2.2 percent in South Carolina. In Mississippi and Arkansas, Blue Cross was virtually nonexistent. With only 3 percent of the population having "anything approximating comprehensive insurance protection," it seemed clear that the private sector could not meet these needs. The only solution was to mobilize "the group purchasing power of the people" through national health insurance. National health insurance would "help build a more effective organization for providing the best in prevention, diagnosis and treatment, largely solve the individual's problem of paying for medical care . . . and create a stable and assured financial basis for health services."[61]

Ewing's emphasis on inequality in access to care posed a direct challenge to the South, where racial discrimination permeated the health care system.[62] Truman had taken the strongest stance on civil rights issues of any president to date. He had issued an executive order banning racial discrimination in the armed forces and had created the President's Committee on Civil Rights. In so doing he had asserted that it was the duty of the federal government "to act to preserve liberty when state or local authorities abridge or fail to uphold these guarantees."[63] If federal officials attempted to increase access to care through national health insurance, might they not then also confront the inequality in access posed by racial segregation?

Ewing's report also made him the enemy of Republicans, who viewed him as a partisan, liberal ideologue.[64] After all, the National Health Assembly had not endorsed national health insurance. So why was he "spending untold millions in tax money to spread its erroneous 'facts' and false conclusions—forming a government lobby to sell Compulsory Health Insurance to the people of America"? Ewing's report demonstrated the "insidious infiltration of left-wing Democrats into high places." Ewing had become a dangerous man. He had sold the president on the idea of the National Health Assembly and now had "the funds, field organization, and personal staff in Washington to put over his scheme of State Socialism."[65]

To halt Ewing, Republicans launched an aggressive probe into administration efforts to promote national health insurance. They set out to prove that members of the executive branch had ventured into the realm of legislative salesmanship and that tax dollars had been spent to influence public opinion on this communist-inspired measure. On May 28, 1947, Republican members of the obscure House Committee on Expenditures in the Executive Department formed a nominally bipartisan subcommittee of Republicans and southern Democrats to investigate workshops organized by the Social Security Board, the AFL, and the Congress of Industrial Organizations (CIO), the union of industrial workers. The workshops, they charged, were devised "to build up an artificial federally stimulated public demand . . . for enactment of legislation for compulsory health insurance."[66] Federal bureaucrats on the Social Security Board were trying

to impose a nation-wide scheme of socialized medicine upon the United States. Wherever some form of dictatorship prevails in government, there we also find some manifestation of socialized medicine. The brand name of dictatorship makes no difference— Communism, Fascism, Nazism, Socialism—all are alike in that they enforce a system of State Medicine.

Great Britain's Labour Party had just created the National Health Service, an event that was widely publicized.[67] If the United States pursued the same course, "the medical profession and all our hospitals can be taken over by the federal government and forged into a new and gigantic health bureaucracy . . . it would only be a matter of time until Washington likewise moved into the field of education, religion, the press, the radio. Freedom soon would be in total eclipse."[68]

Subcommittee members also used the investigation to demonstrate that national health insurance was an insidious communist plot: "American communism holds this program as a cardinal point in its objectives; in some instances, known Communists and fellow travelers are at work diligently with federal funds in furtherance of the Moscow party line."[69] One of these "fellow travelers" was Ernst Boas, chairman of the Physicians' Forum, an organization of a thousand maverick physicians who supported national health insurance. Boas reportedly had been identified by HUAC as a member of eight communist-front organizations. Another was Jacob Fisher, a young Social Security Board staffer, who ostensibly was an associate of "various Communist-front and fellow traveler organizations" that were involved in "avowedly sponsoring the Moscow Party Line in the United States."[70] Hazel Huffman, an investigator for the subcommittee, went to see Maureen Mulliner, acting commissioner of the Social Security Board, regarding Fisher's alleged infractions. Mulliner asked what the charges against Fisher were: "Were they that he is a Communist?" Huffman replied that she wouldn't say that, but rather that he was "communistic."[71] Fisher's crime? He had published a report on socialized medicine in New Zealand in the *Social Security Bulletin.* The Social Security Board immediately called off a scheduled trip by Fisher and ordered an FBI investigation into the matter. Fisher was later cleared of any communist affiliation.

When the hearings ended, the subcommittee voted to turn the evidence over to the FBI for prosecution, but since no crime had been uncovered, no action was taken.[72] The hearings had accomplished their objective. National health insurance had been discredited as part of a communist plot to spread socialized medicine, threaten liberty, and undermine the democratic way of life. National health insurance proponents had been smeared as agents of this plot, either communists themselves or "fellow travelers." As Falk recalled,

There were some members of Congress who tried to make a big shindig out of an attempt to show that we were behind these workshops and the inclusion of some very leftish people in them. We were not responsible. . . . That was a phony performance from beginning to end. . . . It was a smear business, that's all.[73]

Republicans also called hearings to promote alternative health insurance proposals. Ohio senator Robert Taft, a dour, unbending man devoid of personal charm, was the leader of the conservative wing of the Republican Party. A complex man who aspired to capture his party's presidential nomination in the 1948 elections, Taft was dead set against government intervention on most issues, yet he was willing to support a federal housing program and federal funding for hospital construction. As a result of the Republican gains in 1946, Taft now chaired the Senate Labor and Public Welfare Committee, which he used as a forum to convince the public of the dangers of national health insurance and to promote his alternative plan for federal aid to the states for medical care for the poor. During committee hearings, Taft called 29 friendly witnesses but only a single opposition witness, a representative of the International Workers Order, a well-known communist organization. The hearings became an inquisition into "socialized medicine."[74] Witnesses testified that Taft's proposal would allow states to develop their own programs "under minimum federal safeguards," while the Truman plan would "socialize the practice of medicine in the United States" and "abolish free enterprise in the medical field."[75] Taft also used the threat of national health insurance to court physicians, his natural political allies. In an address to the Wayne County Medical Society, Taft warned his audience that the Truman plan would be the first step toward a British-type national health service.[76]

In the months preceding the 1948 presidential election, Truman's popularity hit an all-time low, and polls predicted his certain defeat. His own party was splintered into warring factions, with one contingent supporting former vice president Henry Wallace and his Progressive Party candidacy and another faction supporting Senator Strom Thurmond (D-S.C.) and his States' Rights Party. Thurmond had formed the States' Rights Party after southern delegates walked out of the 1948 Democratic National Convention when a civil rights plank was included in the party platform. Black voters rewarded Truman's support for civil rights by providing the swing votes in key northern states.[77] Truman lost four southern states but won the presidency, and the Democrats regained control of both houses of Congress.

During the election Truman had campaigned for national health insurance. Public interest was at its peak. Now was the time to act. As AFL official Nelson Cruikshank explained, "The high tide of the pressure was in '48 right after the dramatic victory of Truman."[78] Three months after his inauguration, a new national health insurance bill (S. 1679) was introduced. The bill included a ban on racial discrimination in health care but made a concession to the South. Southern states would be allowed to provide "separate facilities for persons of different race or color" as long as they were of "equal" quality to white facilities.[79]

That provision did not reassure southern Democrats, who in the 1948 Democratic victory had regained the control of the key congressional committees through which all social welfare legislation had to pass.[80] If national health insurance succeeded, it would be without the support of the South. Instead, Alabama senator Lister Hill introduced his own bill for federal assistance to the states to subsidize Blue Cross coverage for low-income people.[81] The program would be administered by state health departments, which in most instances were "deeply influenced by the state medical societies."[82]

Truman versus the Medical Lobby

As the Truman administration geared up to promote national health insurance, the AMA launched the National Education Campaign to prevent its implementation and to encourage the spread of private health insurance. Oscar Ewing, the Federal Security Administration chief, was the first target.

At the start of the National Education Campaign, the AMA assessed each member $25, then hired the public relations firm of Whitaker and Baxter. A husband-and-wife team, Clem Whitaker and Leone Baxter had worked for the California Medical Association to help kill a state health insurance bill promoted by Governor Earl Warren. In the California battle, they had sponsored radio broadcasts criticizing the Warren proposal, developed a newspaper distribution network that provided local papers with free editorials, and gathered dirt on health experts who supported Warren's plan.[83]

Whitaker and Baxter now applied the tactics they had honed in California to the national political scene. A massive amount of campaign literature was produced. Posters, pamphlets, leaflets, form resolutions, speeches, cartoons, and publicity materials for state medical societies all had one goal: "to keep public opinion hostile to national health insurance."[84] As Whitaker explained to a reporter:

All you have to do is give it a bad name, and have a Devil. America's opposed to socialism so we're going to name national health insurance "socialized medicine." And we've got to have a devil. We first thought of making President Truman the devil, but he's too popular. But this man Ewing is a perfect Devil and we're going to give him the works.[85]

Addressing the AMA convention in Atlanta in 1949, Whitaker sought to motivate his audience with a call for action:

This fight that American medicine is waging is a fundamental struggle against government domination. . . . The trend toward State-ism in America has become unmistakable . . . it is only a short step from the "Welfare State" to the "Total State," which taxes the wage earner into government enslavement, which stamps out incentive and soon crushes individual liberty.[86]

AMA national headquarters told state medical societies to organize every county society "into a hard-driving campaign organization" with battle orders going out by "letter, telegraph and telephone." State organizations were given form speeches to "get laymen for medicine in this fight." They were instructed to approach local newspapers to get the "real facts" before the editors. Every newspaper in the country should be called on, "preferably by a doctor who knows the editor and has his confidence." The book *The Road Ahead*, describing how Great Britain's national health service was leading toward socialism, was widely disseminated.[87] A special assistant was hired to coordinate publicity with the AMA's Department of Press Relations. Doctors received copies of the pamphlet *The Voluntary Way Is the American Way* to place in their reception rooms and colored posters with the caption "The Doctor: Keep Politics Out of This Picture" to display in their offices. Auxiliaries of physicians' wives organized the National Women's Campaign to distribute literature, win endorsements from women's clubs, and help build a national speakers bureau for community events.

Every venue promoted the message that national health insurance was part of a communist plot to destroy freedom. Editorials in the *Journal of the American Medical Association*, articles, and pamphlets all decried the threat to liberty. National health insurance would "regiment doctors and patients alike under a vast bureaucracy," doubling or tripling the cost of medical care.[88] The administration of such a "colossal plan from Washington" would create hundreds of new federal employees to operate the system, handle paperwork, check on physicians, and investigate "real or imaginary infringements" of federal, state, and local regulations. It would also require hundreds of regulations.[89] Patients would surrender liberty and receive in return "low-grade assembly line medicine."[90] There would be long lines in doctor's offices, and the close doctor-patient relationship would be destroyed.[91]

Any physician who deviated from the AMA line chanced being expelled from membership and thus risked losing hospital appointments and referrals. Dr. Caldwell Esselstyn ran the Rip Van Winkle Clinic in rural Hudson, New York. One of the small group of physicians who publicly supported national health insurance, he fully understood the potential costs:

> If anybody, like a surgeon whose ability to support his family depends entirely on the referrals that he gets from the other physicians in the county medical society, this lifeblood can be shut off very effectively by physicians who . . . will find a reason never to refer a patient to you, simply because you don't follow the party line. And this goes for your social life in the community where you're really ostracized by the other people in your medical profession, and it also goes for the way your kids are handled in school. . . . For somebody who depends on referrals, the economic sanctions that can be lowered by organized medicine are tremendous.[92]

The AMA also initiated an "all-out drive to provide the American people with voluntary health insurance coverage."[93] Doctors were advised to "encourage patients to get good, sound voluntary insurance for their own protection and the protection of their families."[94] A group of physicians headed by the director of the Michigan Medical Service Plan recommended that every state adopt a voluntary, nonprofit health insurance program organized like Blue Cross.[95] The group asked the AMA to finance the necessary organizational work in the states: "If the voluntary machinery can be put in motion simultaneously in all states and the plan can be given publicity in the press, in magazines, on the air and by speakers before civic and other groups, . . . [national health insurance] will be effectively blocked." Private insurance already covered more than 55 million people, either through commercial insurance plans or through "the great Blue Cross Hospital System." It was "one of the most rapid and spectacular economic developments in our time."[96] In just the past two years, more than 15 million additional people had been covered.[97]

To enlist the support of other organizations, the AMA invited local Chamber of Commerce chapters, real estate boards, Farm Bureaus, American Legion chapters, women's clubs, Parent-Teacher Associations, and insurance companies to meet with its leaders "with a view to gaining their support and having additional outlets for informative materials. . . . These organizations could offer strong opposition to the nationalization of medicine and could aid in promoting voluntary insurance."[98] Blue Cross, the Insurance Economic Society, and the Chamber of Commerce all took a public position opposing national health insurance and endorsing private insurance. Edward O'Connor, managing director of the Insurance Economics Society, testified that private insurers were "writing a large volume of disability, hospital and medical care insurance." A federal program that intervened in the private market would be "un-American."[99] Insurance industry executive Ray Murphy explained:

> In contrast to the Federal compulsory plan, voluntary insurance plans are diverse in origin and sponsorship. They are dynamic, experimental, and progressive. The proposed Federal Government model is monopolistic as well as compulsory. The principle of competitive selection between plans is discarded and voluntary choice is abolished.[100]

The U.S. Chamber of Commerce released its own pamphlet, *You and Socialized Medicine*, charging that "top administrators of the Federal Security Agency have a plan for socialized medicine in America."[101] To those who see in the "compulsory insurance program of the Democrat planners another step toward further state socialism and the totalitarian welfare state prevailing in foreign lands, there is an alternative in keeping with the freedom-loving policies of a free nation"—voluntary health insurance for the majority of Americans coupled with federal aid to the states for medical care for the poor.[102] Chamber publications told employers they should explore the possibilities of group insurance plans to help their employees pay their health care costs.[103] After all, "in 1947 the American people [had] spent $10 billion for liquor, $4 billion for tobacco and over $2 billion more for cosmetic items."[104] If they cut down on unnecessary purchases, they could easily pay for their own health care.

The pharmaceutical and drug manufacturers were initially neutral, but Ig Falk, an excellent technician but a poor judge of politics, made a tactical error by insisting on including a provision that would allow the government to set drug prices. That stirred up the entire pharmaceutical industry against the bill.[105]

The American Hospital Association was less hostile to the Truman plan, but hospital administrators could ill afford to buck the AMA. As Dr. Michael Davis, a liberal physician who worked for national health insurance, explained:

> The hospital administrators are both the bosses and the servants of the medical staff of the hospital . . . their medical staffs derive their income from the private practice of medicine. . . . Well, a hospital administrator who gets the antagonism of his medical staff because he's an advocate of socialized medicine, will generally speaking, not carry the job in that hospital very long. The board of trustees, who has the ultimate control, will get rid of him if he's unpopular with the medical staff.[106]

The AMA campaign brought national health insurance to a standstill. As Ewing admitted:

> Our proposed legislation was getting nowhere with the Congress. Many of our representatives and Senators whom we thought would go along with us, wouldn't. . . . You would talk to a Congressman or Senator and so often he would say, "You have no idea what political influence a doctor has in his local community, and I don't want to get them stirred up against me."[107]

In 1945 75 percent of Americans supported national health insurance; by 1949 only 21 percent favored President Truman's plan.[108] A frustrated Truman wrote to his old friend Ben Turoff, "I can't understand

By the end of the 1940s the public was increasingly critical of the AMA for abusing physicians' moral authority as healers. Library of Congress, Prints and Photographs Divisions, © *St. Louis Post Dispatch*, 1962

the rabid approach of the American Medical Association—they have distorted and misrepresented the whole program so that it will be necessary for me to go out and tell the people just exactly what we are asking for."[109]

During the campaign the AMA drew heavily upon physicians' cultural authority as experts on health issues. By the end of the decade, the abuse of this authority for such blatantly selfish ends made the public increasingly critical of the AMA, perceiving it as a negative organization that was against everything. The AMA had opposed aid to medical schools on the grounds that federal aid would lead to federal control.[110] The AMA had also helped kill disability insurance and had blocked measures to provide school health programs and medical care to veterans' dependents. People were especially outraged when the AMA paid the Reverend Dan Gilbert $3,000 to mail Protestant clergymen a letter calling national health insurance "this monster of anti-Christ."[111] As one critic complained:

> A lot of us laymen are fed to the teeth with the AMA's methods. With its persistently negative approach to everything. With its unvarying misrepresentation of the efforts other countries are making to solve the problem. With its "crusade" and its "battle" and its vilification of the government, the public, and its own members who speak out.[112]

Some dissident physicians began to criticize the AMA openly. Dr. Esselstyn called the AMA "an inbred group of people who become wrapped up in medical politics and who really become pretty nearsighted."[113] Dr. Bernard Meyer testified before the Senate that "character assassination, intimidation, fear of reprisal, etc. discourage a frank repudiation of many society-sponsored policies." At the annual meeting of the New York Medical Society, 38 percent of physicians attending voted for the candidates who supported national health insurance.[114] Hospital administrators also began to have concerns about their public image as close associates of physicians. One administrator wrote, "Some doctors and their friends do question whether it is right to use the county medical society . . . for political purposes and whether the sacred patient-physician relationship should be subverted to political ends."[115]

Democratic supporters of national health insurance tried to capitalize on public suspicion of the AMA. Representative John Dingell (D-Mich.)

blasted the AMA lobby, calling its anti-health-insurance campaign "one of the most cold-blooded lobbying operations in American history." Oscar Ewing awarded the doctors' lobby first prize among business lobbies for spending $353,990 during the first nine months of 1948.[116] Seeking to take advantage of this split, Senator Pepper invited AHA officers to come to Washington to discuss the issues. Although many hospital administrators said privately that a compromise might be possible, their close ties to physicians prevented them from publicly repudiating the AMA. The hospitals were "not unsympathetic to national health insurance," but they had been "blackmailed into supporting the position of the AMA. . . . [If] the medical profession was opposed to a thing, they felt that it was smart for them to be opposed."[117]

When Republicans held a rally to define their campaign themes for the 1950 congressional elections, they focused on cultivating physicians' fears of national health insurance. Physicians were warned that if Democrats picked up seats in the House and Senate, they would capture the 82nd Congress and "socialize our medical profession and imprison it under the iron rule of a Federal bureaucracy."[118] These arguments were given credence by a series of events that seemed to demonstrate that the communists were indeed intent on taking over the world. In November 1949 the Soviet Union established a communist government in occupied Germany. Then in the final months of the year the nationalist government in China collapsed and the entire Chinese mainland came under the control of communists.[119] A few months later, at a Lincoln's birthday dinner in Wheeling, West Virginia, Joseph McCarthy, an undistinguished first-term senator from Wisconsin, claimed to have a list of 205 Communist Party members working in the State Department.[120]

In the 1950 election physicians provided crucial support for Republicans and targeted for defeat Democrats who had supported national health insurance. In Pennsylvania's 26th District a "Healing Arts" committee organized against the Democratic candidate who had endorsed Truman's plan in 1948. Physicians mailed nearly 200,000 personal letters to their patients, explaining that there were "evil forces creeping into this country" and asking them to vote for Republican candidates.[121] They even posted notices in waiting rooms asking, "Will you please do me a favor by going to the polls on September 13, 1949 and voting for John P. Saylor? If you need transportation on that day, please notify me at once."[122] AMA women's auxiliaries conducted house-to-house calls and ran telephone banks. On Election Day spot radio announcements were made every hour on the hour. In Wisconsin doctors started a Physicians for Freedom campaign to defeat Representative Andrew Biemiller (D-Wis.), a House sponsor of national health insurance. Utah doctors worked against Biemiller's Senate Cosponsor, Elbert Thomas (D-Utah).[123]

In Florida, physicians mobilized to defeat Claude Pepper. A prominent urologist wrote his colleagues asking for money and endorsing Pepper's opponent, George Smathers. He wrote, "We physicians in Florida have a terrific fight on our hands to defeat Senator Claude Pepper, the outstanding advocate of 'socialized medicine' and the 'welfare state' in America. . . . In eliminating Pepper from Congress, the first great battle against Socialism in America will have been won."[124] Another doctor was so agitated that he donated a month's income to the race.[125] When Smathers visited any county, he just called a prominent doctor, "and that doctor would have all the prominent doctors of the city and their wives and several of the most important businessmen there."[126] As Pepper recalled:

> The doctors in Florida agreed that the first three minutes of every consultation with every patient would be devoted to attacking socialized medicine and Claude Pepper. They were so bitter that their wives took to the streets and highways. They tried to paint me as a monster of some sort.[127]

Physicians also ran half-page ads of a photo showing Senator Pepper with the African American singer Paul Robeson, who was a member of the Communist Party. In the primary, six liberal Democratic senators were defeated, including Pepper. In Pepper's view, the single most influential factor in his defeat was the doctors' opposition.[128] But he also had a powerful enemy in Edward Ball, a wealthy businessman who despised Pepper for his support of minimum-wage and tax legislation. Ball organized a group of Florida businessmen who raised millions of dollars to defeat Pepper. They collected every photo of Pepper with African Americans, monitored his "every statement on civil rights" and on the need for the United States to be more tolerant of the Soviet Union, and charged that northern labor bosses were "paying ten to twenty dollars to blacks to register" and vote for him. Pepper later admitted, "I never knew what hit me."[129]

In 1950 Ewing attempted to develop a scaled-down plan that would just cover hospital bills, convinced that the AMA would not object if physicians' services were excluded. In Falk's view, that was a naive tactic that would not succeed:

> The AMA said, "Oh, that's just the camel's nose, and it's a hell of a big nose, getting under the tent. Sure if you get hospital benefits, how long will it be before you tack on medical benefits?" And whenever anybody asked that question, we said: "no comment." Because that was the intent.[130]

Truman did not run for reelection in 1952, and the Republican Party chose General Dwight D. Eisenhower, the former World War II supreme Allied commander, as its candidate. Eisenhower liked to describe himself as a middle-of-the-roader, liberal on social issues but fiscally conservative. He had little sympathy for either Senator Joseph McCarthy's Red-baiting tactics or the conservative old-guard wing of his own party. In the months leading up to the election, the AMA and the insurance industry continued their campaign against national health insurance proponents. *Medical Economics*, a drug trade publication sent to all doctors, declared:

> A number of professions and industries are ready to band together in a massive election-year campaign against all forms of state socialism. Their target will be the national candidates who lean towards schemes like compulsory health insurance. Their techniques will be those exploited so successfully by the medical profession last year.[131]

Eisenhower, who firmly believed that social needs could best be met by the private sector, denounced national health insurance during the campaign as a "vast and unfair government system" that would foreclose future opportunities for private insurers to show they could deal with the problem.[132] He won the election, becoming the first Republican president after two decades of Democratic rule, and his victory was widely interpreted as a referendum against national health insurance. During the eight subsequent years of Republican administration, national health insurance disappeared from the political agenda. For Truman it was his most "bitter disappointment," the defeat that troubled him most "in a personal way."[133]

A Subsidy for Insurers

Throughout his term President Eisenhower remained a foe of national health insurance. In 1954 he consolidated three departments into a new Department of Health, Education, and Welfare (HEW) and charged HEW to devise a private solution to counter mounting pressure in Congress for a program to ease the burden of individual medical costs.[134] Alan Pond, a special assistant at HEW, recalled: "There was a general feeling that unless there was substantial stimulation of the private insurance business . . . there would not be the kind of universal coverage which would be necessary if some form of federal insurance wasn't to come into being."[135] The objective was clear: "promote the private sector in the health insurance business, be sure it keeps moving."

Private insurance had rapidly expanded from covering just 22 percent of Americans in 1946 to over 50 percent by 1952, but its dramatic growth also starkly illuminated its flaws.[136] Although commercial insurance companies had become experienced at marketing group policies and estimating actuarially sound group premiums, they had quickly learned that it was unprofitable to insure high-risk individuals. No insurance company wanted to cover disabled people or people with chronic health problems such as diabetes, arthritis, or heart disease, and they especially did not want to cover the elderly, who might both be disabled and have numerous chronic conditions. The burden of covering these individuals fell to Blue Cross, with its community-rated plans and communitywide mission.

So far the commercial insurers had moved "timidly and slowly in the field of health insurance."[137] The dilemma was how to devise a workable plan that they would not oppose.[138] According to Pond:

> In the Republican party the executives of corporations large and small have played an important role. This was particularly true of the health insurance business. Many of the executives in the health insurance business were very active Republicans. They were convinced . . . that there was no need for a tax supported health insurance scheme for any part of the population except for the very poor.[139]

A Blue Cross administrator from Philadelphia, panicky about increasing demands on Blue Cross to insure the sick and the elderly, concocted a "reinsurance" scheme. Under reinsurance, private companies would cover basic health expenses and the government would pick up the catastrophic costs. If insurers had protection against catastrophic losses, they would be able to experiment with new forms of coverage for these groups.[140]

Eisenhower seized upon reinsurance as a way to derail national health insurance and encourage the development of private plans. Fearing that "the top brass" had not been involved "in any concerted way," he invited the presidents of the 15 largest insurance companies to a White House luncheon to discuss his reinsurance plan and persuade them that he had no interest in becoming involved in private insurance or in regulating the industry. He explained that reinsurance could "accelerate the development of private health insurance . . . and encourage companies to be venturesome and to step forward in untried areas." It was "a hundred per cent endorsement of the principle of private insurance."[141] But the executives were unconvinced. The reinsurance formula required the government to calculate insurers' losses. That meant federal scrutiny of company records, which involved "getting our noses into their accounts." Worse, reinsurance might establish a precedent for federal regulation of the industry, thus undermining the sacred principle of the insurance industry: keep regulation at the state level.[142] Although Eisenhower made a nationally televised plea for the reinsurance proposal and appeared personally before the National Association of Insurance Commissioners to assure them that he had no desire to regulate their products, his efforts were to no avail.

The AMA, ever watchful of government intervention, immediately denounced reinsurance as socialism and lobbied against it in Congress. According to another HEW official, the AMA took the "simplistic and doctrinaire position" that it would be the first step toward a compulsory government program. "As to how it would possibly affect a doctor in and of itself, they couldn't really answer and that wasn't their pitch." Instead they reiterated insurers' arguments that the plan was unworkable, "a hopeless morass."[143] HEW officials tried to persuade the president of the AMA, "a wiry little doctor of stern and unmoving features," that he was wrong on the merits, but "he was unmoved."[144] After meeting with some AMA representatives, they came away feeling the doctors were "not very bright and not particularly helpful and certainly not very forward-looking."[145] Within the Eisenhower administration, the general attitude toward the AMA was one of contempt:

> The AMA presidents all were people who had come up through their hierarchy of committeeships and officerships and who were in a sense captives of the staff. They couldn't really have an independent thought . . . by the process by which they were selected there was almost a weeding out of leadership rather than the contrary.[146]

The reinsurance bill was defeated in the Senate by one vote. Following the defeat, Eisenhower bitterly complained that the AMA hierarchy was "just plain stupid . . . a little group of reactionary men dead set against any change."[147]

Conclusion

For the first half of the twentieth century, physicians drew upon their cultural authority as healers to revive the Red scare of the 1910s and define proposals for national health insurance as socialist-inspired. The most respected and highly paid professional group in the country, physicians were able to insert their parochial interests into the political process to preserve their control over the mechanisms for financing health care through the organizational clout of the AMA. As doctors abused their healing power for self-serving ends, political leaders and ordinary citizens came to believe that they had overstepped professional boundaries. Instead of being viewed as worthy of veneration, they were increasingly perceived as an interest group like any other, self-protective, insular, and negative. Thus they achieved their political objectives but paid a heavy price.

Ironically, what allowed physicians to win these battles was the fact that they had powerful allies among employers and insurers in the private sector and among conservative Republicans and southern Democrats in Congress. As long as physicians' interests coincided with these other stakeholders, they could be assured of success. That coalition began to disintegrate in the 1950s. As the private health insurance system expanded rapidly with large corporations becoming the main financiers of health insurance for the able-bodied, full-time members of the labor force, an unfilled need remained. Who would insure the remainder, the vulnerable individuals that private insurance companies refused to cover—poor single mothers and their children, elderly men and women, people with disabilities? Surprisingly, the labor movement reversed course and led the way for disability benefits and health insurance for the aged, trumping physicians' dominance in health policy debates.

two

Organized Labor's Health Benefits

On April 1, 1946, John L. Lewis, the fiery president of the United Mine Workers, called his miners out of the coal pits. A powerful figure with his massive head, black hair, and bushy eyebrows, Lewis refused to settle the strike until the mine owners met his demand for a desperately needed health and welfare fund.[1] The coal miners, with their black sputum, sunken chests, and emaciated torsos, were in the poorest condition of all the workers. Miners had the highest rates of tuberculosis, pneumonia, and black lung disease.[2] Over the course of the 35 years from 1910 to 1945, more than 2 million men had been mangled in the mines, and 68,842 had been killed.[3] As Lewis pleaded:

> When a man is killed or taken away, or his back is broken or his flesh is burned from his bones, we have no replacements in the mines. . . . Why not remove from their minds the horror that tomorrow they may be killed by the fall of a hanging rock or by the terrible ravages of a burning mine explosion that tears through the galleries of the mines?[4]

Health and welfare benefits would guarantee that injured miners would receive medical care and provide them and their families with a source of income if they were injured or killed.

As the strike wore on, it began to exact its toll on the economy. The railroads laid off 51,000 workers, Ford Motor Company began to shut down operations, and New Jersey declared a state of emergency.[5] With a national crisis looming, Lewis declared a two-week truce but then resumed the strike when the truce date came and went with no settlement. Finally, on May 29, the 59-day strike was settled when mine owners agreed to contribute 10 cents for each ton of coal to set up a health and welfare fund. The fund would provide free medical care for miners and their families, hospital care with free choice of a physician, cash benefits for disabled miners, and survivors' benefits for their widows.[6] Moreover, the fund would not be solely controlled by the owners but would be run by a trusteeship that included a union representative.[7]

The United Mine Workers set a precedent that other unions quickly followed. From 1940 to 1966 the number of people with insurance against the costs of medical care increased from 6 million to more than 75 million, with most of the growth occurring through trade union action.[8] As Beth Stevens noted, "The political pressure exerted by the American labor movement was . . . a demand for a private alternative to state-run welfare programs."[9] Why did the American trade unions pursue private benefits instead of a federal program? One answer is that organized labor was averse to political action, preferring to improve the lot of the working class through collective bargaining agreements. As George Meany, secretary-treasurer of the AFL in the late 1940s, explained, "We certainly don't look to the political structure for our wages and working conditions: we get them our way."[10] Another answer is simple political expediency. Although the AFL supported Truman's plan, when national health insurance appeared to be a lost cause, the unions focused on issues where they had a greater chance of success. But neither pessimism nor a preference for collective bargaining alone can explain why the trade unions fought for private health insurance. The answer lies in the labor-management struggles of the postwar era, when the trade unions, confronted by hostile business and conservative forces that sought to sharply curb their broader ambitions, came to view collectively bargained health benefits as the best weapon for recruiting and retaining members.

The Development of Private Health Benefits

The Second World War ended the debilitating depression that had gripped the nation in the 1930s. Deflation, economic sluggishness, and unemployment vanished in the boom created by wartime industrial expansion. The armed forces drew more than 15 million men and women out of the civilian labor force, creating a serious labor shortage.[11] Tightening labor markets meant higher wages but also inflation, overwork, and work speedups. Although workers were earning higher wages, their gains were eroded by rising prices. Simmering discontent among workers erupted in a wave of strikes that threatened wartime production. Congress repeatedly attempted to quell the strikes with a series of bills restricting unions and outlawing strikes. Once the United States officially entered the war in November 1941, the unions made a no-strike pledge for the war's duration, fearing they would appear unpatriotic if their action threatened production. In return for their cooperation, President Roosevelt created the National War Labor Board to mediate settlements in labor disputes and set policy regarding the scope of collective bargaining.[12]

Two wartime rulings accelerated the growth of private health plans. The first was the Revenue Act of 1942, which to prevent wartime profiteering levied an excess-profits tax on corporate earnings. The tax of 80 to 90 percent applied to any corporate profits that were higher than prewar levels. However, employer contributions to group pension and health insurance plans were excluded from the calculation of profits, because they were considered a tax-deductible business expense. This ruling gave corporations an incentive to reduce excess profits by depositing them in trust funds for fringe benefits.[13]

The second important ruling was a 1943 decision by the National War Labor Board that employer contributions to employee benefit plans would not be counted as wages. The trade unions had been unable to demand higher wages because they were bound by their no-strike pledge. The board's decision gave them the opportunity to negotiate health and pension benefits in their collective bargaining agreements as a substitute for wage increases.[14] Some commercial insurers also recognized the potential of the National War Labor Board ruling and began aggressively marketing group health insurance policies directly to employers.[15] Employers viewed fringe benefits as a way to build a company identity among their employees, separate from the unions' growth.[16]

Together these rulings opened the floodgates to health insurance and pension programs. In nonunionized firms employers purchased generous health insurance packages from commercial insurers, hoping to ward off unionization. In unionized firms employers began offering health benefits, without union input, to convince workers they had no need to join the union. The major business groups encouraged these activities. The Chamber of Commerce urged employers to move quickly to install voluntary health insurance plans. The National Association of Manufacturers (NAM) agreed that "management should not surrender its initiative in this matter to the union."[17] Once the plans were installed, the field of battle shifted to new turf: which party would control these funds? Could employers run the plans unilaterally or would the union participate in decisions about terms and conditions?

The trade unions emerged out of the war in a position of strength. By 1946 nearly one-third of American workers belonged to unions, a proportion equal to that in many European countries.[18] But when President Truman turned to the trade unions in his fight for national health insurance, he received at best lukewarm support. Lewis had initially promised Truman the backing of the United Mine Workers on this issue, but once the miners had won their own health benefits, he withdrew his support.[19] The United Auto Workers had never been an unwavering advocate of national health insurance. When UAW official Clayton Fountain spoke at a workshop organized by the Social Security Board to promote national health insurance, he decried "the dangers of the bureaucratic movement" and declared that "under such a plan one would be considerably kicked about."[20] A few months later, the UAW negotiated its own health care plan with General Motors, the first in the mass production industries. The CIO had been actively involved in writing the Wagner-Murray-Dingell bill for national health insurance in 1942. But once the Republicans won control of Congress in the 1946 elections, the CIO passed an official resolution calling for "Security Through Bargaining." The union would now work to secure health benefits in collective bargaining contracts.[21]

The newly elected Republicans of the 80th Congress, eager to reverse the pro-labor New Deal policies, introduced 65 bills pertaining to unions or collective bargaining. These efforts culminated in the Taft-Hartley Act in 1947. Taft-Hartley rescinded many of the rights unions had won during the 1930s. It prohibited secondary boycotts, permitted states to ban the closed shop (which had made it easier for unions to carve out bargaining units by forcing all covered employees to be union members), and imposed severe penalties for staging unauthorized strikes. A separate clause banned communist members.[22] In the wake of Taft-Hartley, the CIO expelled 11 communist-controlled unions, triggering internecine warfare among the large industrial unions and dramatically narrowing the scope of political debate within the labor movement.[23]

Although Taft-Hartley outlawed independent, union-run welfare funds through a provision that employers had to share equally in the administration of any pension or health plan, it had left unresolved the issue of whether employers had to bargain over fringe benefits.[24] In 1948 the National Labor Relations Board ruled that fringe benefits *were* subject to collective bargaining, a decision that was upheld by the Supreme Court. Then in 1949 the Wage Stabilization Board, whose job was to keep inflation from wage increases under control, determined that fringe benefits were not inflationary. With many options for increasing membership closed off, union leaders made bargaining for fringe benefits a top priority. Collectively bargained benefits obtained on union terms were viewed by labor leaders as the "virtual equivalent of a closed shop."[25] Fringe benefits became organized labor's key strategy for recruiting and retaining members. Over half of strikes in 1949 and 70 percent in 1950 were over this issue.[26]

Between 1946 and 1957 the number of workers covered by negotiated health insurance plans rose from 1 million to 12 million, plus an additional 20 million dependents. Close to 95 percent of industrial workers represented by the CIO were covered, compared to only 20 percent of skilled craft workers affiliated with the AFL.[27] As for national health insurance, most industrial unionists now "gave [it] only lip service." Private health insurance "had taken the heat off."[28]

The expansion of private health benefits divided the working class into those who had health insurance and those who did not, and it transformed the way organized labor mobilized politically. Instead of requiring leaders who could inspire the troops to stand by the barricades, the labor movement needed leaders who could master complex financial instruments.[29] The next battle would be won by policy experts with calculators, not charismatic militants who could issue a call to arms.

Winning Disability Insurance

In 1955 the trade unions shifted strategy. Since 1938 the union movement had been embroiled in internecine warfare over goals and the means to achieve them. The CIO hoped to build on wartime economic measures to craft a corporatist state with unions, employers, and government jointly negotiating broad economic policy. The AFL opposed any corporatist arrangement and demanded a return to free collective bargaining unfettered by federal regulations.[30] In 1952 new leaders who were unburdened by the feuds of the past took the helm of the two organizations. George Meany, a burly Irishman from the Bronx who had begun his career as a business agent for the plumbers' union, was elected AFL president, and Walter Reuther, the redheaded son of German immigrants, was elected president of the CIO. Within 48 hours of his election Reuther called Meany to plan a reunion of the two unions, and in 1955 the warring factions of the labor movement merged into a single organization.[31] They had been fighting each other for nearly two decades. Now it was time to set an agenda to demonstrate what a unified labor movement could achieve.

There were two gaping holes in the welfare state: disability insurance and health insurance for the retired. These were issues where the trade unions could take the lead. The AFL-CIO created a new Social Security Committee and appointed Nelson Cruikshank to serve as director. Cruikshank, a former minister, was known for his ironic sense of humor and his pragmatic approach to union concerns. He was always able to temper his "fervor for social action with a tolerance for the morally ambiguous ways in which Washington worked."[32] The assistant director was Katherine Ellickson, a Vassar graduate who had taught high school in New York city for two years and then became interested in labor issues. She was one of the first employees of the CIO in 1935 and then worked for the Social Security Board until 1940. After taking two years off to have her two children, she returned to the CIO in 1942 and helped prepare the Wagner-Murray-Dingell bill for national health insurance, even though the chances of success were low:

> I don't think we ever thought we had any chance of getting it through in the near future. I think this is something that we were for, just as we were for other things . . . but this didn't mean that we thought we were really going to get it.[33]

Also on board as head of the legislative department was former Congressman Andrew Biemiller (D-Wis.), the labor activist who had lost the 1950 election for supporting national health insurance.

The AFL-CIO decided to tackle the disability issue first. Disability benefits were a union concern because disabled workers had no government benefits until they became eligible for Social Security at age 65. That placed the burden of their support on the unions. Some unions negotiated benefits for disabled members in their collective bargaining agreements but in return had to make concessions on wage increases for working members. Thus the incentive to shift this cost to the government was intense.

In 1956 the AFL-CIO made the fight for disability insurance "a kind of wedding ceremony."[34] Cruikshank and Ellickson wrote a bill to expand Social Security to include disabled workers and immediately won support in the House of Representatives. The bill got hung up in the Senate Finance Committee, however, when the AMA protested "the potential involvement of the federal government in relationships with physicians and determinations of disability."[35] Even though disability benefits involved no medical care, the AMA feared any measure that would allow the government to extend its reach. When the Advisory Council on Social Security had recommended disability benefits in its 1947 report, the AMA had fought it "tooth and nail" in the press and in the halls of Congress.[36] Hoping to appease the AMA, Cruikshank promised that federal officials would set no fee schedules for physicians' examinations of applicants but would accept whatever the state rehabilitation agencies established as the going rate.[37] That failed to dampen AMA opposition. According to Ig Falk, they thought, "Oh, this is just a camel getting his nose under the tent and therefore they opposed it . . . because the next thing you'd have a broader disability program and the next thing you'll be giving medical care to the disabled."[38]

The deadlock in the Finance Committee meant that there would be a fight on the Senate floor. In a "flash of genius," reformers agreed to allow state agencies to administer the program, the formula favored by southerners, and to limit disability insurance to workers age 50 or older, as a concession to the insurance industry.[39] That provision appeased commercial insurers, who had initially opposed disability insurance for fear it would be the first step toward socializing the entire industry. As Edward O'Connor, managing director of the Insurance Economic Society, warned physicians, "If we should be regimented first with compulsory disability compensation, government compulsory medical care will follow. . . . What the Government shall subsidize, it shall control."[40]

Once benefits were limited to older workers, insurers agreed not to lobby against the bill.

To break the deadlock, Cruikshank and Biemiller approached Senator Walter George (D-Ga.), the Finance Committee chairman, who was planning to retire when his term ended. George, one of the southern politicians Roosevelt had tried to purge in the 1938 election, had been saved when the local craft unions held a mass rally on his behalf. That gave the unions special access to him. Cruikshank convinced him that "the disability bill would be the George bill, his valedictory. . . . This would be his last bill." He knew that George's "prestige was so great that . . . if we got him to support us, . . . we could get a majority of the Senate that would support it." Once Senator George agreed to vote for the measure, "immediately, when he attached his name to it, there were six Senators, all from the South."[41] Southern Democrats who had sided with Republicans against national health insurance voted for disability insurance because it would be locally administered and would thus pose no threat to racial practices. The day the vote was scheduled, President Eisenhower sent Vice President Nixon to preside over the Senate in case of a tie vote. The measure carried by a vote of 47 to 45. One more nay vote and Nixon would have been able to break the tie.[42] Conceding defeat, Eisenhower signed the bill into law.

The AMA had depended on southern Democrats to vote against any measure that would affect the medical system but were caught off guard by the disability bill. In the 1956 election campaign the AMA attempted to retaliate against politicians who had voted for disability insurance and defeated incumbent Senator Earl Clements (D-Ky.).[43] The experience conveyed a powerful message, however, by demonstrating that the AMA could be defeated when confronted with a rival with equal organizational capacity and greater political skill. The key to success was to pick off AMA allies with concessions that responded to their concerns.

Insuring Retirees

Health insurance for the aged was next on the AFL-CIO agenda. The idea of government-financed health care for this group had first been broached eight years earlier by Oscar Ewing, Truman's point man for national health insurance, who had been "casting around for something that we might save out of the defeat."[44] One night when Ewing was having cocktails at the home of his longtime friend William Randolph Hearst, the wealthy and influential newspaper publisher, Hearst suggested narrowing the focus to just the elderly. A few weeks later Ewing met with Louis Pink, head of New York's Blue Cross program, and listened to his thoughts about that idea. Pink complained that Blue Cross was rapidly losing business to commercial insurers who experience-rated their premiums to attract young, healthy customers, leaving the Blue Cross plans with the older, sicker individuals. Some plans were forced to raise their rates. Others abandoned community rating, where all policyholders would pay the same rate (regardless of health risk), and started basing premiums on health risk.[45] In Pink's view, here was a situation where government intervention would be legitimate:

> There is one phase of this whole problem where I think the government might be very helpful. It's the over-65 group. We really have no actuarial experience or data upon which we could formulate a program covering them. We can't prophesy what our losses would be, what we ought to charge, what the premiums should be.[46]

Ewing discussed the matter with Social Security Administration officials but initially received a cool reception. They still hoped for a universal health plan and felt this would be "a betrayal of their cause."[47] Ewing finally won over Ig Falk and then approached President Truman, who concurred that the narrower approach should be considered. A bill for federal hospital benefits for the aged was introduced in the Ways and Means Committee in 1952, but it died in committee with the AMA watching warily from the sidelines: "there was no need or chance to express a view but those bills were carefully studied."[48]

In 1956 the AFL-CIO, flush with victory over disability insurance, decided it was time to revive health benefits for the elderly. Throughout the 1950s the trade unions had negotiated better health benefits for current workers in each collective bargaining agreement, but generally these plans excluded retired workers. Worn-out workers had pensions for their leisure years but no health insurance. The situation worsened after 1958 during a fierce contract struggle when the United Auto Workers union was "cajoled" into signing the "never, never letter," promising never again to "demand negotiations for those on retirement."[49] That promise lasted only until 1961, when the UAW wrested an agreement from American Motors to pay half of retirees' Blue Cross/Blue Shield premiums. Then in 1964 the UAW negotiated fully paid premiums for retirees.[50] Winning health benefits for retirees solved one problem but often created another by forcing the unions to give up wage increases. This problem was exacerbated by the practice of experience rating.[51] As Cruikshank complained, "You get an experience rated thing and you get a program loaded with the costs of retirees and it always meant you had to give up something else, you see, if you added this expense."[52] The dilemma of balancing the concerns of active workers against the needs of retirees gave the trade unions a vested interest in turning the financing of health insurance for the aged over to the government. If the government absorbed this cost, then the unions would be able to negotiate higher wages and better benefits for current workers.

During strategy sessions, Cruikshank and Ellickson focused on three issues: how to avoid alienating the hospitals and Blue Cross, what kind of provision might attract nurses, and how to minimize physician opposition. To placate hospital administrators, they conceived a strategy of policy by stealth. Instead of imposing rigid hospital regulations at the start, standards would be brought in incrementally. Initially, "the government would only intervene in hospitals for licensing." Scrutiny would gradually be increased, and "after two or three years" higher federal standards would be imposed.[53]

Cruikshank and Ellickson discussed having Blue Cross and the commercial insurance companies administer the program as a way to gain their cooperation. But they were wary of including insurers because of their experience with the state workmen's compensation programs. These programs, which were administered by private insurance companies, provided income and health benefits for sick and injured workers. In workmen's compensation, insurers "simply met bills that were presented to them without any real consideration of whether the expenditure was necessary or not." Their passivity made it difficult to enforce quality standards or control costs. Further, they had learned that if insurers had a vested interest in a benefit, they "got interested in opposing improvements in legislation." A different concern arose regarding Blue Cross and Blue Shield: "would they be representing the hospitals or the federal government and could they very well represent both?"[54]

To avoid antagonizing the AMA, Cruikshank and Ellickson initially planned to exclude medical services entirely, but the steelworkers' union demanded that surgical care be included.[55] Even though that was not "necessarily the best thing from the point of view of politics," it would help sell the program to the rank and file. How could a cost that was covered under collectively bargained plans not be included in a federal program? As Ellickson explained, "Because surgical charges were so high . . . if you didn't cover that, a lot of workers might feel, Well, this isn't much of a program."[56] Even though a provision was included specifying that the government would exert no supervision over the practice of medicine or the manner in which medical services were provided, the AMA was not reassured.[57] However, there were some physicians who would meet with the AFL-CIO "from time to time." Members of the Group Health Association provided helpful advice too.[58]

In 1956 Cruikshank convinced Ways and Means Committee member Representative Emmanuel Cellars (R-N.Y.) to introduce his model bill, but Cellars' bill for health insurance for retirees died in committee. It was revised in 1957, this time with physicians' services excluded entirely. Cruikshank then approached the two highest-ranking Democrats on Ways and Means, both southerners, to sponsor the revised bill, but they refused.[59] Finally, Representative Aime Forand (D-R.I.), a little-known congressman from Rhode Island, agreed to consider it. Forand "dropped the bill in the hopper," surprising Cruikshank, who thought he wasn't going to do it.[60] Forand's role in promoting the bill was minimal at first: "He didn't really carry the ball in the committee. He introduced the legislation. He had his name on it."[61] But later he became its foremost advocate in Congress. In 1958 Ways and Means held the first hearings on the Forand bill, but no vote was taken. When the committee finally voted in 1960, the tally was 17 nay, 8 yea, with seven southern Democrats siding with conservative Republicans.[62]

For the next five years, health insurance for the aged dominated the AFL-CIO Social Security department.[63] Lisbeth Bamberger Schorr, who had been on the front lines negotiating UAW health plans in the 1940s, recalled: "The AFL-CIO became a sort of headquarters . . . for the people who were trying to get something done about health insurance for the aged. . . . I remember the scene . . . when we were assembling, cutting and pasting a bill." They supplied the technical staff, drafted speeches for Medicare supporters in Congress, and sponsored lunches and meetings. They prepared a "truth sheet" refuting Republican allegations about socialized medicine. They also invited supporters on the House Ways and Means Committee to discuss testimony that might come up during hearings and briefed them on areas where opponents might probe. "Our activities there were directed at two things—one, making a good record, and secondly, at trying to get the committee members to understand what the substantive issues were."[64]

The first presidential candidate to recognize the political potential of the senior vote was John F. Kennedy, the handsome, youthful, politically ambitious junior senator from Massachusetts. Polls showed that medical care for the aged was a leading concern of the public, second only to preventing inflation.[65] As one of his campaign supporters, Madison, Wisconsin, mayor Ian Nestingen later explained, "Of all the issues on which he campaigned . . . the one that constantly provoked the most interest or had the most queries raised of a spontaneous nature was the Forand bill. I don't think there's any question the President noticed this public interest and apparent support."[66] Convinced this issue could help him win his party's nomination, Kennedy endorsed the Forand bill, then asked Cruikshank to draft a measure he could introduce in the Senate.[67] Kennedy also created the Senate Committee on Aging and formed the Senior Citizens for Kennedy organization to cultivate older voters.

As momentum for federal action built, the AMA issued a "legislative alert." More lobbyists were hired, new task forces were created, and a field division was established to involve the state and local medical societies and educate physicians. Educating physicians was especially critical because they could "relate to their representatives in Congress" and build a legislative action program within the states. By 1960 the AMA had 950 people working on political issues, with 75 percent of their time devoted to health legislation.[68]

AMA leaders understood that a fallback position was needed and hatched a plan with Blue Cross wherein the government would subsidize private insurance premiums for the low-income elderly to purchase private health benefits.[69] As Walter McNerney, president of the Blue Cross Association, explained: "Our initial preference was that we would take a risk. We would quote a rate and the government would help the aged pay that rate. It wouldn't be a subsidy to Blue Cross. It would be a payment to the aged."[70]

Although the AMA subsidy plan won the support of Richard Nixon, who was running for president, the Republican Party instead supported a plan to expand existing public assistance for health care.[71] After a lengthy and bitter debate, these activities culminated in the Kerr-Mills Act of 1960, a program of federal grants to the states for health care for the aged poor.[72] Kerr-Mills satisfied southern Democrats because it would provide states with funds without permitting federal officials to intervene in the racially segregated health care system. It also mollified the AMA because payments would be made through state health agencies, which physicians largely controlled. As Social Security Administration actuary Robert Myers explained:

> The Kerr-Mills bill . . . was developed really as a counter-fire against the social insurance approach. . . . Mr. Mills and Senator Kerr didn't want the social insurance approach because of their fear that this would burgeon on out . . . and destroy a lot of private insurance and eventually develop into national health insurance or even socialized medicine.[73]

What the AMA failed to recognize was that Kerr-Mills also established the principle that the federal government had financial responsibility for medical care for the aged.[74]

Yet Kerr-Mills did not have the intended effect of dampening demand for a social insurance program for the aged, because it provided health insurance for only a minuscule portion of the elderly population. When the Senate Committee on Aging investigated the Kerr-Mills Act in 1963, committee members discovered that nationwide only 148,000 older people—fewer than 1 percent—had received any help under Kerr-Mills. Only 28 states had implemented the program by 1963, and only 4 provided the full range of care.[75] Many states that had established programs lacked sufficient state funds to finance them.[76] Even when a program was operating, doctors and hospitals refused to participate because payments were below the prevailing rate.[77] In most states, restrictive means tests excluded many of the aged who needed assistance. Twelve states had "family responsibility" provisions that effectively imposed a means test on the relatives of the aged, deterring many poor, elderly people from applying for support. In Pennsylvania, for example, the elderly had to provide detailed information on their children's finances to qualify for Kerr-Mills benefits.[78] In New York, many older people withdrew their applications on learning that their children would be involved. One man said, "Please kill my application. I don't want my son questioned."[79] Nine states also had "recovery" clauses, providing that beneficiaries' homes would be sold after their deaths to reimburse the state for the cost of care. This was a particularly repellant practice to the elderly, whose self-respect depended on owning their own homes free and clear.

When it appeared that a federal health insurance program for the aged was making headway, the commercial insurance companies decided it was time to get involved politically:

> The insurance industry was a force to be concerned with, particularly with regard to individual congressmen and Senators. They tended to do what they did behind the scenes. More of the insurance company opposition was directed toward that part of the iceberg that didn't show up in public. They did support candidates and oppose candidates based upon their views. They got out a lot of information against the program.[80]

Insurers were able to mobilize political support at the state and local level: "The insurance companies do have tremendous political influence because so many local political machines got involved with insurance. A good many state legislators are said to be insurance agents or are lawyers for insurance companies."[81] In 1958 260 commercial insurance companies joined together to form the Health Insurance Association of America to counter the efforts of the AFL-CIO. According to Ellickson, the insurance companies "provided the technical attacks of costs, the cost estimates . . . And the insurance people would talk against it at the meetings where we were talking for it." Then, "when the legislative issues were hot, they developed these plans that were launched as alternatives." Continental Casualty created Golden 65, the first hospital insurance program for the aged, in 1957. Prudential negotiated a group policy with the American Association of Retired Persons (AARP) in 1958. Mutual of Omaha developed a Senior Security program that same year, and Continental Casualty followed in 1962. Despite the proliferation of commercial plans, most policies covered only a portion of hospital costs and no medical care, leaving old people with many expenses to absorb. For example, Continental Casualty and Mutual of Omaha provided only $10 a day for hospital charges for room and board, less than half the average cost.[82] Furthermore, commercial plans were quite expensive, costing $500 to $600 a year for an elderly couple when the median annual income of people 65 and older was only $2,875. For this reason, fewer than half the people in this group purchased these policies.[83] Commercial insurers also skimmed off the younger, healthier elderly, forcing Blue Cross to raise premiums and add deductibles. As premiums and charges rose, many older people were priced out of the market entirely.[84]

By the 1960 election, the various factions had coalesced into two camps. In one camp were Republicans, southern Democrats, the AMA, and the Health Insurance Association of America. In the other camp were Kennedy, northern Democrats, the AFL-CIO, and senior citizens. During the campaign, the Democratic Party platform included what the press was now calling Medicare, and Kennedy embraced the issue as his own. After Kennedy defeated Nixon in a close contest, the AFL-CIO decided the hour was at hand.

The first task was to educate the unions' own rank and file as well as the general public about the issues. Trade union representatives participated in radio and TV programs, gave speeches, and organized educational conferences.[85] Cruikshank explained their strategy:

> If it was a political campaign, you tried to get it set up right in your platform. You tried to get people who were running for office committed. You tried to get editorials. You tried to get debate. You tried to get time on the radio. There was never any point at which you were not constantly feeling out the opportunity to make a case either to the public or to the people who were going to vote.[86]

Despite efforts to shed the association with socialized medicine, the threat of socialism hovered over the campaign. Clinton Anderson (D-N.M.), the leading Medicare supporter in the Senate, received many letters from constituents such as Martha Botts, who complained,

> I have no doubt that you are most sincere in feeling that Medicare will not lead to socialized medicine, but I still can't help feeling that any insurance that is forced upon me can't help but lead to something else I don't want. What a horrible waste all our wars for Democracy were if we go back to autocratic rule or throw it away on socialism.[87]

Ned Flightner wrote, "Just witnessed your appearance on the Today Show and I must say you sounded more like a Socialist than a Democrat."[88] Mrs. J. L. Flinchum pleaded with Senator Anderson, "You fail to represent me when you advocate government controls for any health care bill. Let Americans remain free Americans."[89] Senator Anderson was forced to defend Medicare, stating

> I have been interested to see how many people have the incorrect impression that the financing of health or hospital care for the aged through the Social Security system would lead to socialized medicine. We are trying harder than the American Medical Association to keep away from socializing American medicine.[90]

Since the Physicians' Forum "had been pretty much discredited and red-baited a great deal" during the Truman era, the AFL-CIO created a new organization, the Physicians' Committee, whose members were not tainted by communist associations. Its leader was Dr. Esselstyn, the physician-reformer who had run the Rip Van Winkle Clinic and who had worked on behalf of the Truman plan in the 1940s. Dr. Esselstyn had witnessed firsthand in his clinic the negative consequences of welfare medicine. He had seen elderly patients who delayed seeking medical care for fear of involving their children in the welfare system. As he recalled:

> I can think of a call one time we got from my next door neighbor. They said that mother was hemorrhaging from a rupture. When I got there—it was in the middle of winter—here was Grandma in the middle of the kitchen. It was a single room house with outdoor toilet facilities, and here was Grandma in the middle of a pool of blood. It turned out that she had an umbilical hernia, that's one that's around the navel, which hung out maybe 18 inches, and about a week before, she hadn't gotten dressed as well as she might have, and she was cooking pancakes for her family, and she leaned over the griddle, and her protruding hernia burned on the griddle. Here it was ten days later.[91]

Dr. Esselstyn had great empathy for hardworking farmers who toward the end of their lives were unable to pay for medical care but who feared going through "the kind of Inquisition they have to go through" to qualify for Kerr-Mills.[92] Esselstyn viewed the Physicians' Committee as a forum for doctors who opposed the AMA to speak out.[93] As Dr. Esselstyn explained:

> When we reached the Forand stage, there were no physicians speaking for the bill except the Physicians' Forum and . . . they might have been the kiss of death as much as anything else. . . . It was a question of the organizations which some of the members had belonged to at some time or another, which were under question. The days of McCarthy were over and dying, but it was in that general frame of reference. We thought we had troubles enough of our own without borrowing trouble.[94]

Many physicians who joined the Physicians' Committee were attached to medical schools or, like Esselstyn, to public health clinics, which gave them the freedom to express their opinions without fear of reprisal. Their goal was to show "that there were some perfectly common sense people with their feet on the ground who were not necessarily involved at that time in banning the bomb or other things of a far out nature."[95] The AFL-CIO remained in the background but furnished the Physicians' Committee with financing and advice on the legislative in and outs on Capitol Hill. As one staff member explained, "Esselstyn used our telephone when he came to Washington. And when he needed a statement mimeographed, we did that and we proofread copy on it."[96] Although many prestigious doctors signed on, including pediatrician Dr. Benjamin Spock, noted heart surgeon Dr. Michael DeBakey, and two Nobel prize winners, they could not penetrate the AMA, whose official stance was to ignore them.[97] When Esselstyn attempted to run an ad in the *AMA News*, the ad was rejected on the grounds that "the wording was misleading."[98]

The AFL-CIO also created a new organization, the National Council of Senior Citizens, to emphasize the support of the elderly. As Cruikshank noted: "What would the whole program have looked like if you hadn't had a Senior Citizen movement? Here is a bill designed for people age 65 and [what] if there hadn't been any Senior Citizen movement?"[99] At first, most council members were retired trade unionists from the clothing industries—first-generation immigrants, mainly Jewish, socialist in orientation but vehemently anticommunist, who in their day had fought fiercely for the right to unionize.[100] The council also recruited members from the retiree departments of the steelworkers' and autoworkers' unions, providing an instant network in key electoral states such as Florida, Michigan, and Ohio. Over 20,000 retired railroad workers subscribed to the union newspaper, *The Voice*, giving the council an immediate audience with that group. The railroaders' strengths were often in states where other senior organizations were weak, such as Tennessee, Nebraska, and Georgia.

The National Council of Senior Citizens was headed by Blue Carstenson, a former HEW staffer known as a salesman and a showman but not as a particularly effective organizer. Former colleagues considered him divisive, someone who would "make alliances and then run around and try to manipulate one group against another."[101] Carstenson attempted to purge members with ties to communist organizations, ostensibly to protect the council from charges that it was "socialistic." When the United Electrical Workers retirees in Philadelphia asked to join, Carstenson explained, "We thought they were probably Communist-controlled. These were the ones at GE who were thrown out of the AFL-CIO. They're still trying to get in." Carstenson did a background check on one member who had refused to testify before HUAC in the 1940s. Although HUAC "had nothing to validate that he was a Communist, that he probably had been back in the '30s but that he was [not] connected at that time . . . we always kept an eye on him."[102] Despite his failings, Carstenson was effective in creating public empathy for senior citizens and drawing attention to their grassroots movement:

> We had to make it a cause and we made it a cause. . . . We charged the atmosphere like a campaign. We tried to create this. . . . We were always jammed in there and there was a hustle and bustle atmosphere. And when reporters came over they were always impressed by telephones ringing and the wild confusion and this little bitty outfit here that was tackling the whole AMA in a little apartment on Capitol Hill. . . . This was news. It used to make every reporter chuckle or smile.[103]

In 1962 Carstenson organized petition drives and letter-writing campaigns among National Council of Senior Citizens clubs. Thousands of senior citizens bombarded their representatives with letters like this one from a retired railroad worker:

I am an old rail who retired in Jan. 1942, we have two retired clubs in San Antonio, Texas and I don't believe any of us understand just what the Medicare Bill would do for the retired people, could you send me something on the Medicare . . . something that would help our cause if we could get one of our daily papers to run it. They give the doctors' side of why they oppose the Medicare bill. Why not give our side of why it's needed.[104]

Whenever congressional hearings were held, council members were on the scene. As AMA lobbyist Joseph Stetler ruefully noted, "They effectively organized testimony at the time of hearings. They had those groups of golden age clubs that would come here and testify. It was effective, I'm sure."[105]

During the 1940s, the AMA had set the terms of the debate and made national health insurance proponents the enemy; now the National

The National Council of Senior Citizens was effective in lobbying on behalf of Medicare. Library of Congress, Prints and Photographs Divisions, LC-USZ62-122433

Council of Senior Citizens turned the tables. Their campaign literature explained that the aged were a deserving group who desperately needed health insurance. Many were in poor health, a high proportion lived in poverty, and few were adequately insured. Commercial insurance would never meet their needs. As Carstenson related:

> In every piece of material and we did this religiously, we spelled out one, two, three, four, what was in Medicare. We put out literally millions and millions and millions of pieces of literature . . . there's been no other bill in history where the details have been as widely disseminated. . . . We did a hard sell, a real hard sell. . . . You can let the AMA interpret it or we can interpret it.[106]

A council pamphlet entitled *Operative Negative* sought "to discredit the AMA on the basis of their record."[107] Other council materials described the AMA as "being against everything."[108] An AFL-CIO briefing paper charged that the AMA was as "opposed as ever to effective action." It was conducting a "cynical campaign with a massive onslaught of distortion, misrepresentation and beguiling promises of something better."[109]

By 1962, when public support for Medicare had reached 69 percent, President Kennedy began a major push to get a bill passed. Even some Republicans favored government action.[110] Yet the House Ways and Means Committee was chaired by fiscal conservative Wilbur Mills (D-Ark.), the cosponsor of Kerr-Mills. Mills' first congressional campaign in Arkansas had been financed by a group of doctors, and his opposition proved to be an insurmountable obstacle.[111] Unable to get a bill out of committee, President Kennedy took Medicare to the Senate floor, attaching a Medicare rider to a welfare bill that had already passed in the House. The measure was defeated 52 to 48, with the majority of Republicans and 21 southern Democrats voting against it. The following year Kennedy sent a new Medicare proposal (King-Anderson) to Congress. Behind the scenes insurers lobbied against it, testifying at Senate hearings that there was no need for a government program, because private insurance among older people had increased from only 2 percent in 1952 to 60 percent by 1963 and continued to grow rapidly.[112] But when Ways and Means voted this time, the results were closer: 13 against, 12 for.[113]

The efforts of reformers neutralized the AMA, which during these years used every propaganda tactic it had employed during the Truman era.[114] The AMA ran newspaper ads and radio and TV spots declaring that Medicare was socialized medicine and a threat to freedom. Doctors were provided with speeches, pamphlets, radio tapes and scripts, and guidelines for using the material. Their wives held afternoon parties for friends and neighbors at which they discussed the evils of Medicare and listened to a recorded talk by Ronald Reagan. "One of the traditional methods of imposing statism on a people has been by way of medicine," Reagan told his listeners.[115] When states held governors' conferences on aging, "the AMA began to organize very effective flying squadrons to come and try to lobby against Medicare."[116] Representative Forand recalled mail he received from a physician who "used his prescription blanks and prescribed tranquilizer pills."[117] The AMA also created a political action committee, AMPAC, to keep from tarnishing its professional image. AMPAC would identify the personal physicians of members of Congress and get their physicians to lobby against Medicare. Then "they went even further and began to hunt down the physicians of people of influence in other organizations."[118]

To refute the argument that the aged had a compelling problem that could only be solved by a government program, the AMA released its own statistics. The aged were not "universally frail and feeble, constantly ill, and doddering from one visit to the doctor to the next." Rather, the vast majority were in good health; only 4 percent of people 65 or older were confined because of chronic illness. Nor were the aged especially needy. After tax obligations and family size were taken into account, aged households had only slightly less income than younger families and fewer financial obligations.[119] Most could afford to pay for their own health care. Why, asked AMA President Ed Annis, should wage earners be forced to pay higher payroll taxes for hospital care for everyone over 65, even those who were wealthy or already had insurance?[120]

When President Kennedy spoke on behalf of Medicare to a crowd of cheering senior citizens in Madison Square Garden, Annis responded the following day. Speaking to an empty arena, still not cleaned up from the previous day's rally, Annis responded point by point to each of Kennedy's comments. AMA lobbyist Joseph Stetler recalled: "We had about four television sets and we broke into teams of two . . . and critically analyzed what he did . . . that night the script was written for Ed

Annis to use the next day. We stayed up all night working on it."[121] Annis then showed a film prepared by a professional writer and television producer. Kennedy's speech was widely viewed as a failure and Annis's response as highly effective. Annis had less success when he attempted to speak to a group of senior citizens in Florida: "They sure scared Dr. Annis. He physically was very concerned at that point because they were very angry, as only Miami senior citizens can get."[122]

Despite this one public relations victory, AMA arguments against Medicare failed to resonate with the public for several reasons. One was that the AFL-CIO had been successful in convincing the public that a real need existed. According to Oscar Ewing, "What brought that public education about was the organization of the Senior Citizens Council . . . their political weight was able to way outbalance the political weight of the doctors. You had 19 million people over 65, and you had 185,000 doctors."[123] Another was that private health insurance now covered 68 percent of the population, making the idea of covering the uninsured both comprehensible and acceptable. As Ellickson explained, "The idea of federal health insurance for those who couldn't afford it or for those who somehow were excluded from private or voluntary health insurance was a perfectly natural . . . thing to do."[124]

How the AMA Was Defeated

On November 22, 1963, President Kennedy was gunned down by an assassin as he rode in an open convertible in a motorcade in Dallas, Texas. His vice president, Lyndon Baines Johnson, still in a state of shock and bewilderment, was sworn in as president that afternoon.[125] In the ensuing chaos, all political decisions were placed on hold.

At his first meeting with Kennedy aides, Johnson asked them to draw together the threads of the fallen president's domestic program. A consummate politician both bluntly honest and calculatingly devious, Johnson could persuade his legislative foes to support his agenda and "outmaneuver them when persuasion failed."[126] With an election just 11 months away, President Johnson chose to mount an attack on poverty, targeting the hard-core poor, those who had no chance to benefit from economic growth. Having grown up in Texas, where he had witnessed the damaging effect of poverty and bigotry, he turned Kennedy's modest proposal for programs to help the Appalachian poor into an ambitious war against poverty. His Great Society would increase funding for education, child health, nutrition, job training, and community action. The capstone would be health insurance for the elderly.

Hearings held by the Senate Subcommittee on the Health of the Elderly in April of 1964 provided a stark illustration of the limits of private health insurance.[127] In just the past year, private insurance rates had increased by as much as 43 percent. Committee members had received thousands of letters from older people all over the country protesting the hikes with "no end in sight."[128] Bankers Life and Casualty admitted that of 76,764 policies issued during 1961 in its plan for those over 65, only 41,130 were still in force in 1963. Some policyholders had died, but more had dropped their coverage because they were unable to pay the premiums. Costs were not the only problem. Insurers threatened that people who filed claims would be dropped unless they agreed to waive future benefits or accept substandard coverage. Furthermore, some companies had provided misleading data to Congress to create the impression that no further action was needed. Tactics included inflating the number of policyholders by including weekly indemnity policies, which paid only a minimal flat amount unrelated to hospital charges or services, or counting someone who held three policies as three separate policyholders.[129]

When the Democrats held their 1964 presidential convention in Atlantic City, members of the National Council of Senior Citizens arrived by the busload. In an impressive show of solidarity, 14,000 senior citizens marched ten blocks down the boardwalk to the convention hotel. That fall the Senate approved a Medicare amendment to a House-passed bill on Social Security benefit increases, thanks to the defection of two southern Democrats, but the measure died in conference committee.[130] Oscar Ewing, now retired, advised the National Council of Senior Citizens, "You'd better make darn sure that your key spokesmen in Congress get back," because the AMA "was too darn powerful."[131] Following Ewing's advice, the council worked to ensure that no Medicare supporters were defeated at the polls, zeroing in on the Ways and Means Committee to pack it with Medicare supporters:

> We knew that we had to defend every single pro-Medicare Senator and Congressman and that we had to try to pick off the key

opponents. . . . If any of these went down, we were in trouble. . . .
Also if members of the Ways and Means Committee who [sup-
ported] Medicare went down to defeat, these, too, would be signs
of the struggle.[132]

When Senator George Smathers (D-Fl.) came out against Medicare, the
AFL-CIO decided to "educate" him by holding hearings in Florida.
Cruikshank explained:

> We really went to work—the National Council of Senior Citizens
> and our unions . . . to really make these demonstrations . . . in Fort
> Lauderdale they had to change the hall three different times.
> Smathers came and looked out over a sea of several thousand old
> people. And while they were orderly and all, there were banners
> all over the place for Medicare.[133]

In the 1964 election, Barry Goldwater, a conservative Arizona senator who opposed Medicare, headed the Republican ticket. He won the
staunch support of the AMA, whose own "almost psychotic fear of
government" meshed with Goldwater's frontier philosophy that the
best government is the one that governs least.[134] Johnson won the election by 61 percent, the largest margin ever received by a president. The
Democrats swept both the Senate and the House by wide margins, with
northern Democrats gaining a majority without the South for the first
time since the New Deal. No incumbent, Republican or Democrat, who
supported Medicare lost.[135] The AMA had put everything into the fight
against former HEW secretary Abraham Ribicoff, who was running for
the Senate. Ribicoff turned to the National Council of Senior Citizens
for support. He ran on a pro-Medicare ticket, printing a million mock
Medicare cards with his photo on the back. Senior citizen clubs passed
out the cards in large quantities, and Ribicoff was victorious.[136]

In his State of the Union address, President Johnson made Medicare
a priority. As it became apparent that some measure would be enacted,
the key interest groups began jockeying to ensure that they had a voice
in the final legislation. The negotiations were conducted by Robert Ball,
a politically skilled tactician who had come up through the ranks in the
Social Security Administration and was widely respected for his expertise and dedication. Even those who opposed Ball's desire to expand
the Social Security program admired his commitment. As Robert Myers,

the actuary of the Social Security Administration, conceded, "Never let it be said that Bob Ball isn't quite intelligent and savvy in the ways of the world."[137] As early as 1961, Ball had had secret telephone conversations with Harry Becker, a Blue Cross official, to try to recruit him as an ally.[138] Ball and AFL-CIO officials also met with AHA representatives, who "would never come in here as the American Hospital Association, but they would come in as individuals who were very knowledgeable in this field and start off by saying, 'Of course, we're against this legislation, but if it's going to pass, it ought to do this.'"[139] The hospitals were carrying a considerable part of the financial burden of care for the aged either through outright charity or by accepting low state welfare payments.[140] From one-third to one-half of their aged patients could not pay their bills.[141] Although AHA representatives "were extremely proper and discreet in their discussions with us, never indicating their own viewpoints . . . we were pretty sure that they were not unsympathetic."[142] In 1962 the AHA adopted a resolution supporting Medicare on the condition that Blue Cross be given responsibility for administering the program, a move that was considered a severe defection by the AMA.[143]

Commercial insurance companies had become resigned to the need for a government program. The aged had proved to be unprofitable clients, forcing insurers to load their costs onto paying customers. Although the commercial insurers never said so publicly, another reformer recalled that privately they had "a great deal of misgiving" about their efforts to insure the elderly. Some of the more farsighted insurance company executives recognized that they were engaged in a self-defeating cause.[144] As early as 1961 the president of the Health Insurance Association of America had begun to discuss how insurers could offer supplemental policies to fill the gaps that would invariably be a part of any government program.[145] Some member companies broke ranks and openly supported Medicare.[146]

A week after the election, Ways and Means Committee chairman Mills indicated that Medicare would be considered as soon as the new Congress convened. The election had threatened his control of his committee. Now he declared he would work out a plan for moving Medicare forward. On January 4, 1965, Medicare bills were introduced in the House and Senate. In a last-ditch effort, the AMA proposed Eldercare, a slightly modified version of Kerr-Mills that would increase federal support to help defray the health insurance costs of the elderly poor.[147] To promote Eldercare the AMA coupled a nationwide newspaper ad campaign with spot announcements on 346 television and 722 radio stations and distributed 10 million pamphlets attacking Medicare. This effort was a total flop.[148] By playing hardball, the AMA not only had lost public respect but also had alienated even their congressional supporters. Elizabeth Wickenden, who was the Washington representative of the Public Health Association, witnessed this gradual erosion:

> While I was working with the Congress . . . there was a total change of attitude toward the medical profession. . . . Part of the psychology of a physician is that he is used to being a very strong authoritarian figure to his patients and a father figure to them . . . he can be authoritarian and still have a conviction that he's doing it for their own good and he can't understand anybody who deliberately goes against him in the doctor-patient relationship. Now in the early period of this battle, it seems to me that the AMA was approaching the Congressmen very much in the same spirit. . . . But over the years . . . this was no longer effective. . . . It was more of a discrediting of the medical profession. It was really a puncturing of this aura of omniscience.[149]

When Ways and Means refused to give Eldercare a public hearing or allow a debate on the House floor, the AMA complained about a brushoff. The House Counsel responded contemptuously that the AMA had testified at length in the 88th, 87th, 86th, and 85th Congresses: "It can hardly be said, therefore, that the American Medical Association has not had an opportunity to present its views on the subject."[150]

A third proposal on the table was Bettercare, a plan for a federal subsidy for the purchase of private health insurance. Bettercare was written by Aetna lobbyists and sponsored by Representative John Byrnes (R-Wis.), the ranking Republican on the Ways and Means Committee.[151] In an effort to prevent deadlock, Mills decided to combine the three approaches—the AFL-CIO hospital insurance plan, the AMA's Eldercare, and Aetna's Bettercare—in one bill, his "three-layer cake." According to Robert Ball, everyone in the room was "flabbergasted."[152] The first layer, Medicare Part A, would pay for hospital care, for skilled nursing care for a limited period, and for some home health care for people recovering from an illness. Part A would not pay for any long-term nursing home care for people with chronic illnesses, a deficiency that would prove to be a big problem in years to come. The second layer was Part B, an optional program that would pay for physicians' services. The third layer was a slightly expanded version of Kerr-Mills termed Medicaid, a program of health insurance for people who were "categorically" eligible for the federal/state cash assistance programs, old-age assistance, and Aid to Families with Dependent Children, the plan favored by the AMA and some conservatives.[153]

Medicare left many health care costs uncovered. Beneficiaries would still have to pay premiums for Part B coverage, co-payments for many services, and the costs for eyeglasses, prescription drugs, and long-term care. Thus the private insurance industry would be relieved of the large, unpredictable costs of serving an elderly clientele but would retain a predictable market for supplemental "medigap" policies.

As a compromise with Blue Cross officials who demanded to administer Medicare (and bolstered that demand by repeated threats of a hospital boycott), federal officials agreed to appoint "fiscal intermediaries" to handle claims, determine payment amounts, and reimburse providers.[154] "You can't stand to talk to a government official? Okay, have somebody else talk for you. . . . If you want a buffer, fine."[155] Although Blue Cross hoped for sole responsibility for administering Medicare, arguing that it "didn't need the false check and balance of a competitive element," at the last minute the commercial insurance companies were also allowed to bid.[156]

AFL-CIO officials were disappointed by many of the features in Mills' proposal, feeling that he had sold out far short of what really could be accomplished.[157] They opposed the last-minute addition of Part B, which they feared would create rampant inflation, and suggested adding some price controls, to no avail.[158] They had also "fought like the dickens against letting the insurance companies into this program," concerned that they would do nothing to keep costs under control.[159] But under the Johnson administration, the labor movement's role had become largely ceremonial. Although administration officials consulted with labor officials, it was largely to keep "the labor boys happy without anything of real substance happening as a result."[160] One AFL-CIO staff member explained: "It was disappointing to be working on this for years and years in every detail and then within a matter of an hour have the entire picture changed totally and be presented with this and not really have had a part in it."[161]

The National Council of Senior Citizens held a rally on Capitol Hill at which more than 100 elected officials endorsed Medicare. On April 8 the Medicare bill passed the House, with 40 southern Democrats opposed. On June 30 it passed in the Senate Finance Committee, 12 to 5. All four southern Democrats and two Republicans who had never before voted for Medicare voted yes.[162] On July 6 it won approval in the full Senate, with southern Democrats and Republicans evenly split. Florida senator George Smathers voted in favor. So did powerful Virginia senator Harry Byrd, who was bullied into it by President Johnson. Medicare was enacted on July 30, 1965, the largest expansion of the welfare state in the second half of the twentieth century.[163]

Politically, Medicare filled the remaining gap that negotiated plans could not cover, removing all pressure for national health insurance. Immediately, as the burden of the older, otherwise uninsured population was removed, Blue Cross began lowering its rates across the country. As Nelson Cruikshank admits:

> What we were really doing was making voluntary insurance viable for almost all of the working population in the country. Now without Medicare, had this burden existed as a threat or had they attempted to meet it, their system would have broken down, which in either case would inevitably have brought on national health insurance.[164]

Soon after Medicare became law, Cruikshank traveled to Independence, Missouri, to visit the Truman Library. Harry Truman warmly welcomed him, holding out his hand and saying, "Hello Cruikshank. Are you still fighting the AMA? Don't give the sons of bitches an inch."[165]

The enactment of Medicare was a turning point for the medical profession. It resulted in the loss of key allies, including the AHA, the Blue Cross Association, and the insurance industry. It also undermined physicians' cultural authority, as the AMA developed a "reputation for intolerance" with the public and politicians.[166] Unlike the insurance industry, whose role was played out behind the scenes, leaving no "residue of anti–insurance company feeling," the AMA's activities were highly visible.[167] AMA general counsel Joseph Stetler ruefully acknowledged, "It doesn't deserve the bad reputation it has and the extensive lack of popularity that it enjoys from the public and even from some elements of the profession and certainly from the government.... They were very unpopular with a lot of people and ultimately with a lot of members of Congress and politicians."[168]

Conclusion

During the 1940s, the American trade unions followed a different course than their European counterparts. Instead of working on behalf of national health insurance, they focused their energies on the right to bargain for fringe benefits in their employment contracts. As a result, there was no labor-sponsored, grassroots initiative to counter the AMA or the commercial and nonprofit insurers, for whom collectively bargained health benefits had opened a large new market of viable employee group insurance pools. Why, then, did the trade unions take the lead in promoting disability insurance and Medicare? That answer is that these programs not only could demonstrate what a unified labor movement could accomplish but also could solve the problem of insuring disabled and retired members, whose high costs raised the stakes when trade unions tried to negotiate wage increases and other benefits for working members.

The AFL-CIO won Medicare by mobilizing its extensive union network of state federations and local chapters, organizing a grassroots senior citizens' movement, and supporting Democratic Party members who served on key congressional committees. Although union leaders were subsequently pushed to the sidelines during Lyndon Johnson's Great Society, there is little doubt that the trade unions paved the way for the final Medicare vote.

The 20-year period between the end of World War II and the enactment of Medicare in 1965 solidified the private health insurance system in several ways. The spread of private health insurance in collective bargaining agreements effectively removed organized labor from the broader struggle for national health insurance and gave the trade unions a vested interest in the private welfare state. Medicare further reinforced private health insurance by providing coverage for a costly group and removing from political debates over national health insurance a constituency considered worthy and deserving.

three

Provider Sovereignty and Civil Rights

As the battle for health insurance for older Americans was waged in Washington, another social revolution of greater magnitude surged up from the South.[1] Beginning with the bus boycotts of the 1950s, civil rights activists engaged in an escalating wave of protests, mass marches, lunch counter sit-ins, and freedom rides. Courageously facing arrests, brutal beatings, and even murder, they demanded an end to segregated schools, restaurants, stores, and public facilities, and insisted on equal opportunity for good jobs.

The legal basis of racial segregation derived from *Plessy v. Ferguson,* the 1896 Supreme Court ruling that "separate but equal" facilities were constitutional. Writing the majority opinion, Justice Henry Brown rationalized:

> Legislation is powerless to eradicate racial instincts or to abolish distinctions based on physical differences, and the attempt to do so can only result in accentuating the difficulties of the present situation. . . . If one race be inferior to the other socially, then the Constitution of the United States cannot put them on the same plane.[2]

At the state level, the "separate but equal" principle was protected by harsh racial codes mandating racial segregation; at the national level, southern congressmen insisted on the primacy of states' rights and used their control over key congressional committees to block any measures that might allow federal authorities to intervene in local racial practices.[3]

Racial discrimination was as rampant in the health care system as in other southern institutions. Some southern hospitals refused to admit any black patients. Others maintained separate "white" and "colored" entrances, water coolers, and bathrooms and reserved certain wards and rooms for black patients only. Segregation also extended to hospital personnel practices, as black physicians were excluded from local medical societies and denied hospital staff privileges.

The sole health care measure of Truman's Fair Deal to be enacted was the Hill-Burton Hospital Survey and Construction Act of 1946. Hill-Burton was a response to a vigorous lobbying campaign by the American Hospital Association for aid for hospital construction, a need that had been deferred by more than a decade of depression and war. To win the votes of southern congressmen, Alabama senator Lister Hill inserted a statute that allowed hospitals to practice racial segregation but still receive federal funds. The statute was justified on the grounds that hospitals were *private* entities whose operations could be regulated only by the states, not by federal authorities. As Hill testified on the Senate floor:

> Who shall practice in the hospitals, and the other matters pertaining to the conduct of hospitals, we have sought in the bill to leave to the authority and determination of the States, and not have the federal government, through this bill, invade the realm of the operation and maintenance of the hospitals.[4]

Senator Hill's statute also appeased physicians and hospital administrators, who might otherwise have rejected the hospital construction program for fear it would "open the door to federal influence."[5] As Ig Falk explained, the Truman administration accepted segregation as "the price we had to pay for getting this legislation through."[6] Despite the concession, AMA officers were chagrined when Congress designated the Public Health Service, one of the numerous agencies within the Department of Health, Education, and Welfare, to administer Hill-Burton. In their paranoid view of the world, the Public Health Service was an agency controlled by left-wingers and Negro sympathizers, a view that could hardly be further from the truth.[7] To placate physicians, Surgeon General Thomas Parran promised that the federal role would be "largely that of guidance," with day-to-day administrative decisions left to local Public Health Service offices.[8]

Hill-Burton did require hospitals to sign a nondiscrimination assurance, agreeing to provide care to people who were unable to pay and to offer care to all persons regardless of race, creed, or color. However,

Section 622 allowed Hill-Burton funds to be used to construct separate facilities for different "population groups" as long as these facilities were of "equal quality." It also allowed racial segregation within a hospital as long as no patient was denied admission if beds allotted to the "other population group" were available. Furthermore, hospitals could deny staff privileges based on race, because these were issues of "internal" hospital policy outside the jurisdiction of the federal government.[9] As long as hospitals were legally defined as private organizations, the federal government would have no authority to intervene in "internal" hospital affairs. That prohibition included administration, personnel, maintenance, and hospital operations.[10]

Hill-Burton and Racial Segregation

Hill-Burton was especially aimed at poor and rural communities that lacked access to health care.[11] Between 1947 and 1974, the Hill-Burton program spread hospital-based care to the rural South. Half of all southern hospitals were constructed in the program's first decade. Some Hill-Burton hospitals admitted black patients but maintained racially segregated wards, even separate nurseries for newborns.[12] Others were entirely segregated, built either solely for whites or solely for blacks. For example, Alabama used Hill-Burton funds to construct racially segregated or separate facilities in all but 2 of its 67 counties.[13] North Carolina built 2 all-white hospitals, 2 all-black hospitals, and 54 hospitals that were segregated by ward.[14] While a few hospitals, such as those in Ahoskie and Greenville, North Carolina, granted admitting rights to black physicians from the beginning, most white hospitals regularly denied staff privileges to black physicians.[15]

In 1954 the Supreme Court overturned the doctrine of "separate but equal," ruling in *Brown v. Board of Education* that segregation deprived minorities of the equal protection of the laws as guaranteed by the Fourteenth Amendment: "Does segregation of children in public schools solely on the basis of race, even though the physical facilities and other 'tangible' factors may be equal, deprive the children of the minority group of equal education opportunities? We believe it does."[16]

The *Brown* decision raised the question whether the "separate but equal" provisions of the Hill-Burton program were constitutional. The

Court had indicated that its decision applied to areas other than education, including public housing, public golf courses, and public audito-
riums. Could federal funds be used to finance hospital construction
projects of doubtful constitutionality? Within the Public Health Service,
attorneys debated how the *Brown* decision would affect agency policy.
They concluded that the Public Health Service could continue funding
segregated hospitals as long as the separate facilities were "of like quality."[17] But Public Health Service officials refused to evaluate whether
segregated hospitals were actually providing a similar quality of care
to all patients. As one official explained, "We are not intending to suggest at this time that we are required to be concerned with relative quality
of segregated services."[18] Public Health Service attorneys also decided
that the federal government had no jurisdiction over internal hospital
policies such as admission practices or room assignments, which fell
under the category of hospital "operation."[19] Until it was "definitely
established that segregation on the basis of race in public hospitals is
unconstitutional, the Surgeon General is certainly under no statutory
mandate to anticipate the outcome of court tests of that issue." Hospital administrators who inquired were informed that "the propriety of
separate hospital facilities for separate racial groups is not directly affected by court decisions to date."[20] The school desegregation decision
did not relieve the Public Health Service of its responsibility to carry
out the Hill-Burton statute as written, even if that meant allowing segregated facilities to continue current practices.[21]

The Civil Rights Challenge to "Separate but Equal"

In the wake of *Brown v. Board of Education*, civil rights advocates organized protests and demonstrations against hospitals and picketed the
headquarters of white medical societies that refused to admit black
physicians. Since most hospitals made membership in the local medical society a prerequisite for staff privileges, this form of discrimination
exacted a double penalty. Not only did it mean that black physicians
couldn't admit patients to the local hospital, it also meant that they
were cut off from patient referral networks. When the NAACP joined
with the National Medical Association, an organization of black physi-

cians, to request admitting rights at Hill-Burton hospitals, some hospitals, embarrassed by the demonstrations, agreed to revise their policies. Greenville's new Pitt County Memorial Hospital, a 120-bed Hill-Burton facility with a 30-bed Negro wing, offered admitting privileges to two black doctors.[22] But many hospitals remained adamantly committed to preserving segregation.[23]

In the face of this resistance, civil rights advocates directed a stream of complaints at the Public Health Service, Congress, and White House officials. The complaints originated from regions where the movement had extensive grassroots mobilization and well-organized networks of activists.[24] For example, Catherine Patterson, from the Gadsden Freedom Movement, objected that the new Baptist Memorial Hospital in Gadsden, Alabama, had separate "white" and "colored" entrances and reserved just 25 beds for Negro adults.[25] Horace Reed, president of the Volusia County, Florida, branch of the NAACP, complained that Halifax Hospital maintained racially separate wards, that "even the most insignificant equipment [was] labeled 'Negro' and 'white,' and that Negro employees were required to occupy a segregated area in the cafeteria."[26] In James A. Walker Memorial Hospital in Wilmington, North Carolina, black patients were segregated in "old sections" of the hospital in a ward that had two toilets for 25 black patients: "The ward was in a building separated from the main hospital so that to reach the operating room, the delivery room, or x-ray facilities, patients were exposed to the elements as they were wheeled across ninety feet of an open yard to the main hospital."[27] In Charlotte, North Carolina, there was "a tacit agreement between the hospital, city police and ambulance operators that black patients be sent to the inferior all-Negro Good Samaritan Hospital."[28] One outrageous incident highlighted the injustice of segregated care. It began when Hughie David, a 34-year-old black man, complained of a severe headache. His white physician, Dr. Richard James, sent him to the emergency room at Charlotte Memorial, the white hospital. When Dr. James examined his patient, he concluded that Mr. David needed immediate hospitalization for a subarachnoid hemorrhage. But since all the "Negro" beds was taken, Mr. David was sent to Good Samaritan Hospital, where there was no neurosurgeon on staff and no facilities where an angiogram could be performed. Mr. David died the following morning for lack of treatment.

In 1963 the civil rights leader Martin Luther King Jr. was arrested for defying a court order to desist from organizing nonviolent protests and sit-ins in Birmingham, Alabama, the most segregated city in the country. During his incarceration, King wrote his famous "Letter from Birmingham Jail," explaining why African Americans had lost patience with southerners' resistance to integration. Following his release from jail, a series of demonstrations by black children was met with brute force by the mayor of Birmingham. As the public witnessed peaceful demonstrators on national television being beaten by police, attacked by dogs, and blasted with high-pressure fire hoses, public opinion turned against white southerners. When Alabama governor George Wallace defiantly blocked the doorway of the University of Alabama as two black students attempted to register, declaring, "Segregation now, segregation tomorrow, segregation forever," President Kennedy determined that new federal legislation was needed.[29]

Hospitals presented a powerful barrier to civil rights objectives because they were still legally defined as private organizations and thus insulated from the legal prohibitions that applied to public entities, including the equal protection provision of the Fourteenth Amendment.[30] Ending segregation required challenging hospitals' immunity from federal oversight. In 1956 the NAACP filed the first of a dozen lawsuits against hospitals, asking the courts to declare the "separate but equal" provision of the Hill-Burton program unconstitutional and to force hospitals to integrate patient care facilities and student training and grant staff privileges to black physicians.

Some suits were dismissed. Others resulted in incremental change as hospitals made minor concessions to ward off more drastic measures. A 1959 suit against the city of Lakeland, Florida, charged that Lakeland General Hospital had received Hill-Burton funds to construct an addition to an existing hospital that had a wing reserved for black patients.[31] When the new wing became overcrowded, the hospital administrator moved all Negro patients to the old building.[32] Although the district court dismissed the case for lack of evidence, the hospital renovated the old building and began admitting patients of both races. The psychiatric and nursery facilities in the new building were also opened to both white and black patients.[33] A 1962 suit against Grady Hospital in Atlanta charged the hospital with racial discrimination in staffing practices, patient admissions, and nursing school admissions.[34] The plaintiffs asked the Court to declare the "separate but equal" provision of the Hill-Burton Act unconstitutional and to issue an injunction against the continued operation of facilities on a segregated basis. In response to the suit, the hospital opened a psychiatric ward for black patients, improved the black maternity ward, and made plans to open a black orthopedic ward. The Fulton County Medical Society admitted to active membership two black physicians who were recent additions to Grady's visiting staff.[35] Another suit, against Lynchburg General Hospital, alleged that even though the hospital had a private board, its practices fell within the scope of civil rights statutes because it was "almost a wholly tax supported institution with tax money coming from the city of Lynchburg and the state of Virginia."[36] In response, the Lynchburg hospital's board moved to transfer the hospital's assets into a private corporation.[37]

Until 1963, court decisions continued to uphold the principle that the equal protection clause of the Fourteenth Amendment did not apply to private institutions. These claims were finally overturned in the case of *Simkins v. Moses H. Cone Memorial Hospital*. The Simkins case was initiated by Dr. George Simkins Jr., a black dentist who had spearheaded a drive to integrate Greensboro, North Carolina's public golf course. When Moses Cone Hospital denied admission to his patient, a man with an abscessed third molar, Simkins called a lawyer who had worked on other integration cases. On further digging, they learned that Moses Cone had received $1,269,950 in federal Hill-Burton funds. Simkins and the NAACP filed a lawsuit against Moses Cone and the other segregated Greensboro hospital, Wesley Long, charging unequal treatment under the law.

For the first time the Department of Justice intervened on behalf of the plaintiffs, arguing that the government had an obligation to protect citizens from unconstitutional action made possible by operation of a federal statute. In 1962 the U.S. District Court, Fourth Circuit, dismissed the complaint on the grounds that the hospital was private in character and therefore beyond the reach of the Fourteenth Amendment. Participation in the Hill-Burton program "in no way transformed hospitals into public agencies subject to federal constitutional inhibitions against discrimination." Simkins appealed the decision, and on March 2, 1963, the Fourth Circuit Court of Appeals ruled that the statute that provided the legal basis for the "separate but equal" clause of Hill-Burton was unconstitutional.[38] Because the hospital received federal funds, it was not a private entity but an "arm of the state" and thus subject to the Fourteenth Amendment. The *Simkins* decision prohibited internal segregation in any facility on the basis of race, creed, or color, banned hospitals and other health care facilities from denying staff privileges on the basis of race, and asserted that all benefits associated with staff privileges had to be available without discrimination.[39] It thus not only challenged the constitutional basis of the practices and procedures that had guided Public Health Service funding decisions for 17 years but also directly contradicted the key premise that had protected hospitals and physicians' sovereign control of the health care system.

The Public Health Service first responded to the *Simkins* ruling by issuing new Hill-Burton regulations that expanded the definition of nondiscrimination. Under the new definition any institution applying for Hill-Burton funds had to prove that it did not discriminate in admissions, room assignments, or staff privileges. The problem was that the Public Health Service had little authority to force hospitals to comply, because the regulations only applied to *pending* applications.[40] Although projects approved on the "separate but equal" basis were unconstitutional, HEW could take action only against a hospital that sought further federal assistance.[41] Hospitals that had violated their nondiscrimination assurances in the past could not be asked to repay federal funds that had been improperly used.[42] The Public Health Service also did not respond forcefully because staff in its local offices had deeply embedded ties to local political structures and were satisfied to leave the resolution of conflicts to local officials.[43]

A June 1964 HEW survey found that all 11 Deep South states still had statutes—enforced through fines or imprisonment—mandating segregation by race.[44] Even though these statutes often violated hospitals' nondiscrimination assurances, Public Health Service officials decided they could not intervene unless a court ruled "the applicable portion of the statute invalid or inoperative." If no court decision existed, the Public Health Service would rely on the opinion of the state attorney general. While these statutes likely would eventually be judged unconstitutional, the Public Health Service could "have little effect on an applicant who may be subject to local enforcement efforts."[45]

By 1964 HEW's cautious approach had created pressures from without and within. As civil rights had moved to the forefront of the national political agenda, members of Congress became openly contemptuous of Public Health Service policies. Senator Harrison Williams (D-N.J.) complained to a Public Health Service official:

> Your description is . . . of an agency following a narrow interpretation of the letter of the law and wholly ignoring the intent of the law. By stating that Hill-Burton does not specifically outlaw segregation once the patient has been admitted into the hospital, you are, in effect, adopting the principle of separate but equal facilities. Considering that the United States Supreme Court, in a unanimous decision, declared this doctrine unconstitutional, I find it hard to accept your position. I cannot think that a Federal agency must continue to operate, some eight years after the Court's decision, in a manner that perpetuates this principle.[46]

Within the Department of Health, Education, and Welfare, new staff members appointed by the Kennedy administration also pushed for change. Lisle Carter, HEW deputy assistant secretary, angrily asked whether segregated facilities could ever be nondiscriminatory.[47] HEW assistant secretary James Quigley argued that it was imperative that the Public Health Service reconsider its position in regard to the Hill-Burton program: "whatever justification there may have been for the original interpretation at the time it was made in the late 1940s, which permitted internal segregation, no such justification exists in 1963." Quigley feared that "if we do not act in this area quickly and effectively, we are going to have pickets outside our door one of these mornings."[48]

The first bill prohibiting any institution that practiced segregation from receiving federal funding had been proposed in the House in 1957 by Representative Adam Clayton Powell (D-N.Y.), a black civil rights activist.[49] The measure was defeated by a vote of 123 to 70, as were bills introduced in succeeding years. The *Simkins* ruling lent the legitimacy of the courts (and by implication the Constitution) to the issue. When Congress enacted the Civil Rights Act of 1964, the watershed racial legislation of the century, the Powell amendment became Title VI. Title VI stated that "no person in the United States shall, on the grounds of race, color or national origin, be excluded from participation in, be denied the benefits of, or be subject to discrimination under any program receiving federal assistance."[50] No longer would racial discrimination by any private organization that received federal funds be tolerated.

Title VI applied to more than 400 federal programs administered by 33 agencies. Next to the courts, HEW became the foremost government agent for changing the nation's racial patterns. HEW had the largest Title VI enforcement office in the federal government. It was responsible for coordinating all compliance investigations in all its programs. Each regional agency in turn was responsible for carrying out day-to-day enforcement activities.[51] This arrangement meant that regional managers and field staff who for decades had complied with local practices that promoted racial segregation now became Title VI compliance investigators.

HEW's task was complicated by loopholes inserted into Title VI by southern congressmen.[52] One provision prohibited federal officials from applying sanctions until they demonstrated that compliance could not be secured voluntarily. Others specified that any regulations adopted had to be approved by the president, that funds could not be terminated to a recipient who ignored the regulations unless the proper congressional committee gave consent, and that the termination applied only to the program that was not in compliance. Title VI also excluded employment practices, which were covered by other titles of the Civil Rights Act and thus administered by other federal agencies.[53]

Within HEW the Public Health Service was given responsibility for desegregating 20,000 hospitals, 2,000 nursing homes, and over 1,000 home health agencies through a newly created Office of Equal Health Opportunities (OEHO). OEHO was headed by Robert Nash, a career civil service employee, who viewed Title VI as an opportunity to use the threat of withholding funds to demand compliance.[54] The problem was that OEHO had only 31 full-time office staff and a field staff of 72. Although Nash could investigate complaints and try to speed up integration, he had no real leverage.[55] A year after the Civil Rights Act was enacted, virtually no progress had been made in hospital desegregation.

Implementing Medicare

The leverage to enforce Title VI came from a different quarter—the implementation of Medicare. During debates in Congress over Medicare, reformers in the Social Security Administration (SSA) had purposely avoided any mention of civil rights. Robert Ball, who was now

SSA commissioner and an expert long-range strategist, recalled, "We didn't want it brought up legislatively. It would have been a big barrier to passage in the Senate, particularly if it had been clear that this was going to be applied. I think everyone knew it, but they didn't want to have to go on record about it."[56] The SSA had just begun planning the process of certifying hospitals and nursing homes for Medicare eligibility on the basis of quality, and now Medicare was swept into the Title VI compliance efforts. To become eligible for federal funds, hospitals applying for Medicare certification also had to prove they were not discriminating.

In fall 1965, representatives from the SSA met with Public Health Service officials to plan the compliance effort. They agreed that the SSA would contribute staff and help formulate rules and procedures to determine whether hospitals would be eligible for Medicare funds. The Public Health Service would take responsibility for large city hospitals and university hospitals, while the SSA would evaluate smaller hospitals, nursing homes, and home health agencies.[57] The SSA regional offices would then review all the compliance reports to see if they were complete and acceptable. About 6,900 small hospitals were immediately cleared on civil rights compliance, leaving 5,500 requiring further follow-up. A hastily assembled staff of nearly 1,000 people, 500 from the SSA and 500 from the Public Health Service, plus medical students on summer internships and outside consultants, was given a three-week crash training program in civil rights and sent south to inspect hospitals and decide if they were complying with the law.

In many respects, the SSA was the ideal government agency to implement Title VI. It had field and regional offices already operating to administer Social Security as well as a large staff of managers and field representatives. It had just issued 19 million Medicare cards, opened 100 district offices, and hired thousands of people to implement Medicare. The SSA was also the only federal agency that was relatively free from both national and local political pressures, because benefits were not provided through local relief authorities but went directly to beneficiaries.[58] The SSA also had a policy legacy that was compatible with civil rights objectives. Its historical agenda was to protect the vulnerable; its clients were the elderly, the widowed, and the disabled. As Robert Ball explained:

From the very foundation of the social security program, our objective has been to provide courteous, efficient service and equal treatment under the law to all claimants. Our training activities have always stressed this. Our legislative proposals . . . have always been prepared with this in mind. . . . The whole process of certifying the eligibility of providers of services, including their compliance with Title VI of the Civil Rights Act, is merely an extension of these principles to a new group of beneficiaries.[59]

The same could not be said of the Public Health Service. Its state agencies, which had been involved in the certification of segregated hospitals for Hill-Burton for decades, now had to confront these same hospitals and demand they change their practices. Said one Public Health Service physician involved in the effort, "I am not sure they were 100 percent enthusiastic about the task. They lived in those communities."[60]

Yet SSA officials had struggled for Medicare for more than a decade. Ending racial segregation while trying to implement a new program that had been resisted by physicians every step of the way seemed a daunting task to Robert Ball:

It seems to me that one of the greatest threats to the successful administration of this pioneering program of health insurance is the fear that hospitals and the medical profession have of federal interference. If our first contact with them, even before the first agreement is signed or the first benefit is paid, is for the Social Security Administration to inspect the hospitals for Title VI compliance, we will be putting an unnecessary barrier in the way of getting . . . off to a good start. . . . I do not believe that we can be asked to do more than what is inherent in the social security responsibility without serious risk.[61]

Using Medicare certification to determine Title VI compliance might damage delicate public relations surrounding the new program. As Ball explained:

The first hard news coming out of implementation of the hospital insurance program would be controversy over whether certain providers of service [discriminate]. . . . Not only would these controversies be aired in the public press long before benefits [were paid], they would be aired at the very time we are making every effort to quiet the fears of doctors and others about the Federal Government's involvement in the areas of hospital and medical insurance.[62]

To counter these fears, early in 1966 the SSA embarked on an aggressive public information campaign. Booklets explaining Title VI requirements were distributed to hospitals, nursing homes, and home health agencies. Talks were presented to labor groups, the insurance industry, religious groups, fraternal organizations, senior citizens' groups, and organizations of hospitals and physicians. The help of the AHA and the AMA was enlisted to prepare hospitals to comply with Title VI.[63] Carlton Spitzer, director of the HEW Office of Public Information, set up interviews with hospital administrators to explain SSA's objectives and allay their concerns, often encountering resistance and suspicion. He also attempted to meet with local newspaper editors to get them to run op-ed pieces on the integration effort. Many refused even to see him, such as the beefy editor who ushered him out of his office after a two-minute conversation, his hand on Spitzer's elbow, almost pushing him down a flight of stairs.[64]

To initiate the process, the surgeon general mailed all hospital administrators a letter informing them that no hospital could discriminate on the basis of race or deny staff privileges to qualified physicians who had been rejected by local medical societies because of race.[65] Satisfying these conditions placed hospital administrators on a collision course with physicians who viewed decisions about where to treat patients as their exclusive purview. As one SSA staffer fretted:

> When, because of Medicare, pressures brought on hospitals' boards for them in turn, to bring pressure on physicians to send Negro patients to what have been predominantly "white hospitals" and white patients to what have been predominantly "Negro hospitals," this can be construed as an interference with the practice of medicine. And having persuaded physicians to use hospitals without regard to race, can we maintain that they should not respect the wishes of patients who prefer to share rooms with only persons of their own race? This would seem to be interference with the practice of medicine.[66]

According to Morton Lebow, public information officer for the OEHO, physicians from the Mobile Infirmary in Alabama continued referring black and white patients to separate hospitals. When that practice was challenged, an alarmed hospital administrator declared, "You don't mean to tell me that you expect us to tell our doctors where they can send their patients?"[67] Despite their misgivings about federal intervention in the practice of medicine, most doctors willingly complied because with Medicare they would be guaranteed payment for treating the elderly, a service they had often performed free.[68]

By May 30, 1966, the SSA had a list of all institutions that were in compliance with Title VI. The next step was to develop an "action list" of hospitals not yet cleared.[69] Ball declared, "I would like to keep the Public Health Service going during the next week in moving into every area where there is a significant problem and pressing quickly for solutions. Or, if we can no longer expect voluntary compliance, to immediately sue."[70] On July 1, 1966, Medicare was put into operation. Still fighting federal intervention, AMA president James Appel suggested that hospitals in communities that opposed integration be allowed to participate in Medicare by "switching the burden of bigotry to the patients. . . . A patient who refused to accept the hospital room offered could be placed in a segregated facility, but he would then lose his Medicare payment."[71] Appel's suggestion fell on deaf ears.

Most hospitals were eager to be approved so that they could begin receiving federal funds.[72] Although they "wanted no part of being watched over by the federal government," they "wanted in because of the financial rewards offered."[73] By July 21, 1966, only 320 hospitals were not certified for Medicare. Some southern hospitals avoided complying with Title VI by doing the "HEW shuffle" during on-site inspections, moving white and black patients into new beds in "integrated" rooms and wards for the study team's visit.[74] In Alabama a local man bragged to an investigator "that they had moved some comatose white patients into rooms with black patients" to fool the investigator.[75] Those who were best at revealing these practices were the local Public Health Service examiners. As the Public Health Service physician quoted earlier explained, "The most feared investigators were white southerners. They knew what they were looking for. We were dealing with deceit at all levels. They sniffed it out."[76]

Establishing compliance in these pockets of resistance was hindered by the difficulty of measuring of racial integration. What constituted an acceptable percentage of black or white patients? In Lynchburg, Virginia, hospital administrators were informed that 13 percent of the patients had to be black before the hospital could win approval. Hospital administrators complained that the quota was too large, given the low percentage of minorities in the service area.[77]

The most controversial issue was biracial room occupancy.[78] In Alabama, several hospitals refused to assign patients to rooms with people of a different race. In Mississippi, the only threats of violence were triggered by this issue.[79] The hospital administrator in Canton was visited by four local Klansmen, who threatened to bomb the hospital if patients were placed in integrated rooms. At another Mississippi hospital, FBI agents investigated allegations of civil rights violations. When the local Public Health Service manager entered the hospital in Meridian, Mississippi (a town where three civil rights workers were murdered), for a minor operation, he shared a room with the head of the local NAACP, a symbolic act that was widely criticized by the community. But after his release the hospital made other biracial room assignments.

The regional assistant commissioner of the SSA in Atlanta, James Murray, suggested ignoring room assignments initially and granting hospitals otherwise in compliance "provisional certification." Not only would this avoid dealing with the stickiest racial issue, it would ward off complaints that the government was interfering in physicians' medical decisions. This compromise was unacceptable to OEHO head Robert Nash, who insisted that "requiring hospitals to assign patients to rooms on a nondiscriminatory basis cannot in any way be considered interference with the practice of medicine."

Tearing down racial barriers did not necessarily lead to integration. Some black patients refused to go to white hospitals, fearing they would not receive proper care.[80] For example, in one Arkansas town, patients continued to go to racially separate hospitals even though both hospitals were officially desegregated. Local administrators begged Public Health Service officials, "Tell us what we are doing wrong and we will make it right. . . . Give us some guidelines . . . give us time . . . don't shut off our hospital beds."[81] This situation created a conundrum for SSA officials, for refusing approval of a hospital could mean denying care to

Medicare beneficiaries. In Mount Bayou, Mississippi, for example, the black hospital could not meet the quality standards for Medicare approval, while the white hospital was having Title VI difficulty.[82] As a result, Medicare beneficiaries had to travel long distances to hospitals in other counties. Further, many insurance companies had canceled hospital coverage for people 65 and older the day Medicare began operating. That meant that Social Security beneficiaries who lived in counties without an approved Medicare hospital would have no insurance coverage at all. This dilemma deprived "the most needy citizens of all—the lowest income, least educated, least resourceful . . . Negro and white alike—of the benefits the law was designed to provide."[83] It also created a public relations nightmare for the SSA. As one staff member explained:

> For a long time the people of this area have been fed a steady diet of anti-government propaganda heightened of course by their deep fears of the civil rights program, but until now they have not largely tended to associate social security . . . with all this. Now I believe there is a very strong feeling that social security has gone over to the enemy.[84]

Despite these problems, significant advances were made.[85] Many hospitals admitted their first black patients, made room assignments without regard to race, removed barriers in waiting rooms, operating rooms, and cafeterias, and offered staff privileges to black physicians for the first time.[86] By October, only 12 hospitals still were not certified.[87] A few holdouts avoided complying with Title VI but received reimbursement from Medicare by billing the government under an "emergency treatment" provision. This provision allowed Medicare patients to receive care from a noncomplying hospital in the event of a life-threatening situation. Instead of using the provision on an emergency basis, these hospitals used it routinely to furnish segregated care. After Mal Schechter, the Washington editor of the journal *Hospital Practice*, publicized the fact that 86 percent of the 21,000 emergency Medicare claims filed in 1967 came from the South (more than half from Alabama and Mississippi), this flexibility was eliminated. Within 18 months nearly every large southern hospital was receiving Medicare funds on a regular basis.[88]

Conclusion

For two-thirds of a century, southern politicians had resisted national health insurance for fear that federal financing of health care services would lead to federal monitoring of racial practices. Their agenda was compatible with the desires of physicians, who had their own reasons for opposing government intervention in the health care system. Medicare realized these fears by requiring hospitals to provide health care services without regard to race. As federal officials began certifying hospitals for Medicare eligibility on the basis of quality, they also forced the hospitals to prove that they were not discriminating. In investigating charges of discrimination, however, federal officials delved into every aspect of hospital operations, from patient room assignments to physician referral networks. Thus the dismantling of racial segregation also allowed federal officials to monitor internal hospital affairs, penetrating the barrier between providers and the federal government and undermining provider sovereignty in the pursuit of racial justice.

four

Don't Rock the Boat

Medicare had to be operating by July 1, 1966. Federal officials had less than a year to notify more than 19 million Social Security beneficiaries that they were eligible for benefits, inform hospitals and physicians of their new rights and responsibilities, and appoint "fiscal intermediaries" to handle claims and process payments. Most Americans knew that Congress had passed a new health insurance program for the elderly, but few understood what benefits Medicare would actually provide or who would be eligible to receive them.

The first task was to win over the AMA, whose cooperation would be crucial to Medicare's success. On July 3 President Lyndon Johnson agreed to meet with AMA officials who had come to complain about socialized medicine. A man of electrifying energy who could be both compassionate and cruel, Johnson was a consummate politician with an "uncanny instinct for the jugular of his adversaries."[1] As the doctors sat around the table, waiting politely for the president to speak, Johnson gave them the "treatment." He first told the assembled physicians, "Your country needs your help. Your President needs your help." Would they be willing to serve in Vietnam, treating wounded civilians? When the doctors immediately responded that they would, Johnson told an aide to get the press. In front of the assembled reporters, the president praised the doctors' willingness to help the Vietnamese. Then when reporters, primed by aides, asked the physicians if they would support Medicare, Johnson replied indignantly, "Of course, they'll support the law of the land." Turning to AMA president James Appel, he said, "You tell him." "Of course, we will," Appel meekly replied. A few weeks later the AMA publicly announced its intention to support Medicare.[2]

94

Although the battle appeared to have been won, in truth it had only begun. Appel was a moderate in AMA circles, and when Dr. Milford Rouse, former speaker of the House of Delegates, assumed office, he was less conciliatory. He made speeches attacking Medicare, refused to accept Medicare patients, and urged other doctors to do the same. On August 12, 1965, the Association of American Physicians and Surgeons published a *New York Times* op-ed piece telling physicians to boycott Medicare.[3] Some physicians defiantly flaunted their disdain for federal officials. Others complied, recognizing, as Ohio doctor Jack Schreiber did, that "Medicare's here to stay. We aren't bitter and we aren't soreheads. But we do plan to protect the doctor-patient relationship from outside interference."[4]

Notifying Beneficiaries

The task of notifying current Social Security beneficiaries as well as the thousands of people who were nearing 65 but not yet receiving benefits fell to SSA officials.[5] Their job was made infinitely more complex by the different requirements for Part A, the hospital benefit, and Part B, physicians' services. Everyone eligible for Social Security benefits would automatically receive Part A, but Part B was voluntary. People who didn't sign up for Part B coverage by March 31 would have to wait for the next enrollment period, which would not be for two years. Getting people signed up was a pressing priority, because most private insurance companies immediately dropped coverage of any services included in Medicare. Some canceled their coverage for people over 65 entirely.[6]

The SSA had had years to plan for Part A, but Part B was added at the last minute. To get people enrolled in Part B, the SSA embarked on a massive public information campaign. Press releases were sent to local newspapers and handed out to newspaper columnists. Posters were hung in Social Security offices, drugstores, and community centers telling people how to enroll. Messages were broadcast on popular radio shows, especially those that appealed to older audiences, such as *Bring Back the Bands* and the *Eddie Arnold Show*. Films were distributed to religious, fraternal, labor, and civil rights organizations.[7] Every Social Security beneficiary received at least three letters as reminders to sign up for Part B. The SSA also worked with the Office of Economic Opportunity, which ran Johnson's antipoverty programs, to do outreach in inner cities and among the homebound elderly. Special mailings were sent to nursing home administrators, urging them to tell their patients about Part B.[8] Most older people welcomed the new program, but some remained suspicious. John Sterusky became so annoyed after he received a sixth letter that he scrawled across it, "Rec'd 6 of these. Are you nuts? For the sixth time, NO."[9]

Despite this effort, thousands of people missed the deadline to enroll. Some discarded the notices, thinking they were junk mail. Others lost the letters or failed to enroll because they incorrectly presumed that their existing insurance policies would still cover physicians' services. Even with these slip-ups, in less than six months 88 percent of the people eligible for Part B had signed up.

Implementing Part A

In designing Medicare, federal officials had agreed that hospitals would be fully reimbursed for their costs, physicians would be paid their "usual and customary" fees, and private insurers would handle claims, inspect providers, and review billed costs.[10] SSA commissioner Robert Ball explained, "By and large, our posture at the beginning was one of paying full costs but not intervening very much in the way hospitals, or at least the better ones, conducted their business."[11] There would be no federal intervention in the sacred doctor-patient relationship. As Section 1801 of the Medicare legislation declared:

> Nothing in this title shall be construed to authorize any Federal officer or employee to exercise any supervision or control over the practice of medicine or the manner in which medical services are provided, or over the selection, tenure or compensation of any officer or employee of any institution, agency or person providing health services; or to exercise any supervision or control over the administration or operation of any such institution, agency or person.[12]

In keeping with this hands-off policy, groups of hospitals and nursing homes were allowed to choose their own "fiscal intermediaries" to administer Part A payments. The fiscal intermediaries were supposed to evaluate claims, determine whether charges were valid and consistent with prevailing rates, and make the payments from federal Medicare funds. To further appease the providers, any hospital that disagreed with the nomination of its group could pick a different intermediary. The SSA then had to negotiate contracts with the intermediaries to cover their administrative costs and work out the operating details.[13]

Medicare reinforced the cozy relationship between insurers and hospitals in several ways. Under the terms of the legislation creating Medicare, the SSA could contract with one national organization that would then subcontract with local organizations, an arrangement tailored for Blue Cross, whose various member plans were represented nationally by the Blue Cross Association (BCA). During the planning period, the BCA was paid a fee to participate in establishing Medicare regulations and contract provisions. When the BCA submitted a huge bill for start-up expenses, SSA officials complained, leading to a "tug-of-war."[14] But SSA officials grudgingly paid the bill. The AHA then nominated the BCA to administer Medicare and urged hospitals and nursing homes to nominate Blue Cross as their fiscal intermediaries.[15] As a result, 80 percent of the fiscal intermediaries chosen were Blue Cross organizations.[16]

During the numerous hearings held on Medicare, Congress had never debated the wisdom of allowing the private insurance industry to perform these critical administrative functions. The only time the issue was raised was on the Senate floor after the Medicare bill had passed both committees, when Senator Wayne Morse (D-Ore.) warned:

> These are non-governmental agencies whose basic commitment is not to the beneficiaries. . . . Blue Cross is essentially a creature and instrumentality of the hospitals. . . . while Blue Cross can legitimately serve as the agent of the hospitals in dealing with the government, it cannot possibly serve as the agent of the government.[17]

As soon as Medicare was enacted, the SSA began secret negotiations with the AHA and Blue Cross to determine the formula for reimbursing hospitals. The AHA "had a large voice" in these negotiations, worrying Senator Clinton Anderson that HEW was "going too far to win broad support."[18] SSA actuary Robert Myers, too, had doubts: "I had thought that Blue Cross, by being our fiscal intermediary, would be on our side in the necessary collective bargaining with the hospitals so as to see that we get an equitable and adequate rate structure. However, the approach . . . seems to be leaning in the other direction."[19] As negotiations proceeded, members of Congress complained that they could not get copies of minutes and reports. Finally, a set of general principles was released on May 2, 1966, just two months before Medicare would begin operating. The principles adopted specified that hospitals would be reimbursed retroactively for all "allowable" expenses plus a 2 percent bonus above their actual costs with no upper limit. Included as allowable costs were basic services, compensation for administrators and physicians who were hospital employees, hospital supplies, drugs prescribed in hospitals, depreciation on buildings and equipment that had been purchased with Hill-Burton funds, and loosely defined public relations costs including dues to professional organizations, professional conferences, lobbying, and even antiunion campaigns.[20] Alarmed, Senator Russell Long (D-La.), chairman of the Senate Finance Committee, expressed "grave concern" that program costs would far exceed original estimates.[21]

Medicare payments for nursing home care were implemented six months after the rest of the program began operating, on January 1, 1967. The legislation specified that Medicare would cover all charges for the first 20 days of skilled nursing care in an extended-care facility following a hospital stay, but only for the condition or illness that led to the hospitalization. For the next 80 days, Medicare would also pay for all but $5 a day. Over the objections of the SSA, the for-profit nursing home industry lobbied Congress and won support for an amendment allowing private nursing homes to be reimbursed for these allowable charges plus a 7.5 percent profit, which they argued was a "reasonable return on equity capital investment."[22] Then for-profit hospitals and nonprofit nursing homes began demanding the same return on their Medicare patients.[23] Unwilling to upset these providers, the SSA agreed. One of the few conditions imposed was that hospitals had to agree to accept the government payment and not charge patients an additional sum. One skeptical federal official noted, "We didn't want a hospital or physician to say, We'll take cost for all the aged that are poor but when we get a nice, juicy one, we'll charge our regular charges which are more."[24]

The sole cost containment provision in Medicare specified that participating hospitals had to appoint a utilization review board to ensure that hospital admissions were medically necessary, a provision that the AMA derided as "an example of governmental interference with the practice of medicine."[25] Since patients only entered hospitals on the recommendation of a physician, that involved monitoring physicians' traditional gatekeeping role. The SSA, reluctant to aggravate physicians, only rarely enforced utilization review standards.[26] Even so, physicians were furious that they could no longer admit patients simply by asking for a bed but now had to sign forms certifying that the admission was medically necessary. One doctor fumed, "The degree and the amount of federal control exerted on a local level through the power of the purse string is simply fantastic to behold."[27] Another doctor complained, "After a while, the federal government will be practicing medicine and doctors will just be the errand boys."[28] But the utilization review committees had no formal criteria for determining whether admissions were necessary and no power to deny payment. In most cases the review committees functioned ineffectively; in some cases they did not function at all.

Although the fiscal intermediaries were supposed to evaluate costs, most plans essentially abdicated this responsibility by subcontracting hospital audits to independent accounting firms such as Price, Waterhouse, which didn't challenge charges submitted for payment.[29] Blue Cross and other insurers simply became administrators, handling claims from patients but exerting no controls. In 1965 alone hospital daily charges jumped 16.5 percent, and between 1967 and 1973 Blue Cross administrative costs for Medicare Part A increased 201 percent.[30] Inflation in health care costs was also triggered by hospital supply companies that charged hospitals five times the regular price for such items as scissors, tape measures, and furniture. Investment analysts began telling clients that hospital supplies were a good investment because they were recession-proof.[31] Actuary Robert Myers decried this "intolerable and deliberate" draining of the Medicare trust fund, to no avail.[32]

Implementing Part B

Like Part A, Part B would also be administered by private insurance companies that would serve as "carriers" to handle claims and pay physicians' bills.[33] One hundred and thirty-six insurers submitted proposals.

Among them were nearly all the large commercial insurers. As a general rule, the SSA selected Blue Shield in areas where it was strong and commercial insurers where they had a large share of the market.[34] By July 1966 19 Blue Shield plans and 9 commercial companies had signed contracts to administer Part B. The commercials included the three power-houses—Aetna Life, Mutual of Omaha, and Prudential.[35] In a few states, the state medical society was allowed to administer Part B. The Rhode Island Medical Society won the contract in its state, but the Mississippi Medical Society was rejected in favor of Travelers Life. Mississippi physicians, who were "disgruntled" by the decision, demonstrated their discontent "by not making much effort to cooperate or even communicate with [Travelers]."[36]

Part B payments were based on a fee-for-service formula that guaranteed physicians full payment for "prevailing" charges.[37] A charge was considered reasonable as long as it was consistent with the doctor's customary charge and not radically higher than the average charge for that service in the area. Each carrier was supposed to keep a file on each participating physician, showing what was charged for a particular service. Some carriers made a real attempt to monitor providers. For example, Travelers Life rejected a claim of $250 for removal of an eye and reduced the payment to $180 as consistent with prevailing charges in the area.[38] Other carriers were less responsible. More than two years after Medicare began operating, 14 carriers had yet to develop procedures for determining physicians' "customary" charges or whether charges billed to Medicare were "reasonable." By the time controls were put into effect, they were too late. As one Senate staffer complained, "They closed the barn door quite belatedly. Because of the length of the delay the carriers no longer have any way of telling what a physician's charges were before Medicare started."[39]

The fact that Medicare contained no controls on doctors' fees was speedily communicated to local medical societies, "not only to prepare doctors for July 1 but to help them adjust fees." As one aide cynically noted, the prospect of Medicare payments based on customary charges was "serving as an incentive to extremely sudden realization on the part of many physicians that their present fees [were] inadequate."[40] In the past, physicians had often charged what they thought a patient could pay. With Medicare they abandoned this practice and charged indigent patients the same as more affluent patients. Dr. Brendan Mylans defended this practice:

I do not represent the ultra-conservative nit-wit branch of the American Medical Association. . . . However, in all fairness one must point out that . . . most physicians . . . even the most grasping, have treated some patients for nothing, or for a nominal sum. . . . However, now that the Government has assumed financial responsibility for the medical care of these patients, it is hardly fair to ask physicians to donate their services to the Government.

As one physician phrased it, "I am very glad to do charity work for my patients, but I certainly do not regard the Federal Government as an object of charity."[41] Some physicians made "gang" visits to nursing homes, seeing large numbers of patients without examining them individually, then charged Medicare for individual exams.[42] Unwilling to rock the boat because of "their preoccupation with having everything neatly in order by July 1," federal officials ignored these dubious practices.[43] Yet there were also legitimate reasons for costs to rise, as many older patients were now receiving medical care that they hadn't been able to afford previously.

Physicians also demanded the right to bill their patients directly and then let the patient be reimbursed by the insurance carrier. They preferred direct billing because there would be no government oversight and thus no limit on fees.[44] SSA officials objected that direct billing could create financial hardships for patients who might have to wait weeks or months to be reimbursed and advocated instead the "assignment" method of billing. Under the assignment method, patients would sign over their Medicare benefits to the physician, who would then be reimbursed by the government. The problem was that physicians who took assignment would not be allowed to charge more than what the insurance carrier deemed to be reasonable. Naturally, physicians objected to mandatory assignment on the grounds that it would lead to government regulation. One doctor mistakenly argued, "When the doctor sends a bill to the federal government [although the bill would actually go to the carrier], it will be scrutinized to see whether it's reasonable or not."[45] To avoid antagonizing doctors further, the SSA allowed direct billing, even though patients often had to pay the difference between what the physician charged and what the carrier allowed.

The entirely predictable result was that average fees for office visits immediately shot up. General practitioners' fees rose 25 percent, internists' 40 percent. Yet the fees of pediatricians, who treated children and thus had no Medicare patients, remained constant.[46] As one physician admitted:

> No health care program has ever strained the ethics of the medical profession as Medicare is doing. The temptation to chisel is enormous. . . . I'll admit that I try to take as much Medicare money from Uncle Sam as I possibly can. From what I've seen and heard, a lot of other doctors are doing the same. . . . Before Medicare I individualized the fee on every case. . . .Those days are gone forever. Now with Medicare patients, we doctors charge our "usual fee" for everything.[47]

With hospitals reimbursed for whatever they charged plus 2 percent, physicians paid their "customary" fees, suppliers totally unregulated, extended care facilities guaranteed 7.5 percent profits, a stepped-up demand for services, and insurance companies simply accommodating, there was neither the will nor the mechanism to contain costs.[48] Concerned that inflation was occurring even before Medicare took effect, in December 1965 Senator Anderson scheduled Finance Committee hearings to investigate the contractual arrangement between the government and the providers.[49] It was the first time Congress had ever conducted hearings on a program before it began. Testimony suggested that SSA officials were being overwhelmed by the provider groups as "Blue Cross, Blue Shield and other carriers . . . rushed to get state approval of increased rates before July 1."[50] When Senator Anderson proposed revising reimbursement formulas, he was barraged with complaints from hospitals and doctors. Four years later an investigation found that Medicare paid more than other Blue Shield contracts and that carrier performance was "erratic, inefficient, costly."[51]

Implementing Medicaid

Medicaid was not really a new program: it was basically an expansion of the Kerr-Mills program, which provided federal grants to the states to fund health care for the aged poor. Medicaid increased federal funds to the states but allowed states to decide how generous benefits would be or whether there would even be a state program. States that established Medicaid programs had to provide hospital care, physician services, and skilled nursing home services, but the amount of services required was not specified. State Medicaid plans had to include the *categorically needy*, which referred to recipients of old-age assistance (OAA), aid to the blind, and Aid to Families with Dependent Children (AFDC). States also could choose to include the *medically needy*, people whose income was too high to qualify for cash assistance but was insufficient to pay their medical expenses.[52] Most often, the medically needy were nursing home residents whose care costs exceeded their income.

Medicaid required the states to designate a single agency to administer the program. Many local Blue Cross plans, encouraged by Blue Cross of America, bid to implement Medicaid and won contracts in 23 states.[53] Other states administered the program themselves through state health departments.[54] Medicaid hospital payments were based on "reasonable costs" and thus completely open-ended. However, physicians were paid a set fee, as they had been in the state welfare medical programs before Kerr-Mills and in Kerr-Mills.[55] States that were already paying the health care expenses of the medically needy through Kerr-Mills could "buy in" to the Medicare program by paying the Part B premium and any coinsurance and deductibles. The buy-in allowed states to shift some of the health care costs of the elderly to the federal government. Since Medicare fees were unregulated, soon the "medical societies [were] plumping for States to buy in" because of the "inviting prospect of Part B fees."[56]

Sensing easy federal money, the states began pressuring HEW to implement Medicaid quickly. In the rush to begin operating Medicaid, some of the same administrative problems that plagued Medicare occurred, but with greater variation across states. Those that had smoothly operating Kerr-Mills programs, such as Pennsylvania and California, had plans ready before the federal guidelines were even written. The California program offered comprehensive benefits, including inpatient and outpatient care and a wide range of preventive and rehabilitative services. In other states the agencies responsible for administering Medicaid failed to determine "customary charges" for services, audit hospital books, or assist hospitals in setting up their utilization review programs. In states where Blue Cross administered Medicaid, auditors noted excessive and unaccountable payments for administrative costs.[57]

Within two years Medicaid was absorbing an increasing share of state revenues, crowding out spending for other social services. In New York, "medically needy" was defined so liberally that nearly half the state's residents could have qualified for benefits. In 1967 Congress sought to rein in costs by severely restricting the definition of "medically needy" to 133 1/3 percent of the AFDC eligibility level. States could continue to provide benefits to higher income individuals would receive no federal match. As a result, the potential number of Medicaid recipients dropped by 750,000 in 1968 and 900,000 in 1969 but also led to howls of protest from the states.[58] In 1971 new regulations allowed states to pay less than full "reasonable costs" for hospital care for the poor.[59] But when the New York legislature attempted to impose a ceiling on Medicaid expenditures, the hospitals sued and won a ruling that they had to be paid the full cost of services provided to Medicaid patients.[60]

Controlling Costs

By the end of the 1960s, the costs of the war in Vietnam and rising prices for energy and health care had created record budget deficits and inflation, ending two decades of economic growth and close to balanced budgets.[61] As the country's economic woes mounted, the health care system came under intense scrutiny for encouraging waste and inefficiency. No one could explain why there was a $49 a day difference in hospital charges between two hospitals in the same community serving similar patient populations, why patients in Philadelphia stayed in the hospital two days longer on average than patients in any other part of the country, or why there was no rational system of planning or coordination of resources with needs. In the Seattle area, for example, occupancy rates in some hospitals were below 50 percent, yet the city planned to build another 500 beds.[62]

When Richard Nixon became president in 1968, he proclaimed that the health care system faced a "massive crisis": "Unless action is taken ... to meet that crisis within the next two or three years, we will have a breakdown in our medical care system."[63] The solution would not come from the commercial insurance companies, who never viewed their mission as cracking down on the providers but simply responded to cost increases by increasing coinsurance and deductibles, reducing the scope of benefits, or raising premiums.[64] Nor would a solution come from Blue Cross, whose primary mission seemed to be protecting the hospitals. When Pennsylvania's insurance commissioner held hearings to determine how hospital charges were calculated, Blue Cross officials refused to release their records: "We do not believe any responsible public purpose would be served by the indiscriminate release of the detailed information relating to salaries, other operating expenses and financial stability."[65]

Some concerted government response was required. The question was what form it would take. Although Nixon was a firm believer in the free market and ideologically opposed to wage or price controls, his economic advisors convinced him that inflationary pressures would continue to mount unless the government intervened in the wage- and price-setting process. Early in 1971 Nixon announced his New Economic Policy. It would involve a mandatory wage-price freeze for 90 days followed by a 2 to 3 percent yearly limit on average price increases and a 5.5 percent cap on wage hikes.[66] Medical care was singled out for special treatment, with physicians' fee increases capped at 2.5 percent annually and rises in hospital charges limited to 6 percent. Within a few months it appeared that the inflationary psychology had been broken. From August to November, the consumer price index rose by only 2.9 percent. But there were pressures to end the freeze from the start. Congress was bent on exempting some areas from control, and commercial insurers argued that the freeze on hospital charges and physicians' fees had halted new sales. More worrisome was that the administration might also freeze insurance premiums.[67] To allay these concerns, Nixon met personally with insurance company executives and promised not to include insurance rates in the price controls.[68]

The question was how to undo the controls without damaging the economy and creating another inflationary surge. In January 1973 the mandatory controls were replaced by voluntary guidelines. Immediately the stock market plunged and consumer prices soared. By April food prices were up 28 percent. Nixon restored the freeze in June for another 60 days, then began a process of dismantling all wage and price controls, industry by industry.[69] When the freeze was lifted for most goods and services, the controls remained on health care and three other key industries. Congress allowed these controls to expire in April, resulting immediately in another sharp increase in physician fees and hospital charges.

Some formal apparatus had to be established to monitor health care costs permanently. The utilization review boards had proved to be largely ineffectual. A second stab at monitoring costs was included in the 1972 amendments to the Social Security Act. The amendments mostly concerned the Social Security program, but they also made several important changes to Medicare. The most notable change was to extend Medicare to people who were eligible for disability insurance, a proposal that had been in the works since 1967 but had been vehemently opposed by the AMA, whose president, Carl Ackerman, argued that disabled persons who were financially needy could be covered under Medicaid.[70] Although the legislation passed both the House and Senate in 1970, it got hung up as part of broader negotiations over Medicare and was finally incorporated into the 1972 amendments. The amendments also allowed Medicare beneficiaries to choose coverage through a health maintenance organization. A little-noticed provision called for professional standards review organizations (PSROs) to be created to review hospital admissions and develop "standard practices."[71] Because the provision was attached to the amendments, it generated less controversy than it otherwise might have on its own.

The concept of PSROs had come out of a series of Senate Finance Committee hearings investigating the implementation of Medicare. During the hearings, it became evident that many of Medicare's problems stemmed from widespread abuses by providers and that Medicare's intermediaries and carriers had failed to prevent these practices.[72] One solution proposed was to create "program review teams" consisting of physicians, health care professionals, and consumers. The review teams would have authority to evaluate the care given to Medicare and Medicaid patients and deny payments for care deemed unnecessary. Upon learning of the proposal, the AMA countered that the monitoring should be done by state medical societies, a suggestion the Senate Finance Committee staff rejected as "totally self-serving." It would, in effect, turn "responsibility for review over to state medical societies with virtually no accountability."[73] Instead the Finance Committee proposed a stricter method of ensuring accountability through PSROs. The PSROs would be responsible for all medical care provided to Medicare patients to ensure that only medically necessary services were provided.[74] To guide the utilization review and identify inappropriate care, the PSROs would establish a set of professional standards or guidelines for medical care. Although the PSROs would include physicians, they would not be operated exclusively by state medical societies.

As the legislation moved through congressional committees, the AMA lobbied vigorously against it and succeeded in watering it down considerably. National norms and mandatory preadmission certification for elective surgery were eliminated, review of outpatient care was prohibited, a requirement was added that the majority of the committee members be physicians, and restrictions were placed on government control of the PSROs data. By 1974 more than 200 physician-staffed PSROs had been established. In most cases, responsibility for review was contracted to hospitals instead of an outside organization, further weakening their effectiveness.[75] Even though the PSROs had the authority to deny payments to physicians, they rarely applied sanctions because physicians generally were reluctant to challenge their colleagues.[76]

The following year, the medical component of the consumer price index rose 15 percent.[77] When HEW suggested more stringent regulations on PSROs in 1976, the Association of American Physicians and Surgeons sued the federal government, claiming the regulations were unconstitutional.[78] Persistent opposition from physicians caused the PSROs to flounder, and five years later no statistical profiles on length of stay for various diagnoses had been established and no sanctions against hospitals that deviated from national standards had been applied.[79]

In 1974 Congress also enacted a new health planning law, the National Health Planning and Resource Development Act. The legislation created a nationwide system of health systems agencies that would be run by consumer-dominated boards, not by physicians. Their task was to draw up three-year plans, review proposals for new projects, and ensure that new federal expenditures be demonstrably beneficial. The exclusion of physicians led AMA president Russell Roth to complain that physicians "had been relegated to a minor role."[80] His concerns were never realized, for although the health systems agencies were supposed to monitor the use of federal funds, they had no decision-making power and ultimately failed to exert any influence on cost increases.

Conclusion

Under Medicare the federal government poured virtually unlimited public resources into financing care for the aged and the poor, turning health care into a profitable enterprise for physicians, hospitals, and insurance companies. As what had been largely a charitable, ostensibly noncommercial enterprise became a growth industry, costs skyrocketed.

With the federal government unable to contain rising costs through price controls, PSROs, or health systems agencies, advocates of national health insurance now argued that the problem could be solved only by entirely revamping the health care system and placing responsibility in the hands of one purchaser, the federal government. However, the reformers' task was infinitely more complex than it had been in the 1940s. The need to contain costs diminished the clarity of the message. What problems would national health insurance solve? It would surely need to rationalize the payment system as well as cover people under age 65 who had no health insurance. It would also need to confront an irrational distribution of physicians across regions and between cities and rural areas. One hundred and thirty-four counties had no doctor. That meant that residents of towns such as Tilden, Illinois (population 1,000), had to go to neighboring towns to get medical care. When a little boy from Tilden was struck by a car while riding his bike, the town's mayor, Lawrence Campbell, personally rushed the child to the hospital, but all three doctors were out on call. The child died the following morning. Mr. Campbell later angrily declared, "I still feel that if that boy had immediate attention," his life might have been saved.[81] And any national health insurance plan would have to revamp a hospital system that had grown haphazardly since World War II, with many hospitals operating like private corporations, pursuing gain and rewarding expansion and utilization.[82] Could national health insurance accomplish all these tasks?

five

Cost Containment versus National Health Insurance

The year 1968 was a tumultuous one. In the first six months, protesters staged more than 200 demonstrations against the war in Vietnam. In April, riots erupted in 168 cities following the assassination of civil rights leader Martin Luther King Jr. In June presidential candidate Robert Kennedy was shot by an Arab nationalist angered over RFK's support for Israel. When Lyndon Johnson announced he would not run for reelection, the Democrats faced a bruising battle among three candidates—Georgia governor George Wallace, who played the race card to win the support of southern Democrats and blue collar workers, George McGovern, who sought to woo new constituencies of women and African Americans, and Hubert Humphrey, the consummate New Dealer. At the Democratic national convention in Chicago, 12,000 police and National Guardsmen waded into a crowd of protestors with rifles, bazookas, and flamethrowers. In the midst of chaos, the Democrats nominated Humphrey, who had to face not only his Republican challenger, former vice president Richard Nixon, but also Wallace, who had formed a third party. Wallace captured the Deep South, throwing the election to Nixon, who became president with only 43.4 percent of the vote.[1]

The chaos continued through Nixon's first year in office, with violent anti–Vietnam War protests culminating in May 1970, when National Guardsmen fired on student protestors at Kent State University, killing four and wounding nine. Outraged students on 250 campuses went on strike and then poured into Washington to lobby against the war. A group of construction workers, angry over the campus protests, struck back, attacking demonstrators in New York's financial district and storming City Hall.

With the country in turmoil, this would seem to be an inauspicious time to enact new social programs. Yet, contrary to popular perceptions, Nixon was not adverse to new social spending. During his first term in office, Congress had increased Social Security benefits significantly, added automatic cost-of-living increases, and extended Medicare to the disabled. President Nixon had also endorsed an ambitious welfare reform plan to replace Aid to Families with Dependent Children with a guaranteed annual income for the working and nonworking poor, a plan set up with incentives to encourage work among welfare recipients.[2] That plan was scrapped, but in 1972 old-age assistance was converted into a solely federal program called Supplemental Security Income (SSI), and SSI beneficiaries were granted automatic entitlement to Medicaid.[3]

In this climate, the liberal reformers who had supported Medicare felt cautiously optimistic that national health insurance would be next. Oscar Ewing declared, "Of course, it's inevitable; it's going to come because people need it."[4] Ig Falk remarked, "There is no turning back from the basic goals and policies incorporated in recently enacted public programs for health care; and . . . extension of those programs to more of the population is socially inevitable."[5] Even the director of the National Association of Blue Shield plans conceded, "The remarkable thing is the virtual absence at this point of publicly stated opposition in some form."[6]

Reviving National Health Insurance

The fight to resurrect national health insurance began in 1968 when Walter Reuther made a fiery speech before the American Public Health Association. Reuther charged that the existing health care system was disjointed, antiquated, and obsolete, a nonsystem of care.[7] The only way to remove economic barriers to care and contain health care costs was through national health insurance.[8] Confronting providers with a directness that Medicare reformers never would have dared to employ, Reuther envisioned a program that would strike at the heart of the fee-for-service payment system: "National health insurance must do more than simply pay doctor bills unilaterally determined by the medical profession or simply reimburse hospitals for costs unilaterally determined by them."[9]

Why did Reuther choose this moment to pursue national health insurance? After all, in the 1960s the trade unions had negotiated increasingly generous private health benefits and had won Medicare for retirees, which shored up collective bargaining. Why replace benefits that had been won through negotiations with a government program? One reason is that Reuther, unlike Meany, had never believed that collective bargaining alone could meet all workers' needs. Rather, he felt that many problems could be corrected only through political action. By the late 1960s collective bargaining had reached its limits, as the golden age of automobile manufacturing faded in the face of competition from foreign imports. Yet health care costs continued to rise, taking an increasingly large share of the total wage package negotiated in each new contract, a situation worsened by the expense of retirees' supplemental medigap benefits. Reuther had presumed that employers in the mass production industries would respond to the proliferation of negotiated benefits by turning to the government to assume some of the costs.[10] But he was wrong. Most large firms simply folded their pension and health insurance costs into their product prices and passed them on to consumers. In this context, it made sense for the unions to pursue a federal program.

Reuther also had personal reasons for leading a drive for national health insurance. Ever since the unification of the AFL and the CIO in 1955, Reuther had been at odds with George Meany over union goals and tactics. For example, Reuther believed that the labor movement had to focus on organizing the unorganized. He became a champion of Cesar Chavez, who was trying to bring the poorly paid migrant laborers into the United Farm Workers union. When Chavez organized a boycott of nonunion grapes, Meany made a donation but otherwise refused to endorse the boycott.[11] In the 1960 election Reuther organized a UAW campaign on John Kennedy's behalf, but Meany withheld his full support. Reuther was also more proactive than Meany on civil rights and more strongly against the Vietnam War. These political differences were exacerbated by different personal styles. Reuther led an almost ascetic life. He took few vacations, had little interest in food or drink, and believed that union leaders should share the lifestyle of the workers they represented. Meany drew a large salary, had gourmet tastes in wine and food, smoked expensive cigars, and played golf, a rich man's hobby. He held AFL-CIO annual meetings at a luxurious Miami beachfront hotel and spent his free time nightclubbing, lounging around the pool, and playing gin rummy. Reuther, outraged that labor meetings were held in Florida, refused to stay in the luxurious suite reserved for him and instead moved to a cheaper hotel. Meany's cronies liked to joke that Reuther was sleeping in a linen closet, squeezing his own orange juice.[12]

After a series of increasingly hostile disputes, in 1968 Reuther pulled the UAW out of the AFL-CIO. Although Reuther hoped to enlist other CIO unions in his crusade to revitalize the labor movement, he went alone. Weeks later he tried to create a new voice for organized labor by launching the Alliance for Labor Action. The only partner he could attract was the thuggish Teamsters union, which Reuther had previously tried to expel from the AFL-CIO for corruption and whose president, Jimmy Hoffa, was currently serving a prison sentence for jury tampering.[13]

Now Reuther needed to show what the UAW, marching alone, could achieve. He opened an office in Washington, D.C., and organized the Committee of 100 for National Health Insurance, a top-notch team of trade unionists, social activists, college professors, physicians, and liberal politicians, among them Representative Martha Griffiths (D-Mich.), whose district was the home of the UAW, and Senator Ted Kennedy (D-Mass.), the roguish youngest brother of the Kennedy clan.[14] Kennedy in particular, as a member of the Senate Labor and Public Welfare Committee and widely viewed as the heir apparent to the White House, seemed well positioned to lead the cause.[15] In Reuther's vision, the Committee for National Health Insurance, as it came to be called, would design a health insurance program that would salvage the best features of the current system but overcome the built-in waste and inefficiencies.

In 1969 committee members drafted their first model bill, an ambitious plan that would fold all public and private health plans into a single federal program, called Health Security. Wary of criticism that its plan might be labeled socialized medicine, the committee promised to reorganize the health care system "in an American way" without taking over hospitals or turning physicians into government employees.[16] Instead their plan would provide incentives for physicians to create prepaid group practices, and it would force doctors and hospitals to operate within a set national health budget. Despite the rhetoric to the contrary, the committee's proposal would usurp the market of the health insurance industry by converting private benefits into a public program.

When Kennedy assumed the chairmanship of the Senate Health Sub-committee in 1971, he introduced his Health Security bill. Basic changes were needed, Kennedy proclaimed, "if we are to escape the twin evils of a national health disaster or the total federalization of health care in the 1970s."[17] His grand plan went awry in July, however, when he ran his car off a bridge on Chappaquiddick Island, Massachusetts, while driving a young campaign worker home from a party. As Mary Jo Kopechne lay trapped in the sunken car, Kennedy left the scene, apparently to hide his involvement, leaving his passenger to drown. His power and prestige threatened, Kennedy suffered an instant "political decompression" in the Senate, losing on every key issue in the next ten months.[18]

Kennedy's fall from grace was brief. By spring, polls indicated he could be the Democratic front-runner for the presidency in 1972.[19] Using his subcommittee as a forum to promote national health insurance, Kennedy held splashy hearings in cities all over the country. Everywhere he went, the press slavishly followed. When the tour ended, his subcommittee issued a report entitled "The Health Care Crisis in America." Momentum seemed to be building for some action. That fall the National Governors' Conference endorsed a proposal for national health insurance.

The AMA remained a foe of any government program. Dr. Robert Heidt, president of the Cincinnati Academy of Medicine, wrote Nixon warning that most physicians had campaigned for his election but were discomforted "to hear of your possible plans for implementing national health insurance." He closed by declaring that he hoped the president's deliberations were guided by facts "rather than by self-aggrandizing bureaucrats."[20] But after its bitter defeat over Medicare, the AMA had discovered it was better to help craft a bill friendly to the profession than work against any reform.[21] Instead of launching an advertising campaign against Health Security, the AMA unveiled its own plan, Medicredit, that would enhance the private health insurance system.[22] Under Medicredit, low-income individuals would receive a voucher to purchase a basic health insurance package, middle-income people would get a tax credit for their insurance premiums, and the government would provide grants to the states to cover the very poor, much like Medicaid.[23] But none of the AMA's former allies offered support.

Hospital administrators had benefited from cooperating with the Social Security Administration in the period leading up to Medicare and appreciated the stable source of income Medicare provided. The American Hospital Association announced that it favored expanding Medicare into a national program. As AHA President George Graham explained, "I don't have a fear of government domination. We have to work with government."[24]

The insurance industry also opposed Medicredit, concerned that an infusion of federal funds into the insurance industry in the form of a subsidy would invite federal regulation.[25] Instead commercial insurers drew up their own bill, which ironically was similar to Eisenhower's plan for reinsurance, which they had rejected in the 1950s. Senate Finance Committee chairman Russell Long (D-La.) sponsored the catastrophic coverage bill, which would make each family responsible for covering its own medical expenses by purchasing a private insurance plan. Should these expenses reach catastrophic levels, then the government would pay the excess.[26]

President Nixon opposed any sort of compulsory federal health insurance program, but the deaths of his two brothers and the financial burden his family had to bear from his brother Harold's long illness had made a lasting impression. In 1947 he had surprised party conservatives by supporting a voluntary federal health insurance plan.[27] Now, not to be outdone by Kennedy, whom he regarded as a formidable political foe despite Kennedy's personal troubles, in February Nixon announced his own health program. As White House counsel John Erlichman noted in an internal memo: "I notice . . . that Teddy Kennedy has called for a national, compulsory health insurance program. As you know, this is a demagogic ploy since we can neither afford such a program nor would it be a good thing for the practice of medicine in this country."[28] Nixon's National Health Insurance Partnership Act took a regulatory approach that encouraged the private insurance market. It centered on an employer mandate where employers would either provide health insurance for their employees directly or pay taxes to insure them through a government program. Kennedy immediately fired off a response, labeling Nixon's plan "poorhouse medicine":

> President Nixon's National Health Insurance Partnership is . . . a partnership between the Administration and the private health

insurance industry. For the private insurance industry, the Administration plan offers a windfall of billions of dollars annually. The windfall is not entirely a surplus, since elements of the Administration's proposal appear to have originated with the insurance industry itself.[29]

The employer mandate won the endorsement of the Washington Business Group on Health, an organization whose primary mission was to bring together top-level executives to exchange ideas on cost-management techniques and help firms design benefits packages that could reduce health expenses. An organization with 200 member corporations, the Washington Business Group was headed by Willis Goldbeck. A man acknowledged by both admirers and critics to be ahead of business on most health issues, Goldbeck felt that if all employers were required by law to provide health benefits for their employees, it would help level the playing field between those employers who provided generous health benefits for employees and also subsidized their dependents and those who provided no insurance coverage. Another business group, the National Leadership Coalition for Health Care Reform, composed of executives from Chrysler, Bethlehem Steel, Lockheed, Safeway, Xerox, and Georgia Pacific, also endorsed a mandated benefits approach.[30]

Nixon's plan would also provide planning grants and loan guarantees for prepaid group practices called health maintenance organizations (HMOs).[31] The original HMO idea was proposed by David Ellwood, an "evangelical" Minneapolis physician who directed the American Rehabilitation Foundation.[32] Ellwood argued that the current health care cost crisis was caused by perverse incentives that encouraged costly treatment and penalized physicians who returned patients to health. He envisioned a system where primary care doctors would serve as gatekeepers who would evaluate patients before they saw specialists or received costly tests and high-technology care. Ellwood cleverly repackaged the prepaid health plans that had been in existence since the 1940s, called them HMOs, and sold them as a pro-market solution. HMOs would be nonprofit and would use any revenues saved to improve health care or increase the number of insured patients.[33]

At first glance, it is puzzling that a proposal to increase government intervention into the delivery of health care should come from Nixon, who had had the support of the AMA in the 1968 election and who had campaigned against federal intervention into the private sector. Yet Nixon's plan was a cool political calculation. National health insurance would clearly be an important issue in the upcoming elections, and White House aides needed an alternative to Kennedy's much grander proposal. Ellwood's plan did not require an immediate expenditure of large sums, and it involved the private sector. The White House approved the initiative, and in a special health message to Congress in February 1971, Nixon made HMOs the centerpiece of his health policy.[34]

By July, 22 different bills were on the table. At one end of the continuum was the AMA's Medicredit; at the other was Kennedy's plan to collapse all existing programs into a single government plan.[35] Yet despite all the activity in Congress, there was little public demand for national health insurance. Reformers' proposals couldn't compete for media attention with the war in Vietnam, which dominated the headlines every night, and there existed no grassroots force to carry the message to the public. Nelson Cruikshank had become president of the National Council of Senior Citizens, and the seniors who had supported Medicare were now primarily concerned with issues such as obtaining prescription drug benefits and monitoring legislation that might increase their health care costs.[36] As one Committee for National Health Insurance member conceded, there was no "massive public clamor to rearrange our present health care system."[37]

The trade union movement, in disarray since Reuther withdrew the UAW from the AFL-CIO, also failed to provide a firm base of support. On May 9, 1970, Reuther was killed when the twin-engine jet he was taking to inspect the UAW's new education center slammed into a tree and burst into flames.[38] The torch was passed to Leonard Woodcock, who vowed to continue the fight. Meany endorsed Health Security and devoted several radio addresses to the issue. In a 1969 speech, he blasted the medical profession:

> [T]here is something indecent about a small group of people making a lot of money out of the misery of other people. . . . This profiteering by the providers of medical care has had its worst effects in Medicare and Medicaid. . . . Some doctors and other health care practitioners have pounced on these programs as get-rich schemes for the medical profession. . . . And, instead of controls being placed

on fees and charges . . . the burden has fallen on the disadvan-
taged people the programs were supposed to help.[39]

But health care reform was a low priority for the AFL-CIO, which
was absorbed in a battle with the Nixon administration over minority
hiring in government-funded construction projects.[40] Health care reform could wait.

Reuther's Committee for National Health Insurance, hoping to stimulate public interest in the issues, outlined an ambitious public information campaign. They would prepare educational materials, hold a rally
in Madison Square Garden, run newspaper ads across the country, and
create a national speakers' bureau. They would also hire staff organizers to drum up political support and set up a "war room" where they
would keep a district-by-district breakdown on the position of congressional candidates.[41] The public relations campaign never materialized,
however, impeded by a lack of funds and foot soldiers. Instead the band
of warriors toiled on, invisible, their hopes pinned on the fate of Ted
Kennedy.

Although Congress took no action on any of the 1972 proposals for
national health insurance, a battered, compromised experimental HMO
pilot program was enacted the following year. The AMA did everything possible to block any HMO legislation. AMA lobbyists attempted
to delay the Senate bill and defeat the House bill in committee.[42] Dr.
Malcolm Todd, who was Nixon's personal physician when he was vice
president, had ascended to the House of Delegates and was chairman
of the Physicians' Committee to Reelect the President. Todd warned
Nixon that "this HMO thing" kept coming up when physicians were
approached to contribute to Nixon's campaign reelection fund.[43] However, HMOs had the support of corporate employers, who were disturbed by rising health care costs, and the measure was enacted over
AMA opposition.

The Health Maintenance Organization and Resources Development
Act of 1973 authorized $375 million in planning grants and loans to en-
courage the development of new HMOs. It also required companies that
had 25 or more employees and that provided health insurance to offer an
HMO option.[44] HMOs that received federal support would have to offer
comprehensive benefits, charge their enrollees the same "community
rate," and allow open enrollment at least once a year, regardless of an

individual's health. These regulations made HMOs the most heavily regulated part of the health insurance system, placing them at a competitive disadvantage with other insurance plans and dampening their growth. A provision allowed Medicare beneficiaries to enroll in HMOs, but only two HMOs chose to participate.[45]

In the 1972 presidential race, Ted Kennedy, still uncertain of the effect of Chappaquiddick on his political future, announced he would not seek his party's nomination.[46] After Kennedy withdrew from the race, Wilbur Mills, the powerful chairman of the Ways and Means committee, began his own quixotic quest for the presidency, claiming in television interviews that he could defeat Nixon by sweeping the South and border states and winning the support of organized labor. Mills believed that segregation was a "dead issue" and was convinced that he could attract the African American vote. As he explained to a national audience, "I voted as I did over the years [against civil rights] because it was necessary to vote that way if I was to stay in Congress."[47]

During the 1972 election campaign, Kennedy and Mills announced that they would develop a joint national health insurance program in the spring.[48] When one of Nixon's informants leaked the news of the Kennedy and Mills plan, Nixon ordered HEW staff to meet with the Health Insurance Association of America and the AMA to devise an alternative proposal.[49] National health insurance might help the president: "Our media activities, once we find out what Mills is going to do, should start urging enactment of our health insurance proposal."[50] Nixon considered making his own major health policy statement in response but decided against it.[51] Instead he decided to emphasize the success of his wage and price controls in reducing inflation. His antiinflation measures had made "heartening progress in our fight against the increase in health care prices."[52] His staff agreed that this message was "fresher, more positive," giving the nation "one more reason why it would be wise to stay on our present course and not veer off in the directions offered by those who want a nationalized health program."[53] When Kennedy retorted that Nixon had done nothing for health care, Nixon reminded physicians that he had "introduced government action only when not to do so would result in no action at all." Further, he had "never involved the government in a manner that would seek to displace or in any way stunt the tremendous thrust and amazing ingenuity of America's traditionally private medical profession."[54]

Mills never won more than 5 percent of the vote in the primaries, and dropped out of the race after it was revealed that he had accepted $100,000 in illegal campaign contributions secretly funneled to him by Electronic Data Systems, a major processor of health insurance claims.[55] But Mills hinted that if a "draft Kennedy" movement materialized, he would be willing to run as vice president.[56] Although Kennedy and Mills got a plank included in the Democratic Party platform advocating compulsory national health care, the liberal George McGovern won a sufficient number of delegates during the primaries to capture the Democratic nomination.[57]

An astute observer of the national mood, Nixon recognized that the conservative Sunbelt was a growing force in American politics. During the campaign, he developed his "southern strategy," wooing former Wallace voters—white suburbanites, blue-collar workers, and ethnic middle-class Americans, especially those upset over school busing as a way to achieve racial balance. He appointed conservative justices to the Supreme Court, delayed school desegregation in Mississippi, and even courted the isolated Teamsters union by withdrawing his support for antistrike legislation that Republicans had been pushing.[58] One of Nixon's staunchest sources of support came from the AMA. Nixon's ally Malcolm Todd, now AMA president, advised him on how to mobilize physicians, who, he assured Nixon, were "not yet committed to socialized medicine for the U.S."[59] Nixon demolished McGovern in the election, winning 61 percent of the votes and carrying the entire (once solidly Democratic) Deep South as well as a majority of urban votes in traditional Democratic strongholds.

As Nixon embarked on his second term, an event that had occurred the previous June consumed his administration and eventually cost him the presidency. On June 17, 1972, police had arrested five men for breaking into the Watergate apartment complex in Washington, D.C. The men were in the process of attaching listening devices to telephones in offices of the Democratic National Committee. One of the men arrested was the security coordinator of the Committee to Re-elect the President. Another served on the staff of the White House Domestic Council. Although the burglary went almost unnoticed by the public, it generated furious activity at the White House, where incriminating documents were shredded and thousands of dollars paid in hush money.

When the burglars were tried in the spring of 1973, one of them, James McCord, implicated the administration. Further inquiry by the Senate indicated that there had been a cover-up at the highest level. One aide gave the shocking news that Nixon's conversations about the break-in had been tape-recorded. Hoping to quell growing public concern, Nixon appointed Harvard law professor Archibald Cox as special prosecutor. When Nixon ordered the Attorney General, Elliott Richardson, to deny Cox's request for the tapes, Richardson refused to carry out the order and resigned instead. Then the Solicitor General Robert Bork fired Cox. Outrage over what became known as the "Saturday Night Massacre" forced Nixon to appoint another special prosecutor, Leon Jaworski, who took him to court when he still refused to turn over the tapes.[60]

By the end of the year, Nixon's support on legislation in Congress had dropped to the lowest point of any president recorded. On 310 legislative votes taken that year, the White House won on only 51 percent.[61] Nixon might have weathered the scandal were it not for the seemingly endless war in Vietnam and the sorry state of the economy. Price increases ordered by the Organization of Petroleum Exporting Countries (OPEC) caused oil prices to rise 350 percent in 1973. Inflation shot up to a frightening 11 percent, causing a recession in the auto industry that then spread nationwide. As the Watergate scandal enveloped the administration, HEW secretary Caspar Weinberger was charged to draft a new health insurance bill to prove "that the government is not paralyzed."[62] Congress was likely to include health care on the agenda, Weinberger argued, and Nixon would be shut out if he did not have his own plan. At the end of 1973, Weinberger submitted a new proposal to the president, urging him to send it to Congress so that the administration could "regain the initiative in the health area."

Weinberger's plan had two parts. Both gave the insurance industry a central role. The first was the Comprehensive Health Insurance Plan, which involved an employer mandate and would be administered by private insurance companies. The second was the Assisted Health Insurance Plan, where states would contract with private insurance companies to cover low-income and high risk individuals.[63] Although administration officials worried about alienating their natural friends, "doctors, nurses, hospital administrators, insurance companies," they also did not want to appear to be "in their pocket."[64] One HEW staffer warned:

We should keep a low profile in dealing with the health special interest groups. . . . We don't want to publicly identify closely with organized medicine or the insurance industry. The key here is to work closely with these groups in developing an overall strategy for handling Congress.[65]

Nixon announced his national health insurance program in his 1974 State of the Union address. His nemesis, Ted Kennedy, labeled the plan a potential windfall for private insurance interests and announced he would oppose it.[66]

Behind the scenes, Committee for National Health Insurance members, undeterred by their failure to develop their public relations campaign, worked to formulate what they presumed would be Kennedy's new plan, one they understood had to be palatable to the private insurance industry. Conceding that it was politically impossible to exclude the insurers completely, they worried about how to control them so that they could not abuse the public interest. Ig Falk, who chaired the Technical Committee, suggested allowing private insurers to serve as fiscal intermediaries, as they did with Medicare.[67]

As the Committee for National Health Insurance toiled away in obscurity, Kennedy met secretly with Mills, and on April 2, 1974, with much fanfare, they announced their own plan, one that differed in some aspects from what committee members had in mind. Kennedy-Mills would replace the current system with a single national health insurance program that would provide a basic benefit package but otherwise preserve most aspects of the traditional health economy. It would include co-payments and deductibles, allow private insurers to serve as fiscal intermediaries, and leave room for lucrative supplementary benefits. Not unexpectedly, the AMA decried the "socialist" measure.[68] The National Federation of Independent Business called it "nothing more than a first step towards socialized medicine."[69] The AFL-CIO, furious at being excluded from the process, also denounced Kennedy-Mills as a sellout of fundamental principles. What was hardest to swallow was that Kennedy-Mills gave Blue Cross and commercial insurers a permanent role.[70] Even more odious was the sizable coinsurance and deductibles, which would place a heavy burden on low- and middle-income families.[71] The AFL-CIO told union members to press their elected representatives to delay voting on national health insurance until the following year, when they presumed a more liberal and veto-proof Congress would be in office, a reasonable hope given the toll Watergate was taking on the prospects of the Republican Party.

Nixon had his own problems with Watergate now escalating out of control.[72] In late April he finally released an edited version of the tapes, a move that satisfied neither the public nor the House Judiciary Committee. The House of Representatives began drafting articles of impeachment. By summer, new Watergate disclosures had become increasingly alarming. On July 24, the Supreme Court ordered Nixon to surrender the full tapes. Despite the uncertainty over the president's future, in August the House Ways and Means Committee met to mark up a compromise health bill, a plan Nixon seemed willing to consider to distract the public from the scandal. As White House staffer Frank Carlucci wrote to Nixon, "Last Thursday Secretary Weinberger described to you the general outlines of a proposed compromise health insurance bill offered by Chairman Mills. He understood that you wanted him to proceed to negotiate a bill within the compromise being offered."[73]

According to some observers, "The momentum for national health insurance in the Congress was greater than in virtually any other session . . . in American history."[74] The Nixon administration was eager to enact a popular program that could deflect attention from Watergate, and congressional support for health insurance was less partisan and ideological than it had been in the past. In May, an editorial in the *Washington Post* proclaimed, "The question is not *whether* the United States should have national health insurance, but *what kind* it should have."[75] Even insurance agents seemed resigned to the inevitable. In an address to members of the New Jersey and New York Insurance Associations, association president Charles Boteler told them, "We all know that national health insurance is inevitable."[76] These predictions turned out to be incorrect. On August 5 Nixon handed over the complete tapes, knowing they would damn him. Four days later he resigned.

Nixon's resignation left his successor, Vice President Gerald Ford, a nation whose faith in the presidency had been shaken and an economy headed toward recession. Still, in his first address to Congress, Ford singled out national health insurance as the major piece of domestic legislation Congress should pass that year. Senate Finance Committee chairman Long promised, "If the House sends us a bill, we will pass it."[77] Although Mills attempted to keep the ball rolling, Ways and Means became a target for lobbyists and contributions from special interests. When the committee met, AMA representatives attended the meeting and mustered 12 votes for an alternative plan similar to Medicredit with vouchers for the poor and tax credits for the middle class.[78] Labor leaders, who expected to unseat antireform Republicans in the 1974 elections, refused to support any compromise plan.[79] The insurance industry was opposed to several aspects of the measure. Further, few politicians were receiving mail on the issue from constituents, suggesting a distinct lack of public interest.[80] Unable to form a clear majority, Mills announced that the compromise measure would be tabled and that the committee would not resume consideration of national health insurance in the fall.[81]

If there were to be a future for national health insurance, it would no longer be negotiated by Mills. On October 7, the police stopped his Lincoln Continental, which was speeding with the lights off at 2 a.m. Mills staggered out, bleeding and drunk. Then his passenger, Annabel Battistella, a stripper who performed as Fannie Fox, jumped out of the car and leaped into the Tidal Basin. Mills won reelection to the House in November despite the scandal, but Democrats divested Ways and Means of its power to delegate committee assignments. Soon after Mills appeared drunk onstage at Fannie Fox's first appearance at a Boston strip club, he lost his chairmanship.[82]

During Ford's brief turn in office, the economy continued its tailspin with negative economic growth, inflation close to 12 percent and rising, and unemployment over 7 percent. The stalling economy forced Ford to retreat from his commitment to national health insurance.[83] By the end of the year, the campaign to whip inflation dominated. Following the collapse of national health insurance, Committee for National Health Insurance members regrouped to plan a strategy for the future. Gone were the grand ideas. Instead, conceding to political reality and abysmal economic forecasts, they agreed that a practical alternative would be a plan that would include all Americans but phase in benefits to various groups in a piecemeal fashion.[84] A phasing in of health insurance coverage might begin with mothers and children, then be extended to older workers and finally to the nonworking poor.[85]

In the 1976 election President Ford won the Republican Party nomination only after a bitter and divisive struggle with Ronald Reagan, the former actor turned politician and champion of the party's right wing.

Jimmy Carter, an obscure peanut farmer and one-term governor of Georgia, captured the Democratic Party nomination. The mild-mannered Carter beat Ford by a bare 2-million-vote margin. Now the economic problems that Ford had failed to address were in Carter's hands.

Shortly after he assumed office in 1977 Carter unveiled a timid anti-inflation program that relied almost exclusively on voluntary restraints by business and labor but included no mandatory controls or even any voluntary targets. Carter's modest goal was to reduce increases in the cost of living index by 2 percent. When these measures failed to have any effect, Carter waited until the end of 1978, then issued some toothless anti-inflation guidelines. The following month OPEC boosted oil prices by 14.5 percent. Gas prices soared, and by 1979 inflation hit 13 percent.[86]

Jimmy Carter Confronts the Hospital Industry

During the early months of his presidential campaign, Carter ignored health care. Later, as his candidacy appeared to be gaining ground, he met with labor leaders, whose support he would need to win the election.[87] The AFL-CIO, suspicious of Carter's credentials as a southern farmer and businessman, refused to support him, but he did win the endorsement of the UAW.[88] From the sidelines, Kennedy pushed the unions to get as much as they could from Carter, who reluctantly promised to pursue national health insurance.[89]

Shortly after Carter was sworn in as president, Kennedy began badgering him to fulfill his campaign commitment.[90] Carter promised Kennedy, "If you come up with a program, that's fine and you'll have my support if it preserves a role for the insurance companies."[91] Committee for National Health Insurance members, who would draft Kennedy's new measure, clearly understood the ground rules. The new technical director of the committee, Harvard professor Rashi Fein, acknowledged, "Private insurers had to have a role in it, and it was more than an intermediary or carrier."[92] Despite Carter's promise to Kennedy, inflation and energy costs remained the overriding issues on the national scene. Since 1966 the consumer price index had increased by 79.7 percent, hospital expenses 237 percent.[93] Before national health insurance could be considered, health care inflation had to be slowed.

The Carter administration's first attempt to rein in health care costs began in 1977 when Carter's HEW secretary, Joseph Califano, developed a seemingly simple plan for an across-the-board cap on hospital charges. One of those idealistic liberal reformers who had entered government service with the idea of making a revolution, Califano had served as Lyndon Johnson's chief advisor on domestic affairs during the 1960s. An intense and driven man who loved power and smoked four packs a day, Califano had been there to escort to class James Meredith, the first black student to be admitted into the University of Mississippi; he had worked with the Defense Department to dream up ways to bring down Fidel Castro. By comparison, hospital cost containment seemed a modest goal. The plan Califano devised would limit yearly rate increases to one and a half times any rise in the consumer price index, with a cap of 9 percent.[94] So that hospitals couldn't just shift costs from Medicare patients to privately insured patients to compensate, the cap would also apply to all private payers as well. As soon as the plan was announced, the hospital lobby began gearing up to thwart what one industry leader called its "most serious challenge."[95]

The AHA, which represented nonprofit community hospitals, formed its first political action committee and set aside a million-dollar advertising campaign fund. Then the for-profit hospitals swung into action. Investor-owned hospitals had expanded rapidly since Medicare had made hospitals such lucrative enterprises, and they were the biggest beneficiaries of inflation in the hospital sector. In just one year, from 1977 to 1978, the Hospital Corporation of America's profits rose 23.4 percent, the Medicore Company's 25.3 percent, and American Medical International's 52.3 percent. The Federation of American Hospitals, which represented for-profit hospitals, made hefty contributions to members of Congress who served on the committees that had jurisdiction over the measure, invited elected officials to speak before the group's convention, and featured interviews with favored politicians in its monthly magazine.[96]

The Federation of American Hospitals also formed a coalition with other hospital associations to devise an alternative to Califano's plan. Their Voluntary Cost Containment Program was directed by a national steering committee that, in turn, coordinated the activities of state-level committees. State committee members mailed over 23,000 letters to every hospital in the country warning that if they didn't get behind the

"Senate Emergency . . . Hospital Cost — Containment Bill"

The hospital industry opposed President Carter's efforts to enact hospital cost containment legislation. 1979, Jimmy Carter Presidential Library

voluntary effort, Carter would likely impose "inflexible and bureaucratic federal controls."[97] The Federation of American Hospitals also encouraged hospital administrators to tap the support they enjoyed in their communities. As Representative Willis Gradison (R-Oh.) noted, "Hospitals are where the babies are born and where lives are saved."[98] Hospitals were called on to enlist their network of trustees and state association executives to woo members of Congress who were wary of controls. The response of physicians and hospitals to the voluntary effort was "overwhelming."[99] According to one hospital administrator, "I filled out the forms. But we knew it was all bulls——t."[100]

Hospital cost containment received an equally hostile reception from the business community. All the key business groups—the National Association of Manufacturers, the Business Roundtable, the Chamber of Commerce, and the Washington Business Group on Health—opposed mandatory price controls.[101] The Washington Business Group on Health

prepared a report that concluded that mandatory controls would interfere with voluntary efforts currently under way and would allow the
federal government to undermine local hospital autonomy.[102] Although
preliminary discussions with Blue Cross/Blue Shield officials had indicated "they were prepared to help out," that support never materialized.[103] Carter's only business support came from the Health Insurance
Association of America, which agreed to a compromise plan: hospitals
would be allowed to use voluntary measures to control costs, but a
mandatory cap would be triggered if voluntary efforts failed to pro-
duce results.[104]

Califano's proposal never made it out of the Senate Finance Committee. Hospital opposition certainly was a factor, but equally damn-
ing was a lack of public concern. Although 65 percent of the public
favored the proposed cap, cost containment was not a high priority for
most people. Third-party payments from insurance companies to providers and low deductibles meant that most people did not feel the
impact of higher health care costs with the same immediacy as they
would an increase in the cost of groceries or gas. Secretary Califano did
receive a few letters of complaint. One woman wrote protesting a $29,764
hospital bill for her sister's one-month stay; an uninsured Georgia
woman described a $60,000 bill she had received for care of her prema-
ture infant.[105] But for the most part, no group that supported the
president's bill lobbied legislators. Representative Bill Gradison noted,
"I haven't received a single letter [on the subject]."[106]

Hospital cost containment also failed because there was dissension
even among Carter's own team about whether a ceiling would achieve
the desired result. Economists on the Council on Wage and Price Stability believed that a cap on hospital costs would not work, even if legislation could be enacted. One senior economist wrote, "The HEW proposed
standards stand virtually no chance of being accepted either by physicians or by hospitals and will almost certainly be met with opposition."[107]

Although Carter seemed headed for defeat, he made hospital cost
containment his number one inflation-fighting measure in his 1979 State
of the Union address: "We must act now to protect all Americans from
health care costs that are rising one million dollars per hour, 24 hours a
day, doubling every five years. We must take control of the largest con-
tributor to that inflation: skyrocketing hospital costs."[108] This time he
made a concerted effort to enlist support from the hospital industry

and business community. HEW officials held White House briefings for the major business organizations and a few sympathetic hospital organizations. One naively optimistic staffer was convinced that "business was more inclined to support hospital cost containment that year."[109] But even though business leaders were worried about health care costs, they were more concerned that hospital cost containment would lead to mandatory cost controls in other parts of the economy.[110] The administration also tried to win over the AFL-CIO, which had opposed the previous effort for fear that hospital cost containment might interfere with the newly won right to collective bargaining in the hospital industry.[111] To allay labor's concerns, Carter added a provision for a "wage pass-through" that would exclude wage increases of hospital employees from compliance measures, but union support remained lukewarm.[112] One staffer noted, "I get the feeling that even though some of these people said they would make calls, their heart is not really in the issue."[113] Finally, a compromise bill was hammered out in the Senate. The bill would allow the hospitals to pursue a voluntary strategy but would cap costs if they failed to reach their goals.[114]

The Senate victory caught industry lobbyists by surprise. One lobbyist who thought cost containment was dead had to scramble: "I was going to get a good night's sleep. I was going to get my clothes from the cleaners, but instead I'm up in the middle of the night to get a plane to Washington."[115] By noon the following day, hospital lobbyists were camped out in the capital, shuttling between offices. Carter's blitz of Congress, meetings with insurance industry executives and business leaders, and concessions to the trade unions proved to be no match for the hospital lobbyists.[116] The much weakened cost containment plan was defeated in the House by a resounding majority. Of the 234 House members who voted against it, 202 had received contributions from the AMA and the hospital organizations.[117] Bill Cable, who served as a congressional liaison under Carter, recalled: "Hospital cost containment was the toughest one I ever had to work on . . . we were so vehemently opposed and so successfully opposed by the hospital association and the hospital industry."[118] While the plan was under consideration, hospital charges rose just over 14 percent. After the industry killed the legislation, costs jumped 22 percent.[119]

Califano ran afoul of the hospital lobby again when he tried to solicit competitive bids for demonstration projects to find more efficient ways to operate Medicare. After bidders offered to process Medicare claims for half of what HEW was currently paying the preferred carriers, Blue Cross sued to stop HEW from awarding the bids. Blue Cross lost the suit but succeeded in blocking Califano's efforts to permit competitive bidding on a routine basis by working the crucial congressional committees. Then, when Califano attempted to force the Blue Shield plans that administered Medicare Part B to add board members who were not physicians, Blue Shield lobbied Congress and halted the order.[120]

"Staging In" Universal Coverage

While pursuing hospital cost containment, the Carter administration initially avoided any tie-in with national health insurance. Indeed, administration officials feared that opponents of national health insurance might view cost containment as a first step toward greater government interference.[121] When Ted Kennedy, brooding about Carter's inaction, spoke before the UAW convention in 1977, he told the cheering crowd that health reform "was in danger of becoming the missing promise" of the Carter administration and urged the president to get a proposal to Congress that year.[122] The next day Carter spoke to the same group, promising to have a bill ready before the end of 1978.[123] After consulting with his advisors, however, he decided against getting involved in too many issues at once. With school integration and welfare reform at the top of the political agenda, it would be at least a year before he could lay out principles for a national health insurance program.[124] When Califano finally began to craft core principles, the task proved to be a more daunting than anyone had expected. As Califano later admitted, "I did not anticipate how unprepared HEW was to develop a national health insurance proposal."[125]

Finally, more than a year later, Califano provided Carter with four options.[126] Carter discussed these options with Kennedy and labor leaders, who insisted that any plan include universal coverage, comprehensive benefits, and tough cost controls. Otherwise, the UAW would not back Carter in the 1980 election.[127] Carter countered with a more modest plan that would achieve universal coverage in stages. Phase 1 would cover all low-income children and provide "catastrophic" care for the aged for the expenses Medicare didn't cover. Other groups would be included later. Kennedy didn't object to phasing in as long as the decision to do so was made in advance. Otherwise, there would be a fight with Congress each time a new group was considered, a politically difficult maneuver. As Carter's advisor, Stuart Eisenstadt, recalled:

> I negotiated for days with Senator Edward Kennedy. . . . We agreed on virtually every program detail. . . . The unbridgeable difference was that President Carter and his economic advisors insisted that each subsequent phase after the first would be triggered only upon a presidential determination that inflation and fiscal conditions permitted it.[128]

Carter's decision was unacceptable to Kennedy, who scheduled a press conference to accuse Carter of a failure of leadership. With cameras rolling and supporters applauding, Kennedy announced that he would introduce his own proposal soon. Labor leaders condemned Carter's plan and vowed to assist Kennedy in enacting a real national health insurance bill.[129] Days later, five Democratic congressmen started a "Dump Carter—Draft Kennedy" movement, and a month later Kennedy announced that he would challenge Carter for the Democratic Party nomination. Kennedy lost early primaries in Iowa and New Hampshire but then won six primaries in the East and in California. Still, he lacked the delegates to beat Carter, and fellow Democrats worried that he was splitting the party and hurting Carter's reelection chances in 1980.

In May Kennedy staged another media event in the Senate Caucus Room, again crowded with supporters and television cameras. National health insurance, Kennedy announced, was "the last, best chance" to bring the health care system under control.[130] His Health Care for All Americans Act (written by the Committee for National Health Insurance) would guarantee universal coverage by requiring employers to pay health insurance premiums either into a quasi-public corporation, to a private insurance company, or to an HMO. The elderly and the disabled would continue to receive Medicare, and the federal government would assume responsibility for the poor.[131]

In response Carter announced his own national health plan, called HealthCare. The Carter proposal would require employers to offer private health insurance to full-time employees (and their dependents) for catastrophic health care expenses. It would also provide a subsidy for small businesses and expand Medicaid for low-income families. However, Carter's plan fell far short of meeting Kennedy and labor's criteria. It was premised on the passage of separate cost containment legislation, it did not guarantee universal coverage, and it preserved too large a role for private insurance companies.[132] Carter and Kennedy continued to negotiate behind the scenes and finally agreed on a compromise plan that would create two national consortia of insurance carriers, one consisting of Blue Cross and Blue Shield, the other of commercial insurers. These consortia would control costs through a national health budget, financed from premium payments, consumer payments, or government payments. As Ig Falk explained to Senator Kennedy, "skillful drafting" had resolved the problems and they now had a bill in sight "well worthy of your introduction."[133] The compromise plan would retain a viable role for the private sector but remain faithful to the essential principles of the Health Care for All Americans Act.[134]

As the economy continued its tailspin, Carter took drastic action to demonstrate that he was still in control. On July 17, 1979, he told members of his cabinet that their performance had been unsatisfactory. All offered to tender their resignations, and by the following week, he had accepted five. Among those fired was Califano, who Carter suspected favored Kennedy. Instead of demonstrating that he was in control, the firings suggested that Carter could not take criticism and was subject to emotional whims.[135]

National health insurance was now a dead issue. Even if it had an advocate within the administration, it could not compete for public attention with a crisis that began in November when Iranian militants overthrew the shah of Iran, stormed the United States Embassy in Tehran, and took 70 Americans hostage. Four days later, a blindfolded hostage was paraded on the embassy grounds near surging crowds chanting anti-American slogans. In retaliation, President Carter ordered a halt to oil imports from Iran and froze all Iranian assets in the United States. Gasoline prices again soared.[136] Carter's popularity temporarily surged as Americans rallied round the flag, then plummeted as the crisis dragged on with no solution in sight.

In the 1980 election, Ronald Reagan captured the Republican Party nomination by appealing to the old right of fiscal conservatives and the new right of social conservatives concerned with abortion, the Equal

Rights Amendment, and school prayer. In his campaign, Reagan promised to reverse the stresses of the Carter years. Carter had failed utterly to whip inflation. Unemployment, which had been low for most of his term, was on the rise. The hostage situation was unresolved.[137] If elected, Reagan would cut taxes, reduce unemployment, contain runaway social spending, strengthen free markets, and balance the budget. Two days before the election, the Iranian parliament voted to release the hostages if the United States accepted four conditions set down by their leader, Ayatollah Khomeini. Although Carter scurried to secure the hostages' release, no deal was struck.[138] Carter won only six states. Reagan's sweep was nationwide.[139] The hostages were finally released on January 20, the day Reagan was sworn in as president.

Discouraged Committee for National Health Insurance members conceded that national health insurance was dead. As Rashi Fein glumly concluded:

> Now that Ronald Reagan was President, there was absolutely no chance that he would buy into it. It did not behoove us to continue to support something [the compromise] which was not all that good, and whose great claim to fame was that it perhaps could be enacted. . . . If we stayed there, the next move would be further to the right, because this would now be the standard from which we would negotiate.[140]

Policy by Stealth: The Prospective Payment System

After his landslide victory President Reagan declared, "In this present crisis, government is not the solution to our problem, government is the problem."[141] His first year in office, he unveiled his own national recovery plan based on supply-side economic theory (or what critics called "voodoo economics"). The core idea of supply-siders was that tax cuts would generate economic growth.[142] Reagan kept his promise to reduce taxes, which instead of eliminating inflation tripled the national debt and ushered in a recession. He also kept his promise to reduce government spending. In his 1981 budget he eliminated the public service jobs program, cut 400,000 people from the food stamps program, reduced the federal subsidy for public housing residents, eliminated the minimum Social Security benefit, and ended benefits for older children of deceased workers.[143]

Medical costs, seemingly unresponsive to the forces that governed other parts of the economy, continued to outpace the consumer price index. President Reagan's first stab at health care costs was in keeping with his pledge to reduce government. His administration folded 22 separate health programs into four block grants for the states (maternal and child health, mental health, primary care, and preventive health).[144] Reagan also proposed capping the growth of the federal share of Medicaid funds at 5 percent, but Democrats felt that a 5 percent cap was too severe. In the end the administration retreated entirely from any Medicaid cuts.[145] From 1981 to 1982 the consumer price index increased by only 3 percent but hospital charges rose 20 percent and doctors' fees nearly 11 percent.[146] Still choosing not to confront the hospital lobby, the Reagan administration's only response was to increase the deductibles paid by Medicare beneficiaries.[147]

In 1982 Congress enacted the Tax Equity and Fiscal Responsibility Act (TEFRA), which contained several measures to control Medicare costs. Included were strict limits on Medicare reimbursement to hospitals and new incentives to encourage HMOs to enroll Medicare beneficiaries. The legislation also replaced the ineffectual PSROs with a second generation of peer review agencies, called peer review organizations. When the hospital industry and the AMA later convinced the Reagan administration that the peer review organizations should be dismantled in favor of a free market approach, the Washington Business Group on Health lobbied Congress and rescued them from the budget axe.[148] But the peer review organizations produced much the same results as the PSROs, rarely sanctioning physicians and generating no significant savings.[149] The sleeper in TEFRA was a requirement that HEW submit to Congress, within five months, a new prospective payment system for Medicare. This requirement was met by an indirect route via Social Security reform.

Since the late 1970s the Social Security trust fund had been teetering toward bankruptcy. In 1981 new projections indicated that there would be insufficient funds to pay benefits in just a few years.[150] To restore Social Security to solvency, President Reagan proposed an immediate cut of 31 percent in early retirement benefits (which would hit people ages 62 to 65) and a 10 percent cut in future benefits, even though polls showed that 65 percent of the public opposed further reductions in health and social welfare programs and even though more than 60 million people would be directly affected by the proposals.[151]

Reprisals from the public were swift and harsh. Hours after Reagan's proposals were announced, senior organizations began mobilizing. The National Council of Senior Citizens fired off 10,000 "seniorgrams" to activate its network of clubs. The AARP sent a legislative alert to 14,000 volunteer leaders, asking them to write their congressional representatives and to tell their friends and relatives to do the same. The Gray Panthers, a small intergenerational, antiestablishment organization, held candlelight vigils in the park across the street from the White House and staged rowdy public demonstrations around the country. Save Our Security, a coalition of 141 senior organizations, held a press conference to demonstrate seniors' opposition to the cuts.[152] Congressional offices were swamped with letters, cards, and phone calls.[153] Within days Reagan's public approval rating plummeted 16 points. Emboldened by the public outcry, Democrats who had acquiesced to Reagan's budget cuts railed against him, while Republicans, worried about the political costs of offending senior citizens, joined Democrats in attacking the proposals. That October, Congress restored the minimum Social Security benefit, promising never again to reduce benefits for current recipients, and Reagan abandoned all plans for benefit cuts in the near term.[154] Instead, he created the bipartisan National Commission on Social Security Reform to devise a politically feasible, long-range solution.

The National Commission on Social Security Reform began meeting in 1982. At each meeting senior citizens demonstrated in front of the hotel and lobbied individual commission members behind the scene. By November a crisis was declared when Social Security was forced to borrow from the Medicare and disability insurance trust funds to pay benefits on time. If some resolution was not reached, benefit checks would be delayed for the first time in history. Medicare had its own problems, however, with projections indicating that the Medicare trust fund would be depleted within five years.[155] The commission waited until after the 1982 congressional elections to hold its final meeting, but the meeting ended in a stalemate when members could not agree on a package of benefit cuts and tax increases.

Instead five commission members (among them Robert Ball and Alan Greenspan, who had served as President Ford's economic advisor) began meeting in secret with no records kept and no transcripts recorded. In January the five presented their recommendations to the full commission.[156] Their plan included delaying Social Security cost-of-living increases for six months, taxing benefits of upper-income Social Security beneficiaries, and raising the age of eligibility for full benefits from 65 to 67. The retirement age increase would be phased in incrementally, starting in 2000, 17 years in the future, so there would be no short-term political cost.[157] The Ways and Means Committee passed the bill by a large majority, and the final legislation was hammered out by a conference committee in March 1983.

The 1983 amendments to the Social Security Act also included a little-noticed provision that was slipped into the Ways and Means Committee bill at the last minute by members of the Health Subcommittee. With all the attention focused on the Social Security crisis, it elicited no debate and generated no controversy, even though it meant a radical restructuring of Medicare. As Paul Light noted, "It would have been a difficult fight on its own but had a free ride on the Social Security bill."[158]

The hospital cost control provision in the amendments would introduce a prospective payment system for Medicare. Instead of reimbursing hospitals after the fact, hospitals would receive a predetermined amount based on what treatment was provided. Prospective payment had been tested in a series of experiments in several states with large Medicaid populations.[159] The plan federal officials finally adopted for Medicare began as the New Jersey experiment. In New Jersey, as in many states, Blue Cross premiums were subject to the approval of the insurance commissioner. Every proposed premium rate increase met with public resistance and unfavorable publicity. Frustrated by having to pay rising hospital charges but forbidden from increasing premiums, Blue Cross turned against its former master, the hospital industry, and asked the state legislature to impose limits on hospital charges. The New Jersey Hospital Association vigorously lobbied against Blue Cross and instead promised to institute a "voluntary" review of hospital budgets. When the voluntary review had no effect on costs (because the reviewers were beholden to the Hospital Association), the legislature empowered the commissioners of health and insurance to actually set rates for Blue Cross patients. But hospitals circumvented the fixed rates by shifting costs to the commercial insurers, whose rates were not regulated. Within five years hospital charges paid by commercial insurers were 30 percent higher than Blue Cross charges. Commercial insurers were forced to raise their premiums and thus lose their competitive advantage over Blue Cross. As commercial insurers began to clamor for more regulation of hospital rates, the New Jersey Department of Health proposed an alternative—hospitals would be paid by the type of case treated, not by the number of patient days.[160] The plan antagonized both the hospitals and Blue Cross—the hospitals because they opposed any departure from cost-based reimbursement, Blue Cross because it gave commercial insurers an edge.

The 1983 amendments to the Social Security Act replaced the cost-plus hospital reimbursement system with this prospective payment system. The prospective payment system created fixed payment schedules for various diagnosis-related groups, called DRGs, regardless of the actual cost of treatment.[161] Hospitals could keep the difference from any cost savings but would not receive additional funds if their costs exceeded the limit. The American Hospital Association embraced prospective payment as a preferable alternative to the strict limits in TEFRA. According to an officer of the association, "Prospective payment was one of the things the hospitals went along with. . . . It was not a bad thing if the federal government did a good job of establishing the rates."[162] Although the prospective payment system only applied to Medicare, many states adopted it for their Medicaid populations as well. After 1983 the Washington Business Group on Health also helped some private companies adopt similar accounting procedures for their own health plans.[163]

The first year the prospective payment system was in operation, the average length of a hospital stay for Medicare beneficiaries declined by over 15 percent.[164] Within a few months, however, hospitals began reporting more high-cost cases, an example of what was called "DRG creep." As the hospital administrator quoted previously explained, "We were always one step ahead of the government."[165] Congress attempted to close the loopholes that allowed DRG creep, but hospitals objected, claiming that they were treating sicker patients, and the government backed down.[166] A few years later, in response to continued complaints from the AHA about the stringency of the DRG system, Congress boosted DRG rates.[167]

The prospective payment system not only changed the incentives in Medicare payments to hospitals but also rearranged the political coalitions within the health care system. Under the old cost-based reimbursement system, hospitals and physicians both benefited when more care was delivered. Now if the revenues expended in caring for patients exceeded the DRG limit, physicians were still the winners, but hospitals were the losers. Thus prospective payment placed hospitals at economic risk for the treatment decisions of physicians.[168] Prospective payment also indirectly put hospitals on a collision course with large, self-insured employers. The prospective payment system did not prohibit hospitals from shifting costs from Medicare patients to other payers, a decision that was bound to raise problems down the line. As hospitals compensated for limits on Medicare charges by increasing charges to younger patients, corporations wound up paying the bills. Once this practice became evident, the business community revolted. The National Association of Manufacturers began demanding that prospective payment regulations be tightened to prevent hospitals from "gaming the system." John Motley, lobbyist for the National Federation of Independent Business, argued, "Greater discipline on physicians is expected to have some spillover effect to the private sector."[169]

Although physicians' fees had increased at three times the rate of hospital payments during the 1980s, they aroused less concern because they represented a smaller portion of total costs. However, Dr. Arnold Redman, editor of the *New England Journal of Medicine*, warned physicians that the reprieve was temporary: "Doctors have to realize that they are the essence of the problem. Though they only get 20 percent of every dollar spent on medical care, they determine most of the other costs. And if they continue to dodge their responsibility, more government regulation is inevitable."[170] Sure enough, in 1984 Congress instituted a temporary freeze on Medicare payment increases to physicians. Then in 1985 Congress created a commission to develop a permanent fee schedule for physicians' services. Anticipating reform, the AMA decided that it would be better to be a part of the process than attempt to block any change. The AMA participated in the commission that drafted a plan and in 1989 agreed to replace fee-for-service payment with a predetermined fee schedule that would be phased in over a five-year period.

Under the new system, medical services were analyzed in terms of their complexity and time demands and then converted into fee schedules for office and hospital visits. Initially the fee schedules were set high, and physicians rallied against any proposed reductions. When the government proposed a 16 percent reduction in 1991, the AMA and other physicians' organizations created such a "firestorm of protest" that the regulation was revised.[171] Following complaints from physicians in 1998 that fees were too low, a more liberal fee schedule was adopted.[172] Even though the medical profession has had a continuing influence on the committees that set fees, both the prospective payment system and the new doctors' fee schedules were essentially "blunt instruments of prospective budgeting and price regulation" that shifted the balance of power from the providers toward the federal government.[173]

Conclusion

At the beginning of the 1970s, universal health insurance was at the forefront of national policy debates, but any chance it had was rapidly diminished by concerns about rising costs. For the next decade cost containment took center stage as the main issue on the health care agenda. As federal officials sought in vain to wrest control over charges and fees from providers, the medical lobby fought back, lobbying legislators and rallying local hospitals and community groups to fend off caps. The providers had important allies in their effort to defeat cost controls. They included business groups, who feared that controls in the health sector would lead to controls in other parts of the economy, and the trade unions, which had just won the right to bargain over wages for hospital employees and saw price controls as an antiunion measure.

A significant shift in power relations occurred with the introduction of the prospective payment system for Medicare, which restructured Medicare but did not tamper with wages or levy an overall cap on charges. But the gains of prospective payment were short-lived, as hospitals found ways to circumvent the controls and shift costs to other payers. When it became apparent that the federal government was incapable of restraining costs, corporate purchasers took matters in their own hands, rising in revolt against the hospitals and doctors.

six

The Revolt of the Corporate Purchaser

For nearly a century hospitals had viewed physicians as their main clients, and physicians accordingly made most of the decisions about what took place in hospitals. They admitted patients whenever they chose, kept them hospitalized for as long as they felt necessary, and ordered whatever tests they wanted. More was better. The longer patients stayed, the more tests were run, the more revenue hospitals took in. Stanford economist Alain Enthoven asserted, "Most physicians have no idea of the cost of the things they order—and no real reason to care."[1] Some people did care. Opal Burge of Hebron, Indiana, was shocked when she received a 208-page hospital bill with charges of over $250,000 for her husband's stay in an intensive care unit as he battled the emphysema that eventually took his life.[2] But most patients didn't object because they weren't paying the bill, at least not directly. Patients entered hospitals when they were sick and in pain, fearful of death, or elated over new life. Most were satisfied with the care they received, and if they thought about costs at all, they believed they were paying for receiving the best care in the world.

That arrangement lasted until the late 1970s. Then the actual customers, the employers who were paying the bills on behalf of their employees, began asking why patients faced long hospital stays for simple procedures, whether it was necessary to run so many expensive tests, and why a box of Kleenex cost 49 cents at Kmart but $19 on a patient's bedside table.[3] In the business world, the market ruled. When corporate executives made a business decision, whether about purchasing supplies or hiring personnel, they drove a hard bargain. Suppliers had to offer the lowest price to win a contract; prospective employees had to provide a resume listing their qualifications and prior experience. In making decisions about health care, however, these same businesses, now in the position of corporate purchasers of health care goods, were stymied. They had no way to determine whether physicians performing services were the best qualified or whether a charge for surgery, a birth, or emergency room care was reasonable. In fact, it was difficult to learn what the exact cost was. When employers sought answers to these questions, the insurers who were supposed to represent their interests refused to cooperate. In the 1980s, corporations decided it was time to use their purchasing power to challenge the providers' dominance over the health care system.

The Origins of the Corporate Revolt

By the early 1980s, the business community had become truly alarmed about the rising cost of health care. Between 1970 and 1982, while the gross domestic product grew by 208 percent, employer expenditures for health benefits grew by 700 percent.[4] Federal expenditures for Medicare slowed somewhat after the prospective payment system was introduced in 1983, but that had no effect on employers' expenditures. Indeed, the opposite was the case, as hospitals compensated for lost Medicare revenues by shifting costs onto private payers.[5] Every effort to cut Medicare payments translated into an increase in corporate costs.[6]

These trends affected small employers differently than large employers. Small firms had to purchase health insurance coverage for their employees in the small-group market. Some insurance carriers avoided this market entirely.[7] Those that did operate there used sophisticated forms of underwriting to skim off the more desirable employee groups and avoid paying for high-risk individuals. Insurers aggressively competed for groups of young and healthy employees, forcing many small firms, especially those with an older workforce, to cut back on coverage.

When the National Federation of Independent Business, the leading organization of small firms, surveyed its members in 1989, the most frequently voiced complaint was the rising cost of health benefits. Consider Ray Morgan, who owned a business in Algona, Iowa, with seven employees. Between 1988 and 1989, Morgan's premiums more than tripled, increasing from $837 to $2,685 a month, even though none of his employees had filed a major claim. Richard Ludwig, president of Lavelle Aircraft Company, a manufacturer with 150 employees, faced a similar dilemma. After premiums doubled between 1986 and 1989, he reluctantly cut benefits. Ludwig explained that, at $396,000 annually, "this is the single most expensive element of our business."[8] As health insurance became less affordable for small-business owners, they began curtailing benefits or dumping their employee health care coverage entirely.

State taxes on insurance premiums and state mandates requiring insurance companies to include certain services in all policies exacerbated the problem. By the mid-1980s there were more than 690 such mandates, ranging from wigs to mental health services to podiatry to acupuncture.[9] According to the National Federation of Independent Business, these mandates "seldom surfaced as a result of constituent demand" but rather were initiated by "well-organized special interest groups including the providers of services." With each new mandate, the number of providers performing the mandated services increased. For example, in Wisconsin after outpatient mental health services were included in state mandates, the number of mental health clinics grew from 40 to more than 900 in ten years. If state mandates were reduced, small firms could purchase a "catastrophic, bare bones policy."[10] Until that happened, the only option was to reduce benefits or drop coverage.

Blue Cross had once been a haven for small-business owners, but competition from commercial insurers had forced many Blue Cross plans to abandon community rating (where every subscriber paid the same rate) and adopt the underwriting practices used by commercial companies. One employer who had held a Blue Cross policy for more than a decade was notified that his group would now be "medically underwritten." Under the new contract terms, Blue Cross reserved the right to refuse coverage for any preexisting condition:

> Your group has been classified as medically underwritten for the contract period. . . . any participant from your group whose coverage becomes effective during the new contract period will be required to fill out and file a medical history questionnaire with us before qualifying for covered services . . . these subscribers may be permanently excluded from receiving . . . benefits for conditions which existed before they enrolled.[11]

In some states Blue Cross began selling stock and branching into the more lucrative life insurance business.[12] In recognition of the changed practices of the organization, in 1986 Congress removed Blue Cross' nonprofit tax exemption, ending its pretense of being a charitable community service organization.

Large firms had an alternative, thanks to the Employment Retirement Security Act of 1974 (ERISA). ERISA was the landmark legislation that created national standards for employee fringe benefit plans.[13] A provision added at the last minute exempted employer-provided fringe benefits from state laws governing these benefits, since fringe benefits were not technically "insurance." That gave firms with sufficient cash reserves or borrowing power an incentive to self-insure instead of purchasing coverage from an insurance company. Self-insured plans did not have to include any of the mandated benefits that ran up the costs of insurance in the small group market. Nor did they have to pay taxes on premiums. Self-insured firms also were exempt from state laws that regulated insurance companies and thus were free from liability in state court if their decisions regarding benefits harmed the people they insured.[14] What that meant was that patients could not sue if the company withheld payment for any health problem. When employees challenged these practices, the courts typically ruled in favor of the employer, as was the case of the Texas employee whose employer cut his health benefits from $1 million to $5,000 after he was diagnosed with AIDS.[15] In some instances, employers that self-insured were able to cut their overhead costs by 50 percent or better.[16]

In 1975, the year after ERISA was enacted, only 5 percent of employees were covered by self-insured plans, mainly those negotiated by labor unions; by 1985 that figure had climbed to 42 percent.[17] By the mid-1990s self-insurance covered nearly half of all workers and a much higher percentage of employees of large companies.[18] Employers, not insurance companies, had become the leading risk bearers.

Downsizing the Private Welfare State

Although being self-insured placed large firms in a more favorable position than small firms that had to purchase coverage from insurance companies, it did not immunize them from rising costs. So in the

1980s, as Marie Gottschalk noted, "business . . . set off on a long march to downsize the private welfare state."[19] Some employers dropped coverage altogether. In 1980 97 percent of medium and large employers offered health insurance benefits; by 1990 the figure was just 92 percent.[20] But dropping health insurance as a fringe benefit was not an option for most firms. In unionized industries, employers were locked into collective bargaining agreements with organized labor that prevented drastic cost-cutting measures. Nonunionized firms that stopped providing health benefits faced a tax penalty, poor employer-employee relations, and negative publicity. Most firms instead sought ways to reduce their costs.

One of the business leaders of the cost containment effort was Lee Iacocca, the brash and outspoken CEO of Chrysler. Iacocca, the son of Italian immigrants, had begun working for Ford after he completed his master's degree at Princeton University, working his way up to president in 1970. After the 1973 oil crisis, Ford experienced its first losing quarter since 1946 as the buying public turned to smaller, more fuel-efficient Japanese cars. Once the gas shortage eased, Americans resumed their love affair with large gas-guzzlers, and Ford was again operating in the black. But Iacocca had had a falling-out with Henry Ford when he insisted that the less profitable smaller vehicles had to be part of Ford's product line in the future. After being demoted twice, on July 14, 1978, he was summarily fired. His old friend Joe Califano called from his office in HEW to comfort him: "Lee, these things have a way of turning out okay. This just could be one the best things that ever happened to you."[21]

At first Iacocca didn't see it that way. But a few months after he left Ford, depressed and angered, he was approached by the Chrysler Corporation, which was in deep trouble as a result of decades of poor management. That year Chrysler posted losses of $160 million. Iacocca accepted the job of chairman and CEO and immediately began to survey management practices to determine how to turn the company around.[22] He didn't like what he saw. Chrysler was set up as a "cluster of little duchies" like Italy in the 1860s, each run by a prima donna.[23] Each of the 35 vice presidents had his own turf with no committee setup, no organizational chart, and no communication between departments. Iacocca fired 33 of the vice presidents, hired new accountants, and reorganized the way the company interacted with its dealerships. But before any of his innovations could take effect, the shah of Iran was deposed, the Americans were taken hostage, and the price of gas doubled—from 65 cents a gallon to over $1.30 a gallon—within a few weeks. People waited in long lines to fill their tanks. There were gas riots at some New York service stations. The market for station wagons, vans, and recreational vehicles dried up almost instantly.

Ideologically, Iacocca had always been "a free enterpriser, a believer in survival of the fittest."[24] With Chrysler close to bankruptcy, Iacocca reconsidered his lifelong opposition to government intervention in private business. He pleaded his case before Congress and won $1.5 billion in loan guarantees from President Carter. Sacrifices were in order. Iacocca first reduced his own salary of $360,000 to $1 a year, then cut other executives' pay by 10 percent. That made it easier to ask the rank-and-file workers to do their share. He put UAW president Doug Fraser on Chrysler's board of directors and wrested several concessions from the union. Autoworkers agreed to a $2-an-hour pay cut and promised not to strike when unprofitable plants were closed. Iacocca then turned to fringe benefits. Pensions took a huge share of the total wage package but were a non-negotiable item. Health care required close scrutiny. As Iacocca examined company records, he was amazed to discover that Blue Cross/Blue Shield was Chrysler's largest supplier, billing more than the company's suppliers of steel and rubber. Overall Chrysler paid about $600 million a year in health care costs, adding about $600 to the sticker price of each car.[25]

Iacocca determine he would find a way for Chrysler to exert its clout as a large purchaser of health services to weed out high-priced, inefficient providers. He first call was to his buddy Joe Califano, the man Carter had fired as HEW secretary. "Joe," Iacocca told him, "being fired by Jimmy Carter is the best thing that ever happened to you."[26] Iacocca invited Califano to his Waldorf Towers suite, and they talked for hours. Over dinner at Romeo Salta's on West 56th Street, Iacocca asked Califano for help. "You say you want to do something about health care costs. Why don't you chair the new health care committee of Chrysler's board of directors?"[27] Califano was hooked. Chrysler's was the first board of directors to appoint such a committee. If he couldn't get a handle on costs as HEW secretary, maybe he could do it through one of the largest corporations in the country.

To start the process, Califano asked Blue Cross/Blue Shield to provide detailed cost information, but Blue Cross stonewalled. When it became clear that Califano would persist, Blue Cross finally hired the Health Data Institute to audit Chrysler's health care expenditures. According to Califano, the audit revealed an "appalling degree of unnecessary care, inefficient practices and outright fraud." Some podiatrists were working on feet one toe at a visit and prolonging time off for employees on disability. Califano recalled the case of one employee certified as disabled because of foot surgery who was apprehended after a lengthy foot chase while attempting to steal parts from a Chrysler plant. Among the more egregious findings were that insurance payments to dermatologists were twice those to general practitioners and 25 percent higher than those to chest surgeons, that hospital stays for normal births were nearly double the national average, and that two-thirds of hospitalizations for "bed rest" for lower back pain were unnecessary.[28] Prescription drugs were also abused. One Chrysler employee received 51 prescriptions for 6,030 Valium pills over a 12-month period. Another got 136 prescriptions for 4,255 Percodan pills filled. As Iacocca complained, "As the system works now, the doctors and hospitals are killing us."[29]

Chrysler's first point of attack was services that could be easily monitored. Chrysler demanded that pharmacists substitute cheaper generic drugs for brand-name products, shifted business to laboratories that charged the lowest prices to run tests, and told physicians to drop their prices or lose Chrysler's business. Chrysler also won an agreement with the UAW for a hospital admission screening program and a "preferred provider" plan wherein workers would only see physicians on an approved list.[30] However, the UAW refused to accept co-payments and deductibles, which members would interpret as a reduction in benefits but which Iacocca saw as the heart of the problem: "The attitude [of workers] is always to let Uncle Lee pick up the tab. So what if you're charging me too much for the tests or the surgery—*I'm not paying for it.*"[31]

Other employers followed Chrysler's lead. In companies without unions, employees were forced to pay higher deductibles and co-payments and share the costs of premiums. Some employers resorted to "churning," switching policies just as the waiting period for employees with large medical expenses expired.[32] They also reduced benefits for expensive diseases such as cancer and AIDS or eliminated coverage for these conditions altogether. In 1980 72 percent of employers paid the total cost of their employees' health insurance; by 1990 just 51 percent did, and only 34 percent fully financed family coverage.[33] Cost sharing had a minimal impact on expenditures overall, however, because the majority of employees used few health care services. Those with serious health problems who used the most services were too concerned about their own health to be deterred from seeking care by high deductibles and co-payments.[34]

Employers also began to organize to use their purchasing power to negotiate better deals with providers. In Minneapolis a coalition of firms organized a purchasing cooperative in 1988 to bargain over prices. By 1992 the Buyers Health Care Cooperative had more than 400 employer members covering 380,000 employees. Co-op members conducted a computer analysis of hospital charges and then demanded that local hospitals implement clinical guidelines to reduce costs.[35] In California, the vice president of Plantronics took state data on hospital costs in his plant's hometown with him when he met with local hospital administrators, and he was able to negotiate a substantial discount. Hospitals were not always so cooperative, of course. In Lake County, Illinois, when a group of employers tried to negotiate directly with the local hospital, their actions triggered a reaction "something akin to the Mount Saint Helens' eruption."[36] However, several of the business leaders also served on the hospital board, and they forced the hospital to come to the bargaining table.

Employers also sought to mobilize politically to gain a more active voice in health policy decisions. In Massachusetts the CEO of Dennison organized 60 of the largest employers in the state and brokered changes in the state's rate-setting system that helped slow the rate of growth in hospital charges.[37] In Arizona a coalition of business leaders sponsored a series of ballot initiatives to curb hospital costs. But the hospitals attacked back, decrying "all out corporate warfare," and defeated the measures. The CEO of Meredith, one of the firms involved in the Arizona coalition, later ruefully recalled:

Initially, we attempted to effect change through negotiation, discussion, debate, through participation of all of the interests with a vested stake in health care delivery. I know what the arguments are for a more conciliatory approach because I accepted them. . . . I am now convinced that we should have been more aggressive.[38]

The U.S. Chamber of Commerce, one of the oldest and largest business organizations in the country, had 2,700 state and local chapters, 65,000 member companies, and a staff of 1,400 in Washington, D.C., alone. With its large membership and vast networks, one might have expected it to be an effective voice for cost containment. The Chamber did influence some state policy decisions. For example, in California the Chamber joined forces with the Health Insurance Association of America to prevent the hospital lobby from watering down a new rate-setting system. More often, however, the Chamber was unable to reach consensus because of the clout of its provider members. When the Chamber formed a health policy committee, it was co-opted by the AHA, which then refused to allow consideration of any position contrary to the hospitals' interests. The Business Roundtable, an organization of the largest corporations in the country, experienced similar problems. When the Roundtable founded a Health Care Task Force in 1982, the drug manufacturer Eli Lilly seized control. Instead of focusing on cost containment, the task force dealt only with issues of interest to the pharmaceutical industry.

The Washington Business Group on Health was the one business group that was not beholden to providers. Its head, Willis Goldbeck, refused to allow any provider organizations into the inner circle, antagonizing the insurance companies, the AMA, and the AHA. Goldbeck had the behind-the-scenes support of the National Association of Manufacturers and other business groups that couldn't openly oppose their own provider members.[39] The Washington Business Group on Health had pushed for PSROs and for the prospective payment system for Medicare that changed how hospital charges were calculated.[40] Now Goldbeck turned to the issue of financial disclosure.

Eighteen states, at the urging of employers' associations, had enacted financial disclosure laws that required providers to release data on costs and physician practice patterns. These data helped businesses negotiate lower rates from providers. Despite the state laws, however, businesses found it difficult to get access to the data and even more difficult to interpret what they received. In 1984 Goldbeck helped Representative Ron Wyden (R-Ore.) write a bill that would give the Department of Health and Human Services the authority to make data on statewide health care charges easily accessible. Physicians and hospital groups lobbied against the Wyden measure, claiming that the data would be easy to misinterpret, but in 1985 Congress passed legislation that allowed employers to request information in state databases directly from the federal government. As states began collecting and reporting data on health care costs, the revelations fueled the fire. Analyses of expenditures showed huge regional variations in the number of tonsillectomies, coronary bypass surgeries, and hysterectomies performed for similar diagnoses, as well as significant discrepancies in prices charged by hospitals and physicians even in the same town.[41]

The Washington Business Group on Health also lobbied for a proposal to expand Medicare to pay for the "catastrophic" health care costs for Medicare beneficiaries, a plan that the business community endorsed because it would shift the burden of retiree health benefits from private companies to the government. In the previous decade, retiree health benefits had become a pressing concern for the large manufacturing companies.[42] The first retiree health benefits had been granted in 1953, when the Big Three auto manufacturers—General Motors, Ford, and Chrysler—agreed to provide retirees age 65 and older the same health benefits as active workers if they paid the full cost themselves. In 1961 the UAW won an agreement that the companies would pay the full cost of health benefits for workers and their dependents and half the cost for retirees. The same benefits were granted to early retirees, who were allowed to retire with reduced benefits at age 60 with 10 years of service and at age 55 with 30 years of service. With each new contract came more generous benefits, including fully paid retiree health benefits in 1964, prescription drugs for employees and their dependents in 1967 and for retirees in 1971, and eyeglass coverage for employees in 1976 and for retirees in 1979.[43] The United Steel Workers Association won a similar benefit package for its members.[44] Nonunionized firms followed suit, encouraged by provisions in the federal tax code that allowed firms to deduct retiree health benefits as a business expense. The enactment of Medicare shifted some of the costs of retiree benefits to the federal government, but firms were still responsible for costs for retirees under age 65 as well as the various co-payments and deductibles for retirees 65 and older that Medicare did not cover. In 1984 30 percent of Medicare beneficiaries received medigap coverage for these extra expenses from a past or current employer, with employers paying most of the cost.[45]

In 1967 the Supreme Court ruled that employers could use retiree health benefits to lure older workers into retirement without the risk of

being sued for age discrimination. Following that decision, auto manufacturers responded to each slump in production by waiving the normal early retirement provisions. During the recessions in 1973–74 and
1981–82 "sweeteners" were added to the usual early retirement benefits to encourage older workers who would not otherwise be eligible
to retire to do so.[46] By the 1980s what had been a relatively small business expense, retiree benefits, had grown into a huge liability, as the
manufacturing workforce aged and the proportion of retirees relative
to younger workers swelled.[47] In some industries there were more retirees than active workers. For example, when Iacocca took over
Chrysler, there were three retirees for every two workers. Bethlehem
Steel had 70,000 active workers and 54,000 retirees in 1980 but 37,000
active workers and 70,000 retirees five years later. This dilemma reached
crisis proportions in 1986, when LTV filed for bankruptcy, terminating
health insurance benefits for its 78,000 retirees.[48] The following year,
troubled Kaiser Steel missed a $255,000 weekly premium payment. More
than 4,300 retirees and 200 working employees over age 65 lost their
health insurance.[49]

Congressional hearings were held, and *Fortune* magazine warned
that retiree health benefits were "unfunded, out of control and growing
more than twice as fast as inflation." If left unchecked, they could
threaten not only profits but entire companies.[50] These events caused
the Financial Accounting Standards Board, which regulates employee
benefits, to take a hard look at retiree health plans. In 1987 the board
issued a regulation that forced firms to include promised retiree health
benefits on their balance sheets as a business expense, making these
large and growing unfunded liabilities visible as part of the bottom
line.[51] Not only had retiree health benefits become a huge business expense, they threatened to undermine investor confidence. As corporations sought a way to shed this responsibility, they seized upon a
proposal to expand Medicare to cover many of these costs.

Shedding Retiree Health Benefits:
The Medicare Catastrophic Coverage Act

The Medicare Catastrophic Coverage Act of 1988 is usually seen as a
striking anomaly in Medicare history. It was enacted in the context of a

rising budget deficit during the administration of Ronald Reagan, a conservative Republican who had campaigned on a promise to reduce government spending. Furthermore, it would increase Medicare expenditures and reverse the gains made by the prospective payment system. How, then, did catastrophic care ascend to the top of the domestic policy agenda and evade insurance industry opposition?

According to the accepted wisdom, the Catastrophic Coverage Act was the pet project of Otis Bowen, a warm and gregarious country doctor and former governor of Indiana.[52] Bowen had served on the 1981 Advisory Council on Social Security and had been offered a position as White House liaison to HEW but had declined because his wife, Beth, had terminal bone cancer. After Beth's death, Bowen married a widow who had been a lifelong friend he taught at the Indiana University School of Medicine. In 1985 Bowen was invited to become Secretary of Health, Education, and Welfare and was easily confirmed. Early in his tenure he began lobbying for President Reagan to include a catastrophic care initiative in his State of the Union address. Bowen had witnessed first-hand the distress of his elderly patients facing enormous health care bills after lengthy hospital stays. He also distrusted the insurance companies that sold medigap policies because of instances where they had refused to cover his patients' bills.

With midterm elections less than a year away, polls indicated that the president was particularly unpopular with the elderly. Catastrophic care legislation, Bowen argued, might soften his image.[53] Yet if Reagan wanted to cultivate elderly voters, catastrophic care seemed a curious choice of issues to pursue. By 1986 nearly 80 percent of people 65 and older already had supplemental medigap insurance that paid most of the costs Medicare did not cover.[54] Furthermore, under the prospective payment system the average hospital stay had dramatically declined, as hospitals released patients "quicker and sicker" to nursing homes or sent them home to recuperate. Only a small fraction of Medicare recipients (less than 1.5 percent) would ever stay in a hospital beyond the Medicare limit.[55] And Bowen's proposal excluded the most pressing concern of the elderly, which was long-term care. Instead of introducing catastrophic care legislation in his State of the Union address, which key administration officials opposed, Reagan ordered Bowen to head a study of the issue.

Bowen conducted his study with great fanfare, holding showy, well-publicized hearings all over the country. By October he had a proposal ready for the president to consider. It is not clear what the fate of Bowen's plan would have been had it not been for the Iran-contra crisis. The crisis began in the summer of 1986, when a group called Islamic Holy War seized three American hostages in Lebanon and demanded the release of 17 Kuwaiti prisoners who had been convicted of bombing American, French, and Kuwaiti installations. That October, halfway around the world in a seemingly unrelated incident, an American military cargo plane carrying a CIA operative was shot down over Nicaragua. Rumors spread that the Reagan administration had hatched a cockeyed plot to use funds from the illegal sale of arms to Iran to support the rebel Nicaraguan organization, called the contras. Four days before the congressional elections, the press reported that the administration had negotiated a secret arms deal with Iranian officials despite an official ban on providing arms to Iran. The deal was reportedly concocted by a small group within the National Security Council, led by Oliver North and personally approved by President Reagan.[56] The Iranians would receive 500 missiles in exchange for the release of one of the hostages. The funds from the sale would also be funneled to the Nicaraguan contras. Although President Reagan denied the plot, on November 3 one of the hostages, David Jacobsen, who directed the American University Hospital, was released.[57]

In the 1986 elections, the Democrats regained control of the Senate, an outcome that was particularly damaging to Reagan's image. Only 5 of 18 Republican senators the president had supported were elected. As the president's popularity plummeted, aides searched for an issue to deflect attention from Iran-contra and prove that the administration was not paralyzed. On November 19 Bowen introduced his proposal at a meeting of the White House Domestic Policy Council. Bowen's plan would expand Medicare coverage for acute hospital stays and cap an individual's out-of-pocket costs for physician services. As a sop to administration conservatives, it would also include federal tax credits to encourage the elderly to purchase private long-term care insurance.[58]

Bowen's report met with stunned silence. The chairman of Reagan's Council of Economic Advisors, Beryl Sprinkle, "a short, roly-poly man of single-minded conservative convictions," charged that the Bowen plan "would replace a competitive private market with a government monopoly."[59] Attorney General Edwin Meese complained that it would intrude into a market already served by private companies.[60] Medicare expansion on so grand a scale was a direct assault on the entire conservative agenda. Bowen countered that doing nothing would suggest that Reagan was insensitive to the elderly and the poor. Furthermore, he argued, the small amount of business the private insurance industry would lose would not destroy the market.

The next day Bowen announced his proposal at a news conference. Democrats in Congress applauded. Senator Ted Kennedy called Bowen "a great American" and told Republicans to "listen a little more" to Bowen and a "little less to the insurance industry."[61] If the president did not introduce Bowen's plan, he would do it himself. Four days later Bowen was summoned to the White House to meet with insurance executives. The executives expressed no opposition to Bowen's proposal for the simple reason that insurers had no desire to pay for lengthy hospital stays beyond the Medicare limit. The medigap market was saturated and never had been that profitable to begin with. Expanding Medicare to cover catastrophic illness might also slow the trend toward self-insurance among large corporations. Although the Health Insurance Association of America favored an optional voucher program that would enable Medicare beneficiaries who had no medigap coverage to purchase private insurance, the executives made no attempt to defeat Bowen's plan.[62] According to a Health Insurance Association of America spokeswoman, "The companies can live with it. It's just that we feel the approach is misdirected."[63] Another industry representative noted, "We are not worried about losing the medigap market."[64] When one administration official asked, "How do you beat this proposal with private insurance?" the executives countered, "It's not a good business decision for us to get into that area."[65] There would still be numerous gaps in coverage, according to the vice president of Empire Blue Cross, including $2,000 a year for deductibles and co-payments. Nor would the Bowen plan cover Alzheimer's disease, which was "obviously a market for the private industry," noted Leonard Tondl of Mutual of Omaha, one of the insurers that had begun offering such coverage on an experimental basis. Conservative columnist Peter Ferrara acknowledged, "Insurance companies weren't interested in fighting. . . . Medigap just isn't that profitable."[66]

President Reagan was convinced by Bowen's arguments. He would support expanding Medicare on one condition—that it be financed entirely by the elderly. A bill was sent to Congress on February 24, 1987. What started as a relatively modest proposal expanded as it moved through the Democrat-controlled Congress. The final measure was much more generous than Bowen had originally proposed. It would cap the amount beneficiaries would have to pay for hospital and physician care at $2,146 per year and cover many other costs currently paid by individually purchased medigap policies or by employers, including prescription drugs, mammography screening, hospice care, and even caregiver support for the frail elderly.[67]

A decade earlier the hospital lobby had crushed Carter's proposal to cap the individual health care costs of all insured people, not just Medicare.[68] With the proposal narrowed to include just retirees, the hospital industry was less resistant. The AHA endorsed the measure as long as reimbursements to hospitals were not cut. The AMA supported it as long as fee-for-service was not challenged.[69] Blue Cross and Blue Shield supported it, as did the manufacturers of generic drugs. The Medicare Catastrophic Coverage Act's most enthusiastic boosters were the large manufacturers and the Washington Business Group on Health, which had been lobbying for relief from retiree health benefits.[70] The Catastrophic Coverage Act would solve part of the problem by shifting most of these costs to the federal government or to retirees themselves through higher taxes.

Bowen's original proposal was relatively modest and would be financed by a $59 annual charge, but cost estimates rose as new benefits were added. The one that aroused the most controversy was prescription drug coverage, which the AARP had relentlessly pursued. According to cynics, the AARP wanted drugs covered because it operated as a middleman for the nation's second largest mail order drug supply service, collecting a royalty on every prescription it filled. Adding drug coverage to Medicare would mean AARP would reap huge profits.[71] As one administration official complained, "They run the largest mail order drug operation in the business—they're going to make a fortune on it."[72] In reality AARP would lose business if seniors received prescription drugs for free.

The drug benefit aroused the fierce opposition of the Pharmaceutical Manufacturers Association (PMA). The PMA feared that if premiums failed to cover the program's costs, then the government would slap on price controls. To prevent an open-ended drug benefit from being included, the PMA organized a $3 million lobbying campaign. The PMA hired a public relations firm to phone the elderly and warn them that if the Medicare Catastrophic Coverage Act was enacted, they would be forced to pay higher taxes for benefits they already had.[73] The letter was signed by Dr. Francis Davis, president of Physicians for Quality Medical Care, a PMA front. In the letter Davis warned senior citizens that "if the House version passed instead of the Senate bill, senior citizens would be the losers," because only a few would benefit, "while higher premiums would be charged to all."[74] Seniors were urged to write their representatives supporting a watered-down Senate version that would phase in prescription drug coverage gradually and permit Medicare to stop paying for entire classes of drugs if costs rose too quickly.[75] Representative Pete Stark (D-Calif.) charged the PMA with being involved in "one of the sleaziest lobbying campaigns I've seen in some time." But the PMA had an ally in Bowen, who was dismayed that his bill had become a Christmas tree, with members of Congress vying to add new ornaments. Calling the drug benefit a "cruel hoax," Bowen argued that it would significantly raise the costs of the program. If the drug benefit was retained, he would recommend a presidential veto.

When it appeared that a prescription drug benefit would be included anyway, the PMA demanded a role in the negotiations. Representative Andrew Jacobs (D-Ind.), whose district was home to drug manufacturer Eli Lilly, offered an amendment to strike language encouraging the use of generic substitutes for brand-name drugs.[76] That amendment was rejected, but Jacobs won a victory. The final bill made no reference to cost controls. If prescription drug costs exceeded expectations, beneficiaries would pay higher premiums.

As word of the catastrophic coverage plan spread, most senior citizens' organizations initially supported it. The AARP actively lobbied for the proposal. When administration conservatives tried to convince the president to veto the measure, AARP helped persuade him to sign it.

Despite the positive response from many stakeholder groups usually opposed to government action, there were also early warnings that the proposal might receive a hostile reception. The Chamber of Commerce charged Bowen with "shoving Medicare further along a socialist path" and created a task force to develop a private sector approach.[77] The National Committee to Preserve Social Security and Medicare, an organization that was founded in 1982 to "save Social Security," also raised objections. This group had had a seedy reputation since an incident in 1983 when it had mailed a solicitation to thousands of older people promising that for a $10 contribution they would receive a printout of their Social Security earnings record, something the Social Security Administration provided for free. After its activities became the subject of congressional hearings in both chambers, it was named one of the nation's worst public interest groups by *Washington Monthly* magazine. During the 1986 elections, however, the National Committee had increased its staff from just a handful to more than 50, including 12 registered lobbyists, and persuaded 100,000 senior citizens to become active in local political campaigns.[78] In an effort to scuttle the bill, the group sent letters to more than 1.5 million people in September 1987, warning older people about the tax increase.[79]

As the Medicare legislation moved forward, the National Committee placed an ad in the *Washington Post* warning Congress: "Don't make a mistake that will harm and anger your senior constituents." After the measure passed the Senate in October 1987, the National Committee mailed a "legislative alert" to members of Congress asking them to vote against a conference bill. Most members of Congress discounted the National Committee, convinced that AARP spoke for the majority of senior citizens. Yet congressional staffers had begun sensing intense grassroots opposition. In a prescient statement, Peter Ferrera wrote, "AARP in any event will have its hands full next year as the elderly discover that what the organization has delivered for their dues is a major income tax increase exclusively on them, for benefits that are not the focus of their concern."[80] These warnings went unheeded.

On July 1, 1988, Congress passed the Medicare Catastrophic Coverage Act with huge bipartisan majorities in both House and Senate. President Reagan quickly signed the bill, and it was not until Congress adjourned that people began to understand its implications.[81] The Medicare Catastrophic Coverage Act would be a great benefit for the 20 percent of the elderly who had no medigap insurance and would guarantee that all Medicare beneficiaries had full prescription drug coverage.[82] But it would only modestly improve coverage for most older people, and it would significantly increase taxes for a large minority.[83] All Medicare beneficiaries would pay higher Part B premiums, and more affluent Medicare beneficiaries would pay an additional surcharge, up to $800 for a single person and $1,600 for a couple.[84] The clear winners were major corporations that were saddled with retiree health benefits. They would receive what the UAW called "a windfall reduction in liability," coupled with "a corresponding shift in cost through the increased Part B premium, to Medicare beneficiaries." The Employee Benefit Research Institute estimated that employers' liability for current retirees would drop by 30 percent.[85] Many retirees would now be paying a surtax and higher premiums to fund benefits their employers had formerly provided free. Employers did have to provide a rebate to retirees in the first year, a provision the AFL-CIO and UAW demanded, but only for that one year. After that, employers' expenses would be reduced with no rebate for retired employees.[86]

Retirees who had medigap benefits were furious.[87] Across the country, petition drives and other protests arose almost instantaneously, and their virulence surprised even congressional veterans. Senior citizens bombarded members of Congress with letters and phone calls denouncing the surtax and demanding long-term care benefits.[88] A 64-year-old former airline pilot organized the Seniors Coalition Against the Catastrophic Coverage Act from his retirement home in Las Vegas, claiming to have gathered 410,000 signatures on a repeal petition. Members of Congress were flooded with letters and phone calls. Senator Pete Wilson (R-Calif.) received 3,000 letters, 15,000 postcards, and an uncountable number of phone calls denouncing the surtax. Representative Claude Pepper received hundreds of surly letters from constituents such as Robert Landon, who wrote: "I did not complain when you decided to tax part of my Social Security but I strenuously object to your putting the bite on me again and having the gall to tell me that I can afford it."[89]

Senior citizens were stirred up by the National Committee to Preserve Social Security and Medicare, but other, more respectable seniors' groups whose members had retiree benefits also demanded repeal.[90] Federal employees were especially peeved at AARP. As Thomas Slater wrote, "As a federal retiree, I am furious that the American Association of Retired Persons (of which I am a member) would lobby for such an unfair law and angry that Congress passed it. . . . Repeal would make me happy."[91] Another retiree wrote:

Yes, my wife and I both pay the maximum surtax. But we already are paying $765.60 for Medicare and our gap insurance coverage costs $3,082 annually. Adding in the catastrophic surtax brings the cost for our health coverage to $5447.60 in 1989 and almost $6,000 two years hence.[92]

In an unpopular move AARP fired the head of California's Vote Project for supporting repeal legislation and tried to oust an AARP chapter president in Florida. More than 6,000 older people canceled their AARP membership.

Then the elderly took to the streets, an attention-getting move since people 65 and older are the least likely of all age groups to protest or take part in a demonstration.[93] In a scene replayed over and over on the nightly news, several dozen angry seniors accosted Representative Dan Rostenkowski (D-Ill.), chair of the House Ways and Means Committee, as he attempted to drive away from a meeting. Rostenkowski, a major supporter of the legislation, had maneuvered it through Congress, and now the elderly sought retribution. The demonstrators surrounded Rostenkowski's car, beating it with picket signs, pounding on the windows, and shouting "Coward!" "Recall!" and "Impeach!" A shaken Rostenkowski abandoned his car and fled the scene on foot.[94] As the protest mounted in intensity, members of Congress turned their wrath on the AARP. Representative Harris Fawell (R-Ill.) remarked, "They've clearly lost touch with their membership. Maybe they're too worried about selling prescription drugs to pay attention to costs and duplication of services."[95] On April 12 the Senate voted to hold hearings on the catastrophic law. The AARP refused to testify at the hearing, complaining that the witness lineup was stacked against the law.[96] As one senior citizen after another decried the legislation, a frustrated Senator Bob Packwood declared:

I will tell you who we have heard from. They all live in Sun City and they all have incomes of $30,000. I do not think it is unfair or unethical or immoral or wrong to ask those of us who are a little bit more privileged to give a little extra to take care of those who are a little less privileged.[97]

Senator Alan Simpson warned that members would regret a repeal vote: "We're not confused. We're terrorized. But when the older Americans . . .

find out we've been swung around by our tails by a small group of wealthy senior citizens, my guess is we'll see a firestorm."[98]

On October 4, 1989, in an unprecedented move, the House voted to repeal the program it had approved just 16 months earlier. Two days later the Senate voted to repeal the surtax, retaining only the long-term hospital benefit, which was subsequently eliminated, too.[99] Representative Henry Waxman (D-Calif.) said members voted to repeal the entire program because "the elderly were ungrateful. So let them stew in their own juices."[100] Representative Stark added, "The hell with it.... If seniors want long term care without helping to pay for it, they had better guess again."[101]

The repeal of the Medicare Catastrophic Coverage Act was a setback for the business community. In its wake, many firms began retreating from their commitment to their retirees. In April 1989 Pittston Coal declared it would no longer contribute to the miners' health and welfare funds. The United Mine Workers went on strike until Pittston finally agreed after a nine-month standoff to restore some of the benefits and replenish part of the miners' trust fund. Some firms, such as TRW, Pillsbury, and Quaker Oats, shifted more of the cost of retiree benefits onto current workers or retirees by increasing premiums, co-payments, and deductibles or by capping their own expenditures at a set amount.[102] By 1996 88 percent of employers required retirees over age 65 to pay some or all of the premiums that had formerly been provided for free.[103] Some firms established two-tier systems that provided full benefits for current workers and retirees but not for newly hired employees. Others pushed retirees into Medicare HMOs, a move that virtually eliminated their premium costs and transferred the risks of high costs onto Medicare.[104] The number of employers offering retiree benefits to early retirees, those age 55 to 64, dropped from 70 percent in the mid-1980s to 36 percent by 2000. There was an equally precipitous drop in retiree benefits for people 65 and older, with only 26 percent of Medicare-eligible retirees covered by an employer plan in 2000.[105] Thus, while some older people experienced short-term gains from the repeal of the Medicare Catastrophic Coverage Act, the long-term consequence was the loss of a fully financed prescription drug benefit and erosion of benefits for future retirees.

The decline of retiree health benefits represented a devastating loss for people such as 74-year-old Roman Makarewicz, who had worked for 42 years for the Pabst Brewing Company in Milwaukee. On August 6, 1996, with no warning, he and hundreds of other Pabst retirees received a letter announcing that the company was cutting its workforce by 200 and dropping retiree benefits as of September 1. Beer production had fallen by two-thirds in the past year, and Pabst could no longer afford to provide the coverage. Under Pabst's generous retiree health plan, Mr. Makarewicz had paid only $2 for each prescription. Now his prescription drug costs would soar. As he explained, "I've got high blood pressure. I've got to take a water pill. My medications alone are $114 a month. I've got arthritis in my knees. I can barely walk. Forty-two years you work in a place and then get stabbed in the back." His coworker, 70-year-old Gerald Holtslander, wearily agreed: "What are you going to do when they start changing the rules? A little guy can't do anything."[106]

In 2000 the Third Circuit Court of Appeals ruled that retirees who are eligible for Medicare could have a valid claim of age discrimination under the Age Discrimination in Employment Act if their employers provide them with coverage inferior to that offered to younger retirees, that is, those who are under 65 and thus not eligible for Medicare. In light of this decision more employers concluded that it was safer to eliminate retiree health benefits entirely than to risk being sued for age discrimination.[107]

During the 1980s employers had attempted to reduce their health care expenditures by shifting costs to employees, negotiating lower rates with providers, organizing to gain a voice in policy decisions, and supporting legislation that would transfer responsibility for retiree benefits to the federal government. When none of these tactics succeeded to any significant extent, in the late 1980s corporate purchasers turned with a vengeance to managed care.

The Ascendance of Managed Care

In the 1980s companies began experimenting with various piecemeal approaches to managing health care. Some companies, such as Pillsbury and Berol, began negotiating fees directly with physicians and hospitals before treatment or required employees to get approval for routine hospitalizations and obtain second opinions before undergoing certain operations.[108] Others, including Caterpillar, R. J. Reynolds, Chrysler, and aerospace giant Martin Marietta, began their own internal hospital utilization review programs or penalized employees who refused to switch to an HMO by imposing higher co-payments.[109] Berol built its own medical clinic with its own physicians, laboratory, and pharmacy.[110]

Corporate purchasers then turned to managed care in a more coordinated fashion. The shift began in earnest in 1987, when Edward Hennessy, the chairman of Allied Signal, frustrated by a 39 percent hike in health insurance costs in one year, declared, "Enough."[111] Hennessy asked an aide to show him the "most astronomical health care bills" of his employees, those $100,000 or higher. To his amazement, the aide wheeled in a cart with a three-foot-high stack of folders. That spring Hennessy invited a dozen of the nation's largest insurers to compete for a managed care contract. Cigna won the contract by promising to keep rate increases under 6 percent a year for the next three years.

Allied Signal rapidly became a model for the rest of corporate America.[112] Southwestern Bell adopted a managed care plan in 1987. Sears Roebuck switched to managed care in 1990. In 1989 the head of human resources at Wells Fargo organized a breakfast for dozens of area corporations to develop a managed care strategy. As a result of these efforts, the companies formed the Pacific Business Group on Health and began negotiating cheap managed care contracts.[113] The retreat from fee-for-service occurred rapidly. Between 1983 and 1994 the number of physicians employed in group practices, HMOs, and other organizational settings grew from 23 percent to 37 percent.

Managed care was not a single arrangement but rather involved a bewildering variety of forms. Some companies established HMOs with their own medical staff; others involved preferred provider organizations (PPOs) of independent physicians who contracted to provide services for a discounted rate in return for guaranteed patient volumes. Some self-insured firms created and ran their own managed care plans. Others hired specialized managed care firms to process employee claims. Regardless of the specifics, the central tenet of managed care was that doctors and hospitals should no longer be able to choose whatever treatment they preferred. Under managed care they were no longer solely in charge of medical decisions and no longer in control of the allocation of health care resources. Take Dr. Barry Levine, who taught at Harvard Medical School. One day he received a letter from Tufts Associated Health Plans, an HMO that covered some of Levine's patients. He was invited to what he thought would be a brainstorming session with HMO managers to solicit his advice. Instead Joe Gerstein, Tufts' medical director, informed him that he would have to discharge heart attack patients a half day earlier and use a shorter-acting anesthesia so his patients could go home sooner.[114]

The objective of managed care firms was to wrest control of services from physicians and hospitals and push providers to make "cost-efficient" choices.[115] Computer-generated data on patients' treatment and outcomes made it possible to identify subpar performance. Physicians were pressured to spend less time with each individual patient, to use fewer specialists, and to order fewer tests and procedures. When physicians challenged the decisions, statisticians pulled out their spreadsheets to demonstrate how the doctors' choice of treatment deviated from the norm. Some HMOs tethered physicians' incomes to patient treatment decisions. Physicians who kept costs under control were rewarded with incentive pay or bonuses as high as $150,000 a year, while those who failed to do so were threatened with "delisting." According to one national survey, over 70 percent of managed care plans used some type of physician profiling.[116] For the first time, the major health plans were not just clerks paying bills.

In the power grab by employers, physicians found their authority slipping away. When the House Subcommittee on Human Resources and Intergovernmental Relations held hearings on managed care in 1993, one physician after another decried the intrusion of managed care. Dr. Steven Kanig, a podiatrist from Albuquerque, complained:

> Managing care to ensure high quality and control cost is the avowed mission of these organizations [managed care firms]. Each is pursuing a strategy that is aimed at maximizing its competitive position. . . . Many physicians are concerned that the notion of quality has become just another marketing concept and has nothing to do with true quality of care. . . . It should not be assumed that primary gatekeepers automatically provide the most cost-effective care. And the expense of some of the health care parasite industries must be brought under control.[117]

His colleague Dr. Carol Merovka complimented HMOs for making it possible for more small businesses to afford to offer health benefits to their employees. And she appreciated the information HMOs provided that allowed physicians to practice more cost-effectively:

> I have never, as a training physician, had the opportunity to look at how much it cost to have a gallbladder ultrasound or a C.B.C. done, et cetera. . . . So by getting information from these HMOs, I have been able to now figure out when someone comes into my office how I can make tremendous cost savings that still allows me to provide quality care. And that information was not available to me until I participated as a physician in an HMO.[118]

Yet the information provided by her HMO included only a cost analysis; it had nothing to do with patient outcomes. Thus she declared in frustration:

> I need to get out from the burden of managed care. I find it to be very manipulative. I find it to be very obtrusive in the care that I would like to give to my patients. And I feel also that, for the most part, because it is so cost and HMO administrative driven, that the physicians have lost their voice in the process.[119]

Because HMO physicians are "very, very fragmented and disenchanted," not many of her colleagues "have the guts to stand up and say how intimidated they are, how unhappy they are."[120]

During the 1990s outraged physicians began fighting back against the speed-up of the production process, the loss of control over compensation, and the intrusion of nonmedical personnel into clinical decisions. They pursued their challenge to managed care through the courts, in the states, and in Congress, in many instances forming political alliances with consumers who were angered over the sometimes callous and clumsy treatment they received from managed care firms. Patients were forced to travel across town or further, far from family and friends, when they needed surgery. Sick children were given blood tests by cheaper but unfriendly technicians. Cancer patients had to fight to get costly treatments of unproven merit recommended by their doctors or even in some cases to obtain routine treatment.[121] One third-year medical student at the University of New Mexico described a notorious case in which his university's cancer center had to go to court to force an HMO to provide chemotherapy for a patient:

The unhappy ironic ending was that though the court ultimately ruled in the patient's favor, the litigation dragged so long that, by the time of the rule, the cancer had progressed beyond the point where the treatment could help. The patient died shortly after he won in court.[122]

In another case, Dr. Linda Peeno, who was a medical reviewer for Humana, testified that she had caused a death of a man when she denied a heart transplant:

> I was rewarded for this. It brought me an improved reputation in my job and contributed to my advancement afterward. The patient was a piece of computer paper. The "clinical goal" was to figure out a way to avoid payment. The diagnosis was to "DENY." Once I stamped "DENY" across his authorization form, his life's end was as certain as if I had pulled the plug on a ventilator. Not only did I demonstrate I could indeed do what was expected of me, I exemplified the "good" company doctor: I saved a half million dollars.[123]

By the mid-1990s polls showed that the insurance industry had become public enemy number one, even more despised than the tobacco industry.[124]

The AMA helped physicians in multispecialty groups acquire sufficient capital to organize their own HMOs and negotiate exclusive contracts with employers.[125] In 1996 podiatrists formed a union to bargain collectively with HMOs; other specialties considered the feasibility of starting their own unions. In the war with the HMOs, physicians won some battles but lost others. When a team of New Jersey anesthesiologists sued a hospital over the terms of a contract with an HMO, the hospital played hardball, hiring new anesthesiologists and taking patient assignments for these physicians out of the hands of the medical staff.[126] Some doctors, such as Daniel Fisher, packed up their equipment and quit practicing medicine. He explained his decision in a letter to his 2,651 patients:

> The system of HMOs, managed care, restricted hospitals and denial of needed medications has become so corrupt, so rotten, that I cannot stomach it any longer. The system is controlled by for-profit

HMOS with dividend hungry shareholders and high-salaried administrators. I was beginning to feel the pressure and change my prescription habits from the best medicine I knew to the one that would look best on my profile and hating myself for it.[127]

Physicians also lobbied state legislatures to regulate HMOs.[128] They demanded that managed care companies publicly disclose the criteria they used to determine whether to approve a given service and won rulings requiring that nonmedical personnel could not deny services ordered by a physician.[129] At the urging of physicians' organizations, Rhode Island and Virginia passed laws requiring that an independent reviewer be available to assess HMO challenges to specialist referrals. New York enacted a law requiring HMOs to reimburse patients for consultations with physicians outside their HMO.[130] In response to pressure from physicians and consumers, three states passed laws restricting the ability of HMOs to deny claims for emergency room use. In 1996 alone, 110 bills were introduced in 36 states to extend hospital stays following a normal birth.[131] Physicians also used their influence to get state insurance departments to issue regulations requiring HMOs to disclose financial incentives that encouraged physicians to withhold care.[132]

Following a series of takeovers and mergers in the early 1990s, managed care firms grew rapidly in size and market scope.[133] With their billions in assets and influential lobbyists, these companies proved to be formidable opponents. Recognizing their negative public image, they used surrogates to fight their battles, mobilizing the Chamber of Commerce and the National Federation of Independent Business against regulatory measures physicians proposed in the states.[134] As a result, physicians' efforts to ban capitation payments (where they were paid a flat amount for each patient) through either state or federal legislation failed entirely.[135] When state and county medical societies pushed for rules that would prohibit HMOs from excluding physicians from their networks and force them to include "any willing provider," they were blocked by a coalition of employers and HMOs in every one of 29 states except Arkansas.[136]

Physicians also took their grievances to court in a series of class action suits.[137] They sued HMOs for antitrust relief, charging that insurance company mergers had consolidated power in the hands of a few companies.[138] They brought suit against Cigna, one of the largest managed care firms, on racketeering charges for underpaying patients' health claims, reaching a $50 million settlement in Illinois that was subsequently challenged in Florida.[139] Physicians won a major victory on June 20, 2002, when the Supreme Court upheld a lower-court decision giving patients the right to an independent review for denial of treatment.[140]

Physicians also pressed for "patients' rights" legislation that would allow patients who were denied care to sue their HMO.[141] When a patients' bill of rights was proposed in the Virginia General Assembly, the state's largest insurance company, Trigon Healthcare, a Blue Cross/Blue Shield giant, hired 33 lobbyists, including the governor's chief fund-raiser, the wife of the executive director of the state Republican Party, a former state attorney general, and two Democratic Party campaign consultants. Lobbyists worked the General Assembly and held seminars around the state, targeting a provision that would allow patients to sue their health insurer for malpractice.[142] One legislator complained, "There was a great deal of lobbying, as much as I've seen in 35 years."[143] Although most of the bill remained intact, the key issue—the right to sue—was removed. The same organizations successfully employed similar tactics in Texas. Over the next few years, however, ten states gave injured patients the right to sue their HMO in state courts.[144]

The physicians took patients' rights to Congress, a tactic that antagonized self-insured firms, who opposed any feature that would weaken the ERISA preemption (which prevented self-insured firms from being sued in state courts). The Business Roundtable joined forces with the Chamber of Commerce, the National Association of Manufacturers, the Health Insurance Association of America, and Aetna to undermine public support for this provision.[145] The coalition paid for a $750,000 media blitz, widely airing ads that proclaimed that more federal regulation would increase premiums and cause more people to lose coverage.[146] Viewers first heard pitches from a worker, a small-business owner, and a mother and child and were then urged to call an 800 number to register their opposition. NAM also dispatched a memo to 200 lawmakers warning them against supporting the bill and threatening to stuff notes in workers' pay envelopes urging them to protest if it was enacted.[147] In 1999 the House of Representatives narrowly passed a patients' bill of rights, but the measure died in a conference committee.

The patients' bill of rights reappeared in 2001, when the Senate passed a new bill providing a host of protections for patients in self-insured health plans. The most significant provisions gave patients in these plans the right to sue when denial of treatment resulted in injury or death. AMA secretary-treasurer Donald Palmisano lauded the Senate bill as "a huge victory for patients" that "set a gold standard for protecting patients against managed care abuses."[148] While HMOs had stopped fighting other patient protections, they remained opposed to the issue of lawsuits. The bill appeared headed for passage in the House until President George W. Bush threatened to veto it after his advisors concluded that patients' rights were not a high public priority. Although 70 percent of the public said they favored a patients' bill of rights, patients' rights were ranked only seventh in importance, after education, energy exploration, and conservation.[149] It seemed unlikely that a presidential veto would trigger an explosive reaction. Instead, Bush negotiated behind the scenes for an amendment that would cap damages and move some kinds of lawsuits from state to federal courts. Democrats decried the amendment, claiming it "was slanted at every turn for the HMOs and against patients and doctors." The amended bill passed in the House on August 3, 2001, but died in a conference committee, exactly the outcome the HMOs wanted.[150]

In the wake of the failure of patients' rights, the courts began chipping away at the ERISA preemption of state regulations. In 2003 the U.S. Second Circuit Court of Appeals ruled in *Cicio v. Vytra Healthcare* that HMOs could be held liable if lack of patient care led to injury or death.[151] And although the patients' rights issue was dead in Congress, it was still alive in the states, with ten bills for patients' rights and managed care reform pending in 2003.

The costly wars between physicians and insurers resulted in a strategy shift on the part of HMOs and employers. The Coalition for Affordable Quality Health Care, an organization of HMOs, insurance companies, and trade associations, launched a $9 million campaign to improve the image of the managed care industry. Employers began offering their employees less restrictive managed care plans or giving them a choice of plans, and insurers began seeking less contentious relationships with providers.[152] Bending to the strength of the consumer movement, the American Association of Health Plans, the organization representing HMOs, also loosened restrictions on some of the more contentious issues, such as "drive-by" mastectomies and 24-hour hospital stays following a normal birth.[153]

Conclusion

From the New Deal to the 1970s, the chief obstacle to national health insurance was organized medicine. Then the excesses of the profession produced a counterreaction from the corporations that began to challenge the protected provider markets. Corporations tried a variety of tactics ranging from shifting costs to employees to negotiating with providers to organizing coalitions to influence policy debates. Ironically, the most effective challenge to the medical providers came from the private health insurance system, which physicians had helped to construct as an alternative to government intervention. It took the form of billion-dollar, for-profit managed care firms. Managed care helped to undermine physicians' claims of specialized knowledge by putting them at financial risk for their medical decisions and by placing decision-making power in the hands of nonphysicians.

The managed care wars changed the way most consumers received care. In the past health care had been rationed, but in implicit ways such as having lengthy waiting times to get appointments or being unable to see a specialist. Managed care engaged in explicit rationing by limiting patients' options, reducing their choice of health plans, or forcing them to see a physician who was a plan member. Even though most studies have found few differences in health outcomes between managed care and fee-for-service medicine, the visible constraints on choice created the perception that people were frequently denied access to lifesaving treatment or denied access to hospital care. Yet many people were willing to put up with constraints on choice in exchange for a promise of lower costs—a promise that hasn't materialized.[154]

The arousal of corporations and insurance companies also had consequences for national health insurance. It brought newly mobilized, powerful stakeholders into the political arena whenever health care reform was on the table. While corporations were primarily concerned with containing costs, insurers had a vested interest in preventing the federal government from creating competing products and in structuring any new programs in ways that would preserve the private market.

The true victims of the health care wars of the 1980s were neither physicians nor insurers. Rather, they were the millions of elderly people who did not try to overturn Rostenkowski's car, who did not write angry letters to their congressional representatives, and who did not testify before Congress against the Medicare Catastrophic Coverage Act. Not only did these people lose a benefit that would help defray the cost of the supplemental items that Medicare did not cover, such as prescription drugs (coverage for which employers were casting off with abandon), they also lost the sympathy of the key members of Congress whose support they would need if they hoped for any improvement in long-term care coverage. Since then, the long-term care market has moved in a direction that is similar to the pattern of health benefits for the younger population. That is, a small proportion of people purchase expensive policies on their own in the individual long-term care insurance market, a growing number are offered group long-term care benefits through an employer (but with the employer paying none of the costs), and the rest will do just what they have been doing—spending down their assets to qualify for Medicaid or hiring a smart lawyer to help them protect their estates.

seven

The Insurers Triumphant

The cost inflation of the 1980s proved to be damaging to the insurance industry in a number of ways. Not only did private insurance companies incur billions of dollars in underwriting losses, they also experienced an erosion of their economic base as the majority of large employers stopped using conventional insurance to cover their employees, moving to self-insurance instead.[1] Many insurance companies were forced out of the health care marketplace, leading to a rash of insurance company failures. In 1989 the House Committee on Oversight and Investigations concluded an inquiry into the causes of these failures. The inquiry uncovered "a remarkable record of greed and incompetence by the persons responsible for managing these companies." As evidence was presented, a sordid tale unfolded of "excessive underpricing, ridiculous management, self-dealing, non-existent records, and a general concern only for the welfare of the top corporate insiders." Worse, these activities were hidden "by contrived transactions, creative accounting and fraudulent reports to regulatory agencies."[2] The agencies that were supposed to monitor insurance company practices, the state insurance departments, were largely ineffectual, because in most states they lacked the personnel and authority to track and punish wayward insurers. In states where insurance commissioners were elected, their largest campaign contributions came from insurance companies. As one witness testified at another hearing, "In some cases the industry gets them elected."[3] Only one-third of insurance departments even had written rules regarding how to handle the 23,000 or so complaints that each department received on average each year, and half kept no records on the number of complaints about any specific insurance company.

Yet during the 1990s, the insurance industry emerged as the unchallenged master of the health care financing system, trumping physicians and hospitals and turning back challenges that might undermine their access to core markets. Industry leaders mobilized forces to fend off federal regulation, crush proposals for government-backed long-term care insurance and national health insurance, and spur the development of new private company products. At the century's end, the private insurance industry had vanquished any public sector alternative.

Long-Term Care for the Frail Elderly

In the mid-1980s the House Subcommittee on Health and Long Term Care held a series of hearings that highlighted the plight of the frail elderly. Once people became chronically ill with little hope of recovery, Medicare and most private insurance ended.[4] At that point the only option for most people was to deplete their life savings, then submit to what many considered humiliating scrutiny of their income and assets to determine their eligibility for Medicaid. Medicaid applicants faced a bewildering array of rules and regulations that varied from state to state. In some states Medicaid included the "medically needy," people who had minimal assets, low or moderate incomes (but were not desperately poor), and high medical expenses for nursing home care. Other states, those with no "medically needy" program, rejected applicants if their income was $1 over the Medicaid limit even when they owned nothing.[5] In such states anyone with Social Security benefits and a modest pension would likely be disqualified. For example, Ann Blake, a 55-year-old secretary, moved her incontinent 78-year-old mother from her home in Arkansas to a Florida nursing home, then applied for Medicaid, thinking the state would pay for her mother's care. Although Ann's mother owned no property and had a monthly income of just over $1,300, Florida's Medicaid income limit was $1,158 at that time. Her application was denied.[6] Ann was forced to take her mother out of the nursing home and set her up in a trailer in the backyard of her own modest home. Because most people had no idea what the Medicaid eligibility rules were in any particular state until they needed help, they often learned that they were ineligible when it was too late to make other arrangements.

Even people who were accepted for Medicaid often couldn't find a nursing home that would admit them when they needed care, because nursing home operators favored private-pay patients, who were charged higher rates. One study found that nearly 80 percent of nursing homes discriminated against Medicaid beneficiaries in their admission policies. Medicaid patients were often forced to wait two to three times as many days for admission as Medicare or private-pay patients.[7] As one Illinois nursing home administrator explained, "We refuse admission if someone is on Medicaid even if we have empty beds. It is a calculated risk. We would rather have the bed empty."[8] Nursing homes that accepted Medicaid patients usually provided poorer-quality care than those with higher proportions of private-pay patients.[9]

These problems were exacerbated by Medicare's prospective payment system, which reimbursed hospitals a flat amount depending on a patient's diagnosis, no matter how long the stay. Once the prospective payment system went into effect, hospitals transferred patients recovering from surgery or a heart attack to nursing homes as quickly as they could. Swamped with applications, nursing homes tightened their admission requirements.[10] The practice of releasing patients from hospitals quicker and sicker also placed pressure on the states, which through Medicaid paid for 41 percent of all nursing home care.[11] Rising Medicaid costs drained state coffers, consuming resources that might otherwise be used for education, infrastructure, and social services. In an effort to keep costs under control, some states resorted to freezing Medicaid reimbursement rates, a strategy that only worsened the dilemma for the frail elderly.[12] For example, Tennessee's preadmission screening program made it difficult even for very sick people to get nursing home care. One daughter was incredulous that her mother was deemed medically ineligible for nursing home care:

She has been with me every day since she was sick. During the last two years, she has been in my house seven days a week, 24 hours a day. . . . She was in the emergency room, she had a leg ulcer and fell, which created another ulcer on her ankle. She has been treated for symptoms of congestive heart failure. She is a diabetic. She has had a few mini-strokes. . . . She is confused. She cannot cook for herself or get down into the bathtub. . . . But the hospital said it did not see these things. It is hard to get them into a nursing home if they are not completely bedridden.[13]

In another case, a son who failed to find a nursing home placement for his mother explained his frustration with the system:

My mother had a stroke and was getting where she could not take care of herself. She was paranoid. She could not cook meals very well or take care of her house. . . . If she did try to cook, she would burn things. She had bladder accidents . . . I went by every day after work to check on her. . . . Several times we had to redo paperwork.[14]

Despite his mother's precarious health, she was not considered sick enough to qualify for Medicaid.

As the long-term care system was squeezed to the limit, the elderly and their middle-aged children turned to the federal government to solve the problem. According to a poll conducted by the AARP in 1988, more than 75 percent of people age 45 and older supported a national long-term care program similar to Social Security. Governors, too, began to look to Washington for more help.

Long-term care was a market the private insurance industry had barely penetrated. Until the mid-1980s, the insurance industry had been uninterested in long-term care insurance, because expenses were too unpredictable and the elderly too poor to make the product viable. In 1985 fewer than three dozen companies offered any sort of long-term care coverage. The trend toward self-insurance among large firms had eroded the economic base of private insurance plans and left them with the less profitable business of claims processing and benefits management. To compensate for these losses, insurance companies began aggressively seeking new markets. As we saw in Chapter 6, one solution was to market managed care plans to employers.[15] Insurers also began exploring the untapped but potentially profitable long-term care market. In 1986 the Health Insurance Association of America created a Task Force on Long Term Care. The Task Force surveyed developments in the field and discovered that the generation of people who were approaching old age had higher median income, greater wealth, and "greater assets to protect and preserve" than any previous generation. Long-term care insurance presented a lucrative opportunity, because profits in the insurance industry are generated almost entirely from investment income. Policies that incur benefit expenses monthly, such as health insurance, are less profitable than policies whose payouts may be years in the future, such as life insurance.[16] The longer the duration of the policy, the higher the profits. People in their 50s and 60s who might not make claims for several decades and the upper-income "young" elderly who had assets to protect were the ideal "target market for a long term care insurance product."[17] By 1987 72 companies had leaped into the long-term care market.

At first the market was dominated by smaller, specialty companies that sold individual insurance policies. These individual policies were ripe for abuse. Most purchasers were frail elderly people in poor health, and the product was entirely unregulated. Previous investigations of sales practices in the medigap insurance market had found that agents frequently employed deception in explaining the limits and restrictions of their policies and often sold the elderly unnecessary policies for coverage they already had. For example, Mrs. Z. was sold similar medigap policies from three different agents. One 86-year-old Wisconsin woman bought 19 different policies from six agents representing nine companies.[18] Mrs. M's agent sold her a medigap policy, then changed companies four months later and sold her a new policy. Another agent sold the same client 11 different policies from three companies. As one former insurance agent testified, "The goal is to take advantage of what the older person doesn't know." The practice of paying high commissions the first year a policy was in effect encouraged "switching or twisting where agents get seniors to drop the insurance policy they sold them a short while ago to buy a new policy which is of no more value or less value. The agent is sitting pretty with another big, fat first-year sales commission of up to 60 percent of the premium paid by the victim."[19]

State insurance commissioners responded to complaints but only rarely initiated broader investigations of insurance companies. In most states there was no effort to determine whether fraudulent sales practices were isolated instances or systematic occurrences, and insurance companies were rarely fined or disciplined. To curb these abuses, in 1979 Congress enacted legislation that prohibited certain of the more unsavory marketing practices and allowed states to give a "seal of approval" to companies whose medigap policies met certain standards. The following year Congress established criminal penalties for agents who engaged in deceptive sales tactics and required insurers to provide minimum coverage and set minimum standards for loss ratios.[20] That meant that all medigap policies had to pay at least 60 cents on every premium dollar in benefits.[21] Yet a follow-up investigation in 1986 found that the elderly were no better off than they had been eight years before.[22] The regulatory measures had only been sporadically enforced, and little had been done to stop insurance scams. The majority of states allowed coverage gaps and loopholes to persist, and few states monitored how much of policyholders' premiums were actually paid out in benefits.

In 1991 Congress enacted stricter regulations for private medigap policies.[23] Insurance companies that offered supplemental medigap coverage law were prohibited from refusing any Medicare beneficiary who wished to purchase a policy, regardless of health.[24] The glitch was that older people had this protection only if a medigap policy was purchased within a six-month open enrollment period. When this six-month period ended, they could be denied coverage of a preexisting condition or be forced to pay higher rates.

The federal laws governing medigap policies, weak as they were, did not apply to long-term care insurance at all. As the insurance industry began expanding its offerings for long-term care, similar complaints surfaced. By 1989 20 states had begun investigations of sales practices for long-term care insurance in their legislative sessions.[25] In Congress the House Subcommittee on Health and Long Term Care conducted its own investigation and found numerous problems. Unscrupulous sales agents exaggerated what the policies covered and sold people duplicate policies. Insurance companies delayed paying benefits when people filed claims; some even disqualified policyholders entirely.[26] Most policies provided little protection against the cost of nursing home care, few were indexed to keep up with inflation, many excluded admissions for Alzheimer's disease (the main cause of nursing home admissions), and most allowed insurers to cancel coverage at any time. Some enterprising insurance companies created fictitious "groups" to sell insurance to the elderly. For example, in Massachusetts the insurance commissioner investigated a long-term care plan underwritten by the Pioneer Life Insurance Company through a group deceptively named the Association of Retired Americans.[27] As consumer advocate Bonnie Burns noted, "While there has been an explosion of companies willing to enter this market, there is no regulation to protect the consumer on whom this experiment is being conducted."[28]

Following the flurry of bad publicity, the larger insurance companies began entering the field, building upon their experience in marketing group health insurance to employers to craft better policies. Aetna offered a new plan for retired employees in Alaska that covered nursing home care and home care, the first policy sold through an employer group.[29] Prudential test-marketed a new product for AARP members.[30] As the idea of group long-term care insurance spread, other employers began offering long-term care policies to their employees. These policies were often negotiated by benefits managers who used the leverage afforded large groups to insist on automatic inflation adjusters, cheaper rates, a range of care options, and Alzheimer's coverage.

The insurance industry fiercely resisted any efforts by the federal government to regulate long-term care insurance, preferring to leave regulation to insurer-friendly state insurance departments.[31] In 1986 the National Association of Insurance Commissioners developed model legislation for long-term care policies in an effort to head off federal regulation. The Long Term Care Insurance Model Act and Regulation included inflation protection, a 30-day free-look period, and guarantees of refunds in case of a lapse or cancellation.[32] But only a few states adopted the model.[33]

With the industry seemingly incapable of policing itself and cash-strapped states unwilling to take on more of the long-term care burden, a federal program seemed to offer the most feasible solution. The plan came from Claude Pepper, who after his bitter 1950 defeat in the Senate race by George Smathers had returned to private law practice for a decade, then run for a seat in the House of Representatives when a new congressional district was carved out in Dade County following the 1960 census. As Pepper acquired seniority, he had moved up to become chairman of the powerful Rules Committee, which determined what bills would go to the floor for consideration by the entire House of Representatives. Age 87 himself, Pepper was the leading advocate of the elderly, whose major concern was long-term care. Representative Pepper's records were filled with letters such as the following from Robert Matteson:

When you're cornered, faced with odds so great you don't know how to surmount, the human nature in all of us tells us to seek help from persons who appear to be championing our needs and causes. I am 81, diabetic, faced with the possibility of a nursing home, with its grabbing everything I have left in this world, leaving me and my wife in poverty. This is the plight some witless jerk called our "Golden Years." There were occasions through the years when we paid our taxes more dutifully than willingly, but we paid them. So I'm saying to you, Mr. Pepper, please keep up your efforts to help us unfortunate people in the 80-year-class. Persuade the government, of which you are a part, to help us in extended catastrophic care.[34]

A desperate daughter wrote about her 84-year-old father, Valerio Dimaya, who had been hospitalized for several back fractures, then discharged to her care "with a catheter, a broken clavicle and without his dentures":

He can hardly eat a decent meal nor can he swallow well. Yet he was given huge pills for pain and for an antibiotic. The doctor says he doesn't know if it comes in liquid form. They just told me to find a home by looking in the phone book. No help was given. In the meantime, I'm paying for home care, caring for my three children as a single parent, teaching full time and attending school. Is there no real justice?[35]

Pepper had first introduced a bill to expand Medicare to cover home care services for disabled people of all ages on June 24, 1987. His ambitious proposal would have provided skilled nursing care, home health aides, rehabilitation therapy, and caregiver training.[36] Although the program would initially cover only care in the home, it would eventually be expanded "to cover nursing home care as well."[37] Careful to craft the bill so that physicians would not be threatened, Pepper won AMA support by allowing doctors to be the gatekeepers to the program. Anyone applying for benefits would first have to be certified by a physician as to need. Pepper's bill was killed in the House before it reached a floor vote, but Pepper, a shrewd political operator, threatened to bottle up the Medicare Catastrophic Coverage Act in his Rules Committee unless House Speaker Jim Wright promised to allow a floor vote on his home care bill. Wright also had to promise Pepper that he would appoint a commission to study long-term care and health insurance for the unemployed in the fall.[38]

On November 18, 1987, Pepper reintroduced his home care bill. For the insurance industry, Pepper's bill posed a direct threat to the developing long-term care market. Before the vote, the Health Insurance Association of America sent every member of Congress a letter declaring that "this bill is the wrong medicine for our country."[39] It represented "another example of an expensive government solution . . . that would lead to exploding public sector costs." It would create "an elaborate new layer of government regulation of the health care industry" and "preempt the nascent, but rapidly developing private insurance market."[40] The letter closed with a glowing endorsement of private long-term care insurance, which held "great promise in meeting the nursing home as well as home and community-based long term care needs of the chronically ill."[41]

The home care bill also aroused the opposition of business groups because it would be financed by removing the cap on the Medicare share of the payroll tax.[42] The Chamber of Commerce complained that the payroll tax increase would hurt small businesses and set a "dangerous precedent."[43] The National Federation of Independent Business warned that its members strongly opposed raising the payroll tax to finance long-term care and that it would consider the vote on Pepper's bill as "a Key Small Business Vote for the 100th Congress."[44] The National Association of Manufacturers recommended that Congress take measures instead to "encourage the insurance industry to continue to develop/market innovative insurance products for long term care."[45] The *Wall Street Journal* described the home care bill as "the welfare state on cocaine," supported by "the King Kong known as the senior citizen lobby that muscles in on an ever great share of the nation's wealth."[46]

President Reagan had supported the Medicare Catastrophic Coverage Act because the elderly would pay the costs themselves, but Pepper's bill would be funded by a payroll tax hike. Reagan promised to veto the bill should it reach his desk, declaring it would create "a group of underserved beneficiaries and underpaid providers" who "would constitute a potentially powerful lobby for the expansion of financing for benefits which . . . would add billions of dollars to the federal deficit."[47] In June 1988 99 Democrats joined with 144 Republicans to defeat the measure. Any member of Congress who voted in favor received a letter from the Health Insurance Association of America warning, "We want to take special notice of your vote last week on Rep. Pepper's home care bill."[48]

The defeat of the home care bill left the market open for the private insurance industry, but two problems stood in the way of success. The first was that in a number of states, many of the middle-class people who were the target market for long-term care insurance qualified for Medicaid payments for nursing home care. Many became eligible for Medicaid by "spending down" their assets after they entered a nursing home. For example, Margaret Stetler was in her early 80s and had diabetes and chronic heart failure. When she first entered a nursing home, she had over $40,000 in assets, which disqualified her for Medicaid. However, once she had spent down her assets, Medicaid picked up the cost of her care.[49] In other cases, middle-income elderly became eligible for Medicaid before they entered a nursing home by transferring their assets to their children. Although rules prohibited the transfer of assets three years prior to an application for Medicaid, asset transfers were allowed before then. Even within the three-year "look-back" period, there were loopholes that made it possible to shelter assets. An entire industry of Medicaid estate planners arose to help people find a way to qualify for Medicaid and preserve their estates for their children and grandchildren. In 1989 alone, membership in the National Academy of Elder Law Attorneys increased from 88 to 450.[50] Research found that somewhere between 33 and 40 percent of nursing home residents were eligible for Medicaid upon admission. Some had always been poor, but a significant number of this group had transferred assets to children three years prior to admission, often with the help of an elder-law attorney. In 1993 half of Medicaid applicants had transferred assets during the preceding 30 months. Of those who were ineligible for Medicaid when they first entered a nursing home, only one-third remained private payers. The other two-thirds spent down their savings to Medicaid levels within six months to a year. In 1990 the insurance industry began a campaign to tighten Medicaid eligibility rules to make it tougher for middle-class people to qualify for benefits.

The second reason the insurance industry had difficulty selling long-term care insurance was that the public had no confidence in the product. A Consumers Union study of 94 private long-term care insurance

In the 1990s rising health care costs moved national health insurance to the forefront of the political agenda. Library of Congress, Prints and Photographs Divisions, LC-USZ62-126890

policies found many were highly flawed, a situation made worse by "poorly trained and often unscrupulous agents" who misled consumers about the terms, benefits, and limitations of their coverage. So prevalent were these practices that there was a "need to reevaluate whether an agent-based distribution system [could] work for this product."[51] The House Select Committee on Aging similarly found numerous obstacles for people seeking to purchase coverage and substantial evidence of unscrupulous sales practices. One agent testified about the case of "Bob and Grace," who were frightened into purchasing a worthless policy:

> Bob and Grace didn't have much. They lived off a small pension and Social Security and had no significant savings. The agent pounded away at this poor elderly couples' fears. He told them a story of just having come from Miami where he had been with an elderly couple who didn't have insurance and were now actually living off cat food. Slapping his hand on the table, the agent said, "How would you like to spend the rest of your life eating Kal-Kan?" All the elderly gentleman remembered after that was writing out a check for $2,500.[52]

Another couple found the policy they had purchased to be worthless when they sought to collect the promised benefits:

> Mr. Fiery and I worked hard all our lives and were conservative with our spending. After about 5 years of faithfully paying premiums on the insurance, my husband took ill and had to be admitted to the hospital. After that the doctor said he needed care in a nursing home. While I was upset at the prospect of him not being at home, I was thankful that we had taken out the insurance policy to protect us financially for just this kind of thing. When I submitted the insurance forms for payment, the company said that John's care was not provided in a skilled nursing home as required by our policy. Well, the insurance agent didn't say one word about that when he sold us the insurance.[53]

One disgusted agent told of being approached by a company that specialized in long-term care policies:

> They offered me a guarantee of $50,000 minimum, a new 1987 car and gas to work for them. They told me [to say] that no matter

what people had in the way of insurance, it was trash and what I had was great. Their person told me, "Those old f——ts don't know any better anyway."[54]

When Congress attempted to set uniform federal standards to regulate long-term care insurance, the Health Insurance Association of America objected that federal regulation was unnecessary and that insurers needed protection in this new and risky market. Finally, in 1990 Congress established rules for the timely payments of claims, prohibited insurers from offering coverage that duplicated what Medicare already provided, and required insurance companies to adopt the National Association of Insurance Commissioners model policy.[55]

Although one might discount the home care bill as an overly ambitious publicity stunt that was doomed to fail, that interpretation ignores the fact that during this same period other countries succeeded in finding ways to help the frail elderly pay for long-term care. Germany, the Netherlands, and Australia all established arrangements for public long-term care insurance programs even as they were downsizing other entitlement programs.[56]

Reviving National Health Insurance

During the 1980s Congress had attempted to plug up some of the holes in the private health insurance system with the Consolidated Omnibus Reconciliation Act of 1985 (COBRA). COBRA required employers with 20 or more employees who provided group health insurance plans to offer temporary continuation of coverage for people who would otherwise lose it because of retirement, layoff, divorce, separation, or death. Through a tricky political maneuver the COBRA provision was embedded in the budget process, where secrecy prevailed and filibustering (a tactic used to kill controversial legislation) was prohibited, giving the business groups that opposed it no opportunity to mobilize.[57] But various restrictions coupled with high costs meant that only about 20 percent of people who were eligible for COBRA coverage actually took it.[58]

In the 1980s Congress had also enacted a series of measures that expanded Medicaid coverage for pregnant women and children and loosened the direct link between Medicaid and AFDC. States were allowed to base Medicaid eligibility on family income rather than welfare status and to include children in two-parent households.[59] In 1989 states were required to cover pregnant women and children under age 6 in families with incomes up to 133 percent of the federal poverty level. The following year states were required to cover children ages 6 to 18 in families with incomes up to the federal poverty level.[60] Some states took advantage of these new rules to subsidize coverage for entire families.[61] Oregon extended Medicaid eligibility to all state residents with income below the federal poverty level.[62] Tennessee's TennCare program made Medicaid available to families with income up to 400 percent of the federal poverty level.[63] As the eligibility criteria loosened, Medicaid coverage among children improved significantly.

Despite these efforts, by 1990 37 million Americans—mostly poor and low-income adults and children as well as some middle-income people—remained uninsured. More than twice as many had been uncovered for some period in the past two years.[64] Among the uninsured nearly 80 percent were fully employed, many in low-wage jobs with small firms or in occupations or industries that insurance companies deemed too risky.[65] About 1 million were classified as "medically uninsurable." These individuals could not obtain any health coverage because of poor health, a preexisting condition, or current employment in a hazardous occupation.[66] More than at any time in history, polls showed the public supported health care reform.[67]

Many key stakeholders also believed that some major change was necessary. They had the opportunity to air their views during hearings of the Pepper Commission.[68] Pepper Commission members were a who's who of health care policy, including Senator Ted Kennedy, Representative William Gradison, and Senator Jay Rockefeller, who succeeded Claude Pepper as chairman after Pepper's death in 1989. If commissioners could reach a consensus, much of the political work would have been done. After a rocky start with squabbles between those who wanted to emphasize long-term care and those who were most concerned with access to health care, commission members descended into partisan bickering. They finally split votes on a compromise plan called "pay or play" under which firms would have to either offer affordable insurance to their employees or pay into a federal fund for the uninsured.[69]

Although the Pepper Commission report ended up gathering dust on bookshelves, the testimony presented showed that while providers and business leaders favored some type of reform, there was no consensus among them about what the central problem was or what shape reform should take. The AMA conceded that action was needed to cover the uninsured but argued that it should be provided "to the greatest extent" through the private sector.[70] The AHA was most concerned about private insurers' increasingly rigid resistance to the cost-shifting tactics hospitals employed to compensate for cuts in public programs. To achieve universal coverage, which would make cost shifting unnecessary, the AHA advocated an employer mandate coupled with tax credits for small employers and an expanded Medicaid program for the poor.[71]

Large manufacturers also seemed to be leaning toward national health insurance. Chrysler's CEO, Lee Iacocca, had become less enamored of free markets and more willing to consider a government solution to help American manufacturers better compete in a global market.[72] Having to absorb health care in the sticker price of cars was taking its toll on the auto industry. As Iacocca explained:

> In the United States, employers pay most of the health-care bill. In other countries, that's mainly a governmental responsibility. I like our system better, but it does put a burden on the competitiveness of our products.[73]

John Butler, director of employee benefits at General Motors, expressed similar sentiments:

> At one time the unequivocal answer would be "no" to supporting national health insurance. Faced with a health care bill of $3 billion last year, GM is reconsidering its opposition. . . . In terms of our competition, I would say that is something we are looking at. I'm not saying we are endorsing it, just thinking about it.[74]

A survey of executives from Fortune 500 companies found that 80 percent believed that fundamental changes were needed in the health care system and that over 32 percent favored a public health insurance system.[75] Fifty-three percent of the executives also agreed that "the government should force all employers to pay for their workers' health care."[76] Many of these companies resented being charged indirectly for health care for the uninsured and for coverage of their employees' dependents when spouses worked for firms that did not provide coverage. In 1990 a number of large corporations including Bethlehem Steel, Chrysler, Lockheed, Westinghouse, and Xerox endorsed the idea of an employer mandate as a mechanism to control provider prices and fees.

Small firms mainly wanted the same tax and regulatory advantages as self-insured firms. Although they agreed that changes had to be made to control costs, they vehemently opposed an employer mandate or any measure that would raise taxes.[77] Their position was shared by the smaller commercial insurance companies that operated in the small-group and individual insurance market.[78] Like the small companies that they serviced, they wanted legislation that would level the playing field with self-insured firms regarding state mandates and taxes.[79]

The most important players in the game were the large managed care firms, which had grown rapidly in size and market scope following a series of takeovers and mergers.[80] By 1990 the eight largest insurance companies owned 45 percent of the 25 fastest-growing HMOs.[81] These multibillion-dollar firms did not initially stake out a public position on health care reform but just emphasized that they opposed government regulation of any sort.[82]

In 1991 national health insurance moved to the forefront of political debates when Senator John Heinz (D-Pa.) died in a plane crash and the governor of Pennsylvania appointed Harris Wofford, the 65-year-old former president of Bryn Mawr College, to replace him. Wofford was only supposed to serve until a special election could be held, but he decided to run for the regular Senate seat. The little-known Wofford was trailing far behind his opponent, Richard Thornburgh, the twice-elected, popular former governor and U.S. attorney general, until Wofford raised the topic of health insurance. It was a subject that he knew firsthand. His wife had a chronic medical condition, and each time he changed jobs they worried that she might be denied coverage. At one of his campaign stops, he declared, "The constitution says if you're charged with a crime, you have a right to a lawyer. Every American, if they're sick, should have the right to a doctor." The audience responded with thunderous applause and loud amens.[83] Wofford crushed Thornburgh in the election, and polls subsequently showed that voters identified health care as a key factor.[84]

Following the Wofford victory, dozens of bills were introduced in Congress, and business groups, insurance companies, and presidential hopefuls scrambled to develop their own plans. Senator Bob Kerrey (D-Neb.), the Vietnam war hero who had gained notoriety for his romance with movie star Debra Winger, advocated a program like Medicare for people of all ages. President George H. W. Bush, who until then had shown no interest in health care reform, called for greater regulation of the insurance industry, tax credits to help low-income families purchase insurance, and statewide purchasing pools for unhealthy people who were uninsurable in the private market. The candidate who came to own the issue, however, was Bill Clinton, the handsome, youthful, charismatic governor of Arkansas.

During the 1992 presidential campaign, Clinton promised to contain health care costs and guarantee universal coverage. Although he had endorsed the idea of "managed competition" where Americans would be "covered in big groups," he remained vague about what that would actually entail.[85] Clinton won the election, but with a scant 43 percent of the vote. Now he faced the challenge of meeting his campaign promise. On January 15, 1993, he made his first public announcement about health care reform, one that stunned the nation. He would create a task force to develop a plan and put his wife, Hillary Rodham Clinton, a smart, ambitious attorney, in charge. The announcement surprised White House staffers and heads of federal agencies. Many had been working on health care issues for decades. They understood the legislative process and expected to play a major part in health care reform. But their role would be peripheral. Day-to-day operations would be supervised by Ira Magaziner, an old friend who owned a consulting firm. A tall, unkempt man and a driven workaholic, Magaziner's main qualification for the job was a report on health care costs he had written for his home state of Rhode Island.

Some of Clinton's advisors urged him to get the task forces moving quickly to capitalize on the political momentum created by the election before opponents had time to organize. Others felt the budget deficit should take precedence. The deficit was the legacy of the Reagan administrations' economic policies. During the eight years Reagan was in office, the deficit nearly tripled, transforming the United States "from the world's number one creditor nation to the number one debtor." When George H. W. Bush succeeded Reagan in 1988, he went Reagan one better, racking up a deficit of $355 billion.[86] Clinton's economic advisors warned that health care reform would be expensive and should wait.[87] But Clinton had promised to have legislation within 100 days. Delay was out of the question. Magaziner immediately set to work. He created 8 cluster teams and 34 working groups, in all involving more than 630 health policy experts.[88] Some employees from the various federal agencies were included along with Democratic staffers, academics, and physicians. But the key stakeholder groups—insurance companies, business leaders, and provider organizations—though consulted, were not part of the task forces, leading many to feel resentful of the perceived "secrecy" surrounding the preparations. The first hitch came on February 24, 1993, when three groups from the health care industry sued the task force, claiming that Hillary Clinton was not a government employee and therefore could not chair or even attend closed task force meetings. As the First Lady recalled, "It was a deft political move, designed to disrupt our work . . . and foster an impression with the public and the news media that we were conducting secret meetings."[89] Eventually, the suit forced the release of 250 boxes of task force memos and reports, which proved to contain little of interest.

Despite Clinton's desire to get a quick start, the hundred days dragged on for seven months as other issues took precedence. The first delay came from a fight with the Republicans over the federal budget, followed by a protracted struggle with the trade unions over the North American Free Trade Agreement (NAFTA), which the unions viewed as an effort to shift production to low-wage countries with more lax environmental and labor standards. Before the election, Lane Kirkland, the aging president of the AFL-CIO, had told Clinton that the labor movement would be the "storm troopers" for national health insurance. Instead the AFL-CIO devoted its energies and resources to fighting NAFTA.[90]

Finally, on September 22 President Clinton made a prime-time address to the nation outlining his plan for health care reform. In his speech he decried spiraling health care costs, increasing red tape, and unaffordable prescription drugs and declared that Americans should never be at risk of losing their health insurance. Reforming the health care system was integral to improving the economy.[91] Then in a dramatic gesture, he held up a red, white, and blue "health security card" and promised to enact a program that would guarantee universal coverage and access to quality medical care. The details would follow in

October. Six days after the president's speech, the First Lady testified before five powerful congressional committees.[92] After her testimony, the White House planned a "rollout"—a series of speeches and events where the president would generate attention and support for his plan.[93] Instead on October 3, as the president was en route to California, his attention was diverted by an international emergency. American soldiers on a humanitarian mission in Somalia had been pinned down by factions led by Somali warlords after a botched raid on a warlord's headquarters. Two Black Hawk helicopters had been shot down. In the melee 18 Americans were killed and nearly 80 wounded. As the public watched a jeering mob drag the body of an American soldier through the streets, events planned to publicize health care reform were scrapped.[94] Not until October 27 were the Clintons able to relaunch the effort and regain momentum.

The question was how to proceed. One possibility was to hide health care reform in a budget bill, rather than going through normal political channels, where Senate Democrats would likely have difficulty mustering the 60 votes needed to stop a filibuster. This strategy had succeeded with COBRA, but Senator Robert Byrd (D-W.Va.), who chaired the Senate Appropriations Committee, balked, insisting there should be a public debate about so huge a measure.

Another option was to present Congress with general health care reform principles and work out the details later. But Rep. Dan Rostenkowski (D-Ill.), the "gruff and gritty old-school pol from Chicago" who chaired the Ways and Means Committee, insisted on a detailed bill spelling out every aspect of the plan.[95] Rostenkowski supported the concept of universal coverage but knew that higher taxes would be needed to finance it. The time it took to write the full bill gave numerous interest groups the opportunity to make demands in exchange for promises of support. By the time the final bill was released, it was 1,342 pages long, providing an easy target for Republican opponents to mock "big government."[96]

Health Security was the most ambitious policy proposal since the New Deal. It revolved around the concept of "managed competition." Managed competition was devised by concerned business leaders who began meeting in 1990 in Jackson Hole, Wyoming. Attending the meetings were several interested politicians: Dr. David Ellwood, the Minneapolis physician who had been involved in Nixon's HMO initiative;

Alain Enthoven, a Stanford economist; the president of the Blue Cross/ Blue Shield Association; and the executive vice president of Prudential, who represented the "gang of five," Aetna, Travelers, Cigna, MetLife, and Prudential—the large insurance companies that had moved aggressively into managed care. The Washington Business Group on Health was also brought on board. The Jackson Hole group, as it came to be called, hammered out a prototype for health care reform that was modeled around the existing relationship between corporate purchasers and managed care organizations and that favored the large insurers.[97] Under managed competition providers and insurers would be organized into networks that would integrate the financing and delivery of health care.[98] An independent agency would certify private insurance plans and set guidelines for a standard benefit package that all insurers would have to offer.

The Clintons' Health Security plan adopted many features advocated by the Jackson Hole group. It would establish a quasi-private system that relied on the market to drive down costs. The government would organize purchasing cooperatives called "health alliances" that would have the economic clout and expertise to bargain directly with health care providers. Firms with more than 5,000 employees could self-insure but would have to pay a new payroll tax to expand the public program for the uninsured if they chose this route.[99] But Health Security deviated from the recommendations of the Jackson Hole group in some respects. It would allow a national health board to establish regional and national spending limits, and it would give the board the authority to set limits on insurance premium hikes.

Health Security would solve a number of problems with the health care financing system. It would reform the small group and individual insurance market with its pervasive use of risk rating by prohibiting insurance companies from refusing coverage on the basis of age or health or terminating benefits for any reason.[100] It would end hospital cost-shifting because everyone would be covered. It would ease the burden of retiree health benefits by lowering the eligibility age for Medicare and capping the health care costs borne by any single firm. It would retain for the private insurance industry a market of supplemental products to cover health care expenses that were not included in the basic benefit package. And it would allow the large firms that had shifted into managed care to administer the purchasing cooperatives. But the controls on risk rating could cause smaller specialty insurance firms to lose 30 to 60 percent of their business, and health insurance agents would be put out of business entirely. Since no one would be denied coverage, insurance agents would no longer be selling individual coverage.[101]

The delays over the budget and NAFTA gave Clinton's opponents time to mobilize against him. The Health Insurance Association of America had begun to gear up even before Clinton took office. Eleven days after Clinton was sworn in, the association hired Bill Gradison (R-Oh.), the ranking Republican on the House Ways and Means Committee, as its president and chief lobbyist. A respected and knowledgeable Washington insider, Gradison resigned from Congress immediately to coordinate the opposition campaign, bringing with him the leading health policy counsel on Ways and Means, Charles Kahn, as executive vice president. According to Gradison:

> We had lots of time to get geared up. It gave us a lot more time to refine our message, raise our money, do internal staffing changes, and have training sessions with members of our association as to what they could do with their hometowns and their editorial boards.[102]

Gradison placed two public relations consultants on retainer, hired outside lobbyists, and initiated a $3 million advertising campaign. The first ads, which aired in spring 1993, only made vague statements about health care reform. Rather than denounce reform outright, these ads questioned government involvement in the health care system. The general message was "You will lose control" and, alternatively, that the private insurance industry could cover everyone.[103] In response, Hillary Clinton struck back, lashing out at the health insurance industry for "price gouging, cost shifting and unconscionable profiteering" and charging that insurance companies had brought the nation to the brink of bankruptcy."[104] After a hiatus during the summer, the Health Insurance Association of America unveiled a more aggressive round of attack ads in September. The ads featured a husband and wife, Harry and Louise, sitting at the kitchen table worrying about how the president's plan would affect their coverage. One ad said, "The government may force us to pick from a few health plans designed by government bureaucrats."[105] Another used language such as "mandatory,"

"billion dollar bureaucracy run by tens of thousands of new bureaucrats," and "government monopoly."[106] The Harry and Louise ads generated numerous media commentaries, counterresponses, spoofs, and
cartoons. Although 52 percent of those who saw the ads felt they were
completely untrue or more wrong than right, they helped frame Health
Security in a way that shook public confidence.[107] As Ira Magaziner
complained, "Every place I would go to a town hall meeting, a lot of
people would have received letters or calls from these groups. They
would ask questions like, why are you taking over the hospitals, which
was not true. The same thing would happen on talk shows."[108]

The Health Insurance Association of America also organized the
Coalition for Health Insurance Choices to enlist local business leaders
in the struggle. The coalition printed a thick manual spelling out ways
for insurers to get employees, vendors, and other sympathizers involved,
and it set up a toll-free number to mobilize grassroots support, generating more than 135,000 calls. "SWAT teams" wrote letters, lobbied lawmakers, and held seminars to educate the public and local business
leaders. The Lincoln National Life Insurance company of Fort Wayne,
Indiana, had 150 such meetings.[109] CNA Financial, a Chicago-based
insurer, sent brochures to its 70,000 agents and policyholders telling
them to write to members of Congress, targeting 6 key senators and 11
representatives from five states.[110] Insurance agents proved to be highly
effective allies, because they were located in every congressional district, tended to be active in their communities, and had extensive social
networks. According to one of the targets, "I'm getting more lobbying
from insurance agents . . . they really seem to be targeting the district."[111]

Aetna, MetLife, Cigna, Prudential, and Travelers had resigned from
the Health Insurance Association of America in 1992 over its failure to
support health care reform. These companies formed their own organization, the Alliance for Managed Competition.[112] Although Clinton's
Health Security plan to create purchasing alliances revolved around the
managed competition strategy that Alliance for Managed Competition
members had helped design in Jackson Hole, they opposed certain features.[113] Notably, they feared that the alliances would not merely be purchasing cooperatives but would become regulatory bodies with much
broader authority than the Jackson Hole group had originally envisioned.
They also opposed the creation of a national health board that could have
the authority to cap health spending on a nationwide basis.

Manufacturers with extensive retiree benefit commitments initially supported the Clinton plan because it would lower the age of eligibility for Medicare and cap any single firm's health care costs. One auto industry representative noted, "Absent some remedial measure such as that contained in the administration proposal, market forces will eventually force almost all employers to eliminate early retiree coverage."[114] Later, however, they reversed course and came out against the Health Security plan.[115] The shift in position was partly a response to the apparent success of managed care in containing costs. Employers' premiums had increased by 12 percent in 1990 and 8 percent in 1993; in 1994 they actually shrank by 1.1 percent.[116] Manufacturers also worried that the proposed alliances would be too comprehensive in scope, the basic benefit package too large, and the plan to limit lawsuits by employees too skimpy. Clinton also lost the pharmaceutical companies, who feared that the inclusion of prescription drugs would lead to the regulation of drug prices.

Small businesses opposed the employer mandate from the beginning, claiming it would impose an onerous tax burden. The National Federation of Independent Business joined the opposition campaign, dispatching a stream of faxes and action alerts from its Washington office to tens of thousands of small-business owners. Every week the federation polled its 600,000 members on their attitudes toward Health Security and sent their negative responses to members of Congress. The federation also conducted campaigns in states whose representatives served on key committees. For example, the federation targeted Montana Democrat Max Baucus, who sat on the Senate Finance Committee and whose initial public comments on Health Security had been favorable. After the federation staged public forums in Helena, Billings, and Missoula, Baucus wrote to small-business owners in Montana pledging to vote against any bill that could hurt them.[117] The federation also worked the media, using the powerful radio talk shows to generate opposition. When Hillary Clinton pulled into Portland, Oregon, in the Health Security Express, a bus caravan inspired by the freedom riders of the 1960s, a vocal group of protestors surrounded the bus. As she tried to speak, she was drowned out by booing and heckling. Even though she wore a bulletproof vest, she felt for the first time that her life was in danger:

> The call to arms [of the radio talk show hosts] attracted hundreds
> of hard-core right wingers: militia supporters, tax protesters, clinic
> blockaders. . . . After the speech ended and we were driving away
> from the stage, hundred of protesters swarmed the limousine.
> What I could see from the car was a crowd of men who seemed to
> be in their twenties and thirties. I'll never forget the look in their
> eyes and their twisted mouths as they screamed at me while the
> agents pushed them away.[118]

By mid-fall 1993 Clinton had lost the support of all the major business
groups, not only the National Federation of Independent Business, but
also the Chamber of Commerce, the Business Roundtable, and the National Association of Manufacturers.

Whereas in the 1940s the AMA had been the most vocal political
opponent of the Truman plan, in the 1990s physicians were nearly invisible in public debates over Health Security. One reason was that the
AMA was no longer the sole voice of the medical profession. Rather,
the profession had splintered into hundreds of special-purpose medical associations.[119] Another was that the AMA had become more di-
verse, with women and minorities making up a larger percentage of
the membership. These changes not only made consensus more difficult to achieve but also meant that the threat of being ostracized for
publicly disagreeing was less severe.

Initially, the AMA endorsed the concept of universal coverage as long
as it didn't mean stringent cost controls or regulations that would give
managed care an advantage. Some doctors' organizations, such as the
American Academy of Family Physicians and the American Academy
of Pediatrics, gave the Clinton plan full support. Others, such as the
American College of Physicians, opposed some features but supported
the employer mandate, while the American College of Surgeons supported a single-payer system like Medicare, arguing that it would preserve patient choice and physician autonomy.[120] These disagreements
made it impossible for physicians to convey a clear message about where
the medical profession stood on health care reform. Tellingly, the various accounts of Clinton's failed effort scarcely mention the AMA or
physicians.[121]

Republicans, who had initially cooperated with the Clinton administration, adopted a new hard-line stance in the fall. In October the Re-

publican National Committee released its own television ads, calling Health Security a "costly, bureaucratic nightmare" and flooding the airwaves in every city Hillary Clinton visited. In December, William Kristol, a Republican strategist, wrote Republican congressional leaders urging them to kill health care reform. Kristol argued that the Clinton plan was "a serious political threat to the Republican party." Its demise would be "a monumental setback for the President."[122]

The campaign against health care reform was virtually indistinguishable from presidential campaigns in the scale of field organizing, sophistication, and public relations tactics.[123] Various industry groups hired nearly 100 law and public relations firms to lobby. Among the key lobbyists were some household names, including former senator Paul Tsongas (D-Mass.), former congressmen Tom Downey (D-N.Y.), and Vin Weber (R-Minn.). When Senator Christopher Dodd (D-Conn.), who sat on the Labor and Human Resources Committee, was up for reelection in 1992, he received $375,000 from the political action committees of Aetna, Cigna, MetLife, Prudential, and Travelers, as well as $24,000 in contributions from individual insurance officers. In return, Dodd publicly lambasted a Democratic National Committee television spot that accused the insurance industry of obstructing health care reform.[124] The Alliance for Managed Competition bankrolled reelection campaigns for three Connecticut incumbents, Senator Joseph Lieberman and Representatives Barbara Kennelly and Nancy Johnson. Lieberman, who favored a more conservative, less regulatory approach, collected more than $265,000 from health insurance interests during the first quarter of 1994. Kennelly, who served on Ways and Means, received $101,400 from health and insurance industry PACs. To ensure that Kennelly got the message, Aetna employees were told to contact her and "voice your opposition to . . . price controls."[125] In March 1994, alliance executives met with Representative Jim Cooper (D-Tenn.), who was running for the Senate. In the first quarter of 1994, Cooper raised nearly $2.4 million, with a substantial portion coming from the health care sector.[126] In return Cooper sponsored the alliance's preferred plan, which relied mainly on the private market and the tax code to drive down costs. Overall, the Center for Public Integrity estimated that 650 organizations spent at least $100 million to defeat the Clinton plan. Its supporters raised only $15 million.[127] Hillary Clinton bitterly recalled,

"Even a popular President armed with a bully pulpit could not match the hundreds of millions of dollars spent to distort an issue through negative and misleading advertisements and other means."[128]

Polls conducted shortly after Clinton's first announcement showed that 67 percent of the public approved of Health Security. By February 1994, public approval had dwindled to 44 percent.[129] That summer the Senate Finance Committee voted for a compromise plan, but it was never brought to the floor. As the First Lady wrote, "Health care faded with barely a whimper."[130] In the 1994 elections the Republican Party ran on a Contract with America platform against the welfare state and big government, and the debacle over the Health Security plan was widely credited with giving the Republican Party control of the House of Representatives for the first time in 40 years.[131]

The Aftermath

After the demise of Health Security, health policy making moved toward shoring up the private health insurance system by tightening regulations to make private insurance more secure and by expanding coverage for certain groups, namely, children and the elderly. The policy change that received the most publicity was the Personal Responsibility and Work Opportunity Act of 1996, better known as the welfare reform bill. During his presidential campaign, Bill Clinton had pledged to reform the welfare system. With Health Security in tatters, he needed to show he could fulfill at least one of his promises. The Personal Responsibility and Work Opportunity Act replaced AFDC, the New Deal cash assistance for poor mothers and their children, with Temporary Assistance to Needy Families (TANF). TANF had stiffer work requirements, a two-year time limit, and a cap on benefit amounts regardless of family size; combined, these features made it tougher to qualify for cash benefits.[132] The intent of welfare reform was to discourage long-term welfare stayers and encourage work, not to reduce health benefits for poor families. To prevent mothers who lost cash benefits from also losing their health coverage, TANF was purposely decoupled from Medicaid. States were given greater flexibility to expand Medicaid eligibility beyond the traditional welfare limits. Under the new rules, mothers who left TANF could continue receiving Medicaid for up to 12 months. Then at the end of a year they could be reevaluated to see if they might qualify under some other criteria.[133] Among women who left welfare for work, one-third continued on Medicaid, one-third obtained private health coverage, and one-third became uninsured.[134] In some instances, they lost coverage when they left TANF and failed to provide the information needed to redetermine their eligibility for Medicaid. In other cases, they incorrectly believed that they no longer qualified for Medicaid because they were ineligible for TANF.[135] Sometimes they were just rejected outright.

In 1997 a new child benefit, the State Children's Health Insurance Program (SCHIP), was enacted. SCHIP increased funds to the states to insure low-income children. Under SCHIP states could cover children from families with incomes up to 200 percent of the poverty level, either by expanding Medicaid or by creating a separate program.[136] Since SCHIP was enacted, children's uninsurance rates have decreased sharply. From 2001 to 2003, the percentage of low-income children enrolled in either SCHIP or Medicaid rose from 38 percent to 49 percent.[137] SCHIP rules were later amended to allow uninsured parents to be covered along with their children. While several states extended coverage to low-income parents, federal law prohibits Medicaid from covering people who are not parents. Childless adults are excluded entirely.

Despite these gains, many eligible children remain uninsured.[138] Rates of uninsurance are especially high among Hispanic children, with more than 25 percent lacking coverage.[139] One problem in insuring low-income children is how to inform parents who have never been TANF recipients that their children are eligible for benefits. Another problem is that children may inadvertently lose coverage when a parent leaves TANF or when they "age out" of Medicaid and should be transferred to SCHIP but are not.[140] A third problem is that SCHIP does not offer stable coverage. More children were covered after new regulations were adopted in 2002 that required every state to provide Medicaid coverage to all children under age 19 whose family income fell below the federal poverty level.[141] However, the recession of 2001–2 caused state coffers to dwindle. In response, many states tightened Medicaid and SCHIP eligibility criteria and limited new enrollments.[142] By 2003 three states had halted SCHIP enrollments entirely, resulting in long waiting lists for hundreds of children.[143]

A less publicized health policy event was the Health Insurance Portability and Accountability Act of 1996. The brainchild of Senators Ted Kennedy and Nancy Kassebaum (R-Kan.), the Health Insurance Portability and Accountability Act was intended to make the private insurance market more secure and narrow the conditions under which companies could refuse coverage. In the original version, insurance companies would have to guarantee that people could renew their coverage, new employees would be automatically accepted into currently covered groups, experience rating would be prohibited, and it would be more difficult for insurers to exclude an applicant based on a preexisting condition.[144] It was this feature that aroused the most opposition from insurers. The Health Insurance Association of America strenuously objected that allowing people who lost group coverage for any reason to purchase an individual policy from the same company would trigger a "meltdown of the individual insurance market."[145] Individual enrollment lacked the risk-spreading advantage of large group plans and attracted subscribers in poorer health.[146]

What finally passed was a watered-down bill that eliminated some of the more egregious practices of the small group market. HIPAA did give employees who lost group coverage and exhausted their COBRA eligibility the right to convert these policies to individual coverage. HIPAA also prohibited insurers from charging different premiums for individuals within groups and required insurers that operated in the small group market to guarantee renewal to any group.[147] Upon signing the bill, President Clinton proclaimed that it "seals the cracks that swallow as many as 25 million Americans who can't get insurance or who fear they'll lose it."[148] But HIPAA did not say that these policies had to be offered at an affordable price and contained loopholes that allowed insurers to avoid covering people who might run up expensive health care bills. After HIPAA some insurers threatened to cut commissions of agents who sold policies to undesirable individuals or conveniently "lost" the paperwork for qualified applicants. Some insurers have offered the required coverage, but at prohibitive costs.

HIPAA did not dramatically change the nature of the small group market or guarantee that people would not be rejected for coverage because of health. That left people such as Jody and Matt Miller confronting nearly the same obstacles they faced before HIPAA was enacted. The Millers, a couple in their early 40s, had COBRA coverage for

18 months from a group plan that Matt had held at Occidental College while he was writing a book. Although they could have remained with the group plan, the cost was $1,300 a month. Because Jody was thinking of starting her own business and Matt was a self-employed writer, their insurance agent advised them to purchase individual policies now while they were still young and healthy. It would be much harder to obtain such coverage when they were older. The Millers applied to Blue Cross but to their shock and dismay were both rejected. The reason? Jody had once been treated for minor neck spasms and used a nasal spray for sinus problems when she traveled. Matt had had a speck in his field of vision several years earlier. These minor health problems made them high risks according to the calculation of insurance company underwriters.[149]

The other significant change to result from HIPAA has been in private long-term care insurance. Long-term care insurance had grown sluggishly until the mid-1990s, because most people avoided thinking about the prospect of entering a nursing home until a health crisis forced them to do so. By then they were ineligible for coverage or so old that the cost was prohibitive: a 75-year-old who purchased a standard policy in 1995 would pay $8,146 yearly compared to $2,560 for a 65-year-old.[150] The Republican's Contract with America had included a provision that would make premium expenses for long-term care insurance tax deductible.[151] Using tax incentives to encourage the purchase of private insurance would not only stimulate the market but also signal to consumers that the government considered long-term care insurance a worthwhile product.[152] This provision was included in HIPAA. HIPAA allowed people who itemize deductions on their income taxes to deduct a portion of long-term care insurance premiums. It also made employer contributions toward the cost of group long-term care insurance a tax-deductible business expense. After HIPAA long-term care insurance sales increased an average of 21 percent a year, with the biggest increase occurring in group insurance plans offered by employers.[153] Between 1999 and 2001 alone, the number of employers offering long-term care insurance to their employees increased by 46.8 percent.[154] As insurance companies expanded benefits to include coverage for home care, Alzheimer's disease, and residence in assisted-living facilities, long-term care insurance also became an increasingly important part of retirement planning.

Recent experiences suggest that even with expanded regulation, consumers face uncertainty with this product. Some companies, eager to get a foothold in the new market, offered unrealistically low rates and then had to stop writing policies as expenses exceeded premium revenues. For example, Conseco, after increasing its market share through acquisitions and product launches, decided to discontinue new sales following a class action suit by 700,000 clients alleging they had been misled about the likelihood of premium increases. Although marketing materials had promised that premiums would remain stable, rates increased between 10 and 40 percent a year, sometimes several years in a row. One company representative explained, "It's not like life insurance where there's thousands of years' worth of mortality research. With long term care, the nature of the coverage has changed faster than the actuaries can calculate it."[155] To deter insurance companies from offering unrealistically low rates, insurance commissioners in several states began requiring insurers to disclose the company's history of rate increases to prospective clients.

The expansion of private long-term care insurance is a positive development for more affluent middle-income people, those who make enough money to itemize their tax deductions. Purchasing a long-term care policy not only gives them a tax advantage but also provides alternatives to a nursing home when care is needed. Having a home care option has become especially important since the Balanced Budget Act of 1997. The Balanced Budget Act cut Medicare payments for home care visits and tightened up eligibility criteria, making it more difficult for Medicare beneficiaries to qualify for benefits.[156] Presuming that the companies that sell long-term care insurance stay in business and presuming that these policies pay what they promise, which for middle-aged people may involve a 20- or 30-year wait, they will add an element of protection and predictability for this particular segment of the older population. That these promises will be kept is a better bet for people who purchase their policies through an employer group, where they have the protection of experienced benefit analysts, than for individual policy holders.

The Balanced Budget Act of 1997 also created Medicare+Choice, which allowed risk-based HMOs and PPOs to participate in Medicare. Some policy makers viewed Medicare+Choice as a vehicle to provide richer benefits to Medicare beneficiaries compared to what was available in the traditional fee-for-service program, especially prescription drug coverage; others felt Medicare+Choice would reduce costs by generating competition among various plans or even set the stage for the full privatization of Medicare.[157] By 2001 just 16 percent of people 65 and older had chosen the HMO option, while hundreds of plans, affecting more than 2 million people, withdrew from the program due to low reimbursement rates.[158]

The most recent health policy event was enactment of the Medicare Modernization Act of 2003, which provides Medicare beneficiaries with a prescription drug benefit. Hailed as the biggest overhaul of Medicare since its inception, the new program picks up 75 percent of a beneficiary's drug costs up to $2,250 a year.[159] Then in a confusing twist, coverage stops until a beneficiary has spent another $3,600, creating a "doughnut hole."[160] After that Medicare pays 95 percent of any additional drug costs.

The legislation also offers HMOs new incentives to participate in the Medicare program in the wake of the failed Medicare+Choice program. Medicare Advantage gives HMOs payment rates that are 25 percent higher than those paid in the traditional fee-for-service program. Also included are tax incentives to encourage higher-income elderly to purchase private health insurance policies as a substitute for Medicare and $70 billion in subsidies to employers so they won't drop prescription drugs from their retiree health plans (although many analysts doubt that the incentives are sufficient to have that effect). The final caveat is that the federal government is prohibited from negotiating drug prices, the same hands-off concession that was granted to providers in exchange for their cooperation in Medicare. Who concocted this scheme?

The no-price-negotiation feature came from the Pharmaceutical Research and Manufacturers of America (PhRMA), with its 620 lobbyists. In the first six months of 2003, the PhRMA pumped $8 million into a lobbying campaign against price controls. As PhRMA spokesman Jeff Trewhitt said, "We are lobbying anyone who will listen at the 11th hour, and the message is very clear."[161] The "doughnut hole" was a concession to the American Association of Health Plans, which represents managed care firms. In the past, the elderly who chose Medicare HMOs over the traditional Medicare program were motivated mainly by a desire to have their prescription drugs covered. If Medicare assumed all drug costs, then HMOs would be a less attractive alternative. The result was a benefit that paid some of the costs for low spenders, covered most of the costs for people with catastrophic drug expenditures, and preserved the free market for the middle class.[162]

Conclusion

The 1990s is mostly remembered for the failure of Clinton's Health Security plan. The Clinton plan generated hundreds of books and articles seeking to explain the outcome. Some pundits blamed proximal events: the plan's complexity had fueled opponents' claims that it was a misconceived big government effort; the Clinton administration had been unable to nurture durable political alliances as reformers had in 1965; organized labor failed to mobilize a broad spectrum of support. Others blamed more enduring features of American politics—the institutional structure of the state, antistatist values, or racist sentiments.[163]

The focus on this single policy case has obscured the effect of the less dramatic but equally consequential health policy measures that were enacted. On one hand, public policy moved to shore up the private insurance market through increased regulation of insurers and through tax incentives for the purchase of private long-term care insurance. On the other hand, barriers to coverage for low-income families and children were lowered through a loosening of the eligibility criteria in Medicaid and enactment of a new benefit, SCHIP, for children. Yet variations in eligibility criteria across states, an inherent feature of Medicaid, and low cutoff levels in many states meant that most low-income adults and all childless, poor adults were still uninsured.

eight

Why the United States Has
No National Health Insurance
and What Can Be Done About It

Across the entire span of the twentieth century, all attempts to enact a health care reform plan that would guarantee universal coverage have been defeated. The AALL compulsory state health insurance plan in the 1910s, Roosevelt's proposal for national health insurance in the New Deal, Truman's plan in the post–World War II era, Nixon's National Health Insurance Partnership and Kennedy's Health Care for All Americans Act in the 1970s, and Clinton's Health Security plan in the 1990s met the same ignominious fate. These events had significant consequences for the financing of health care, for the ironic outcome in each instance was federal action that entrenched a private alternative to a public program. In the Progressive Era the failed AALL bill stimulated the first commercial insurance plans. In the 1940s Truman's loss occurred alongside court decisions that encouraged the spread of private group insurance. Nixon's National Health Insurance Partnership Act of 1972 led instead to federal support for private HMOs. The defeat of Claude Pepper's home care bill in the 1980s spurred the development of private long-term care products. The failure of President Clinton's Health Security plan in the 1990s led to regulatory measures that shored up the private health insurance system and stimulated the purchase of long-term care products. Even the enactment of Medicare in 1965 preserved a profitable market segment for private insurers in the form of supplemental medigap policies while removing a needy constituency, the aged, from debates over coverage for people of working age.

The health care financing system that emerged over the past 100 years is a patchwork of public and private programs that provides some people with secure coverage but leaves others with sporadic periods of being uninsured and 45 million with no health insurance at all. The recent decline in the number of employers who offer health insurance to their employees—from 67 percent to 63 percent in just the two-year period from 2001 to 2003—has shaken confidence in the future viability of employment-based benefits.[1] The drop in retiree benefits has been even more precipitous, as I noted in Chapter 6, from 70 percent in 1985 to 36 percent by 2000.[2] My task has been to explain how this unwieldy and inefficient financing system came to be and consider what lessons history provides about how to reverse the tide.

Theories of the Welfare State Revisited

Antistatist Values

Some health policy experts hold that antistatist values have been the principal barrier to major health care reform. Does the evidence support this assertion? Antistatist themes have fueled every proposal for government-financed health care services. In the 1910s the socialist threat hovered over the AALL campaign for compulsory health insurance. In the 1940s the AMA decried Truman's national health insurance plan as an un-American plot that would destroy the doctor-patient relationship, create a large health bureaucracy, and pave the way for a communist takeover. Then in the 1990s the haunting specter of big government reappeared to undermine support for President Clinton's Health Security proposal. But if antistatist values were a potent causal force, then why did the public fail to respond in the 1960s when the AMA promoted the same tired themes against Medicare?

One reason is that Medicare appeared on the national agenda in a supportive political climate.[3] The civil rights movement had legitimated federal intervention for the pursuit of racial justice, the communist threat was no longer a domestic issue but had shifted to a distant war in Vietnam, and President Johnson had declared a war against poverty. In the 1960s government was perceived to be a force that could serve the greater public good. A second reason is that there was an organized counterforce, the National Council of Senior Citizens, to challenge AMA claims and demonstrate that the aged were a worthy and deserving constituency.

The evidence suggests that antistatism does provide enduring symbols that are available in political debates over the welfare state.[4]

Antistatist themes help to dramatize the issues, limit the potential range of options considered legitimate choices, and justify inaction.[5] But alternative values of community and social responsibility can also be invoked to support government intervention. What has mattered more than the rhetoric is the constellation of interest groups vying for power and the organizational strength of the contending groups—the AMA versus the AFL-CIO in the 1950s and again in the 1960s, the Health Insurance Association of America and the National Federation of Independent Business versus senior citizens' organizations in the 1980s, and the Health Insurance Association of America and the National Federation of Independent Business allied against a loosely knit and largely ineffectual coalition of social reformers in the 1990s.

Weak Labor

Other health policy experts attribute the failure of health care reform to a weak labor movement. There is some truth to this assertion. For the first half of the twentieth century, the AFL, the largest trade union, rejected outright the idea that workers should form a separate labor party, a strategic choice that weakened labor's ability to pursue national welfare benefits. Not only did it mean that did the trade unions had no direct way to influence policy decisions, it also meant that they were often divided over labor's proper sphere of influence. On one side of these disputes were leaders such as Samuel Gompers and George Meany, who preferred to pursue the class struggle by negotiating better wages and working conditions in collective bargaining agreements. On the other side were leaders such as Walter Reuther, who believed that the unions could work with government to create a European-style corporate state. These internal divisions over strategy and tactics made it impossible for workers to speak with one voice.

Yet there is also evidence that counters the "weak labor" thesis. Once the AFL and the CIO united into a single union in 1955, they mobilized first for disability insurance and then for Medicare. These programs were important to the labor movement because they shifted the cost of insuring disabled workers and retirees to the public purse and thus allowed unions to pursue wage increases and other benefits for working members in their negotiated contracts. The success of disability insurance and Medicare demonstrates that organized labor does not have to form a separate political party to advance social welfare programs.

This brief historical moment of labor unity and strength was over by the late 1960s, when the trade unions once again split into warring factions, with the UAW going it alone after Reuther withdrew that union from the AFL-CIO. Once the AFL-CIO opposed Senator Kennedy's compromise plan for a basic benefit package that, in retrospect, would have been a wise course to pursue, the unions never again exerted their weight on behalf of universal coverage. When President Clinton proposed his Health Security plan, promised trade union support failed to materialize because of what the unions saw as his unfriendly trade policies, leaving no organized force to counter the opposition.

Racial Politics

A third explanation for why the United States has no national health insurance emphasizes the racial politics of the South. From the New Deal until the 1960s, southern politicians did conspire with conservative Republicans to block national health insurance but, interestingly, not disability insurance. What made disability insurance acceptable to them was a compromise hammered out by Nelson Cruikshank and his colleagues that the program would be run by state health departments, not federal officials. The grip of the South on national social welfare legislation weakened considerably in the 1960s and was broken in the Democratic sweep of the 1964 election. The enactment of Medicare, in turn, gave federal officials the leverage to force southern health care facilities to integrate.

While overt racial barriers such as separate white and colored entrances, wards, waiting rooms and cafeterias were removed in the wake of Medicare, racial dynamics have not disappeared entirely from policy-making processes. As job-based benefits have become a surrogate for national policy, racial inequality in access to benefits has become a secondary effect of employment.[6] Racial politics has also been transmitted through coded messages implying that minorities are undeserving beneficiaries of social programs. Such messages permeated the welfare reform debate of 1996, in which welfare recipients were implicitly portrayed as black, promiscuous, and lazy, even though the majority of AFDC recipients were white. They also provided a subtle subtext in debates over Clinton's Health Security plan.[7]

State Structures and Policy Legacies

A fourth explanation for why the United States has no national health insurance emphasizes the effect of American political institutions and the legacies of past policy decisions.[8] Over the course of the twentieth century, a constellation of interest groups did emerge around the health care financing system, jockeying for position every time health care reform was under consideration—trade unions, small businesses, large manufacturers, senior citizens, welfare recipients, and the privately insured middle class. Thus one might argue that trade unions' weak support for national health insurance in the 1940s was driven by the legacy of wartime and postwar policies that encouraged collective bargaining for fringe benefits. One might also argue that Medicare created a senior citizens' movement that was subsequently primed to oppose any benefit cuts or tax increases, or that the financing mechanism in Medicare gave the hospital industry a vested interest in opposing subsequent efforts to impose price controls. Such an argument cannot explain why the unions pursued disability insurance and Medicare, why the most pressing concern of the elderly—long-term care—was never addressed in the political process, or how a prospective payment system for Medicare was able to transcend hospital industry opposition. By attempting to account for nearly everything, theorists who focus on policy legacies can neither predict the direction of policy decisions (i.e., positive or negative) nor explain how the preferences and expectations of various groups get translated into actual political decisions.

Stakeholder Mobilization

The evidence presented in the preceding chapters shows only one historical constant across every case, namely, that each attempt to guarantee universal coverage has been resisted by powerful special interests who have used every weapon on hand to keep the financing of health services a private endeavor. For the first half of the twentieth century, the antireform coalition was led by physicians, who feared that government financing of medical services would lead to government control of medical practice. Physicians appeared to have the deciding voice in health policy debates because their political goals were compatible with those of key allies. These allies included hospital administrators, who had created Blue Cross in the 1930s as a way to finance hospital

care and dampen demand for a government solution; large manufacturers, who viewed fringe benefits as a way to fend off trade unionism;
and insurers, who viewed compulsory health insurance as unwelcome
competition. Even the trade unions, suspicious of state power, championed the medical societies when compulsory state health insurance was
on the agenda in the Progressive Era.

The support of these groups alone might not have given organized
medicine veto power over national health insurance. Physicians also
needed the backing of key elected officials, those who controlled key
congressional committees and who were willing to convert their preferences into negative votes. For three decades, physicians worked to
secure the victory of friends such as Senator Robert Taft and to vanquish enemies such as Senator Claude Pepper. In the 1950 election, the
AMA's rhetorical pyrotechnics had real political consequences, helping to restructure the balance of power in Congress and reshape the
political landscape in a more conservative direction.

Not only did these early victories convince public officials that physicians were an omnipotent political force, they also lulled physicians
into a false sense of security. It took more than a decade to disabuse
both groups of these beliefs. The first indicator that the AMA could win
only when it had these powerful coalition partners occurred in the 1950s
when the AFL-CIO wooed southern Democrats and co-opted the insurance industry in the fight for disability insurance. Then, in the 1960s,
labor leaders joined with senior citizens to vanquish the AMA, their
victory secured by the defection of hospital administrators and insurance companies. The contest over Medicare helped the Democrats sweep
the House and Senate in the 1964 election and gave northern Democrats a majority without the South for the first time since the New Deal,
shattering organized medicine's power base.

The Medicare triumph made reformers more optimistic about the
prospects for national health insurance. With the AMA licking its
wounds and trying to restore its tarnished image, and with millions of
working-age adults and children without coverage, it appeared that
the 1970s would be a propitious time to act. But as the AMA moved off
center stage, the insurance industry moved to the forefront of health
policy debates. From the 1970s to the 1990s, the Health Insurance Association of America lobbied against national health insurance and long-
term care insurance for the frail elderly, mobilizing small-business

groups such as the National Federation of Independent Businesses and insurance agent associations to their cause. The only significant legislation enacted during this period, the Medicare Catastrophic Coverage Act of 1988, had the blessing of the insurance industry. The changing composition of the antireform coalition, dominated first by physicians and then by insurers, has obscured the persistence of stakeholder mobilization as the primary impediment to national health insurance.

Prospects for Reform

What is the likelihood of achieving universal coverage in the future? Some people argue that the prospects are nil, because universal coverage is inherently incompatible with employment-based health insurance. But Germany organizes and finances health benefits through the labor market yet covers everyone.[9] Past experience suggests that any plan for the federal government to become the single payer of health care services would be certain to elicit the opposition of those who benefit from existing arrangements but that the government's role can be expanded to cover the inevitable gaps that occur when coverage is purchased from an industry that, by its nature, is designed to exclude people with the highest health risks.[10]

The public is not averse to taking action. According to one recent poll conducted by America's Health Insurance Plans, the national trade association for health insurers, 59 percent of respondents agreed that the government could do a better job than the private sector in ensuring that more Americans have access to quality care.[11] Other surveys show that people would be willing to spend more tax dollars to improve health care coverage.[12] The question is what course to pursue.

There is no magic bullet. That much is apparent. Rather, the first step should be to continue the process of Medicaid expansion that began in the 1980s. Medicaid has developed in a piecemeal fashion over more than half a century. It originated with state payments to vendors (doctors and hospitals) for health care for the poor, which were converted into the Kerr-Mills program in 1960. When Medicaid was enacted in 1965, eligibility was tied to receipt of welfare benefits and thus to the rules governing welfare eligibility, as had been the case with Kerr-Mills, but the states retained considerable discretion over benefits and eligibility criteria. Federal guidelines specify that states must cover certain mandatory groups. These include pregnant women and children under age six from families with incomes below 133 percent of the poverty level, older children in families with incomes up to the poverty level, most elderly and disabled recipients of SSI (the federal welfare benefit for the very poor), and parents whose income falls below state welfare eligibility levels. States may also choose to cover people in each of these categories at higher income levels.[13] The result is 50 state programs, all with their own rules, enrollment procedures, and income guidelines.

Due to its historic ties to welfare, Medicaid still bases eligibility on family status. According to federal law, childless couples and single adults are not eligible for Medicaid unless the state has obtained a waiver from the Department of Health and Human Services. As a result, only parents are eligible for Medicaid in 42 states.[14]

Medicaid income cutoff levels also vary according to family status. In most states children are eligible for Medicaid or SCHIP if family income is below 200 percent of the federal poverty level. For parents, however, the income cutoff is 70 percent of the poverty level ($10,835 for a family of three in 2004). The result is that in many low-income families, the children are insured but not their parents, or younger children are insured but not their older brothers and sisters. That's the case with Sara and Oscar's family. Sara used to work cleaning houses, but when her third child was born, she calculated that a babysitter, bus fare, and lunch would eat up all her wages. Now she's a stay-at-home mom. Her husband, Oscar, is a driver for a courier service, but lately competition from other companies has cut into his hours and wages. Sara, her third child (who is now 2), and her fourth child (a 1-month-old infant) are covered by Medicaid, but Oscar and the couple's two older children, ages 11 and 14, are uninsured.[15]

Achieving a uniform level of coverage across the states requires changes in federal law to reduce variation across income classes and family types. The first step is to require all states to base Medicaid eligibility on income, not family status.[16] Such a change would extend coverage to the two-thirds of the uninsured population who are poor or near poor and whose income just exceeds current state eligibility levels. For example, Medicaid could be expanded to include parents and childless adults with incomes up to 200 percent of the poverty level ($38,800 for a family of four in 2003).[17] Only 32 percent of this group were insured in 2003.[18]

Medicaid modernization is the direction policy has been headed in the past two decades anyway. The chief obstacle to further expansion is cost. With state budgets periodically in crisis and shortfalls in 2004 totaling nearly $70 billion, governors are unlikely to welcome additional federal mandates unless they are accompanied by fiscal relief.[19] That relief might take the form of an exchange where the federal government would pick up all the costs of covering children if the states would expand coverage of low-income adults, or it could involve a change in the way the federal match is calculated.

Medicaid expansion would improve coverage among some of the uninsured but would do nothing for low-income families above the cutoff point, who live paycheck to paycheck. Patty, a mother of two who cuts pork in a meat processing plant, rotates her bills from month to month:

> What we do is call this one and say "I'm going to be late" and pay that one. Then we'll skip this one, two or three times and pay that one, and then I'll call you back and make arrangements with this one, and we do it like that every month.[20]

In families such as Patty's, where housing, food, child care, and transportation expenses consume the entire household income, health insurance is an unaffordable luxury. Nor would Medicaid expansion help middle-income people who have been labeled uninsurable by medical underwriters. Coverage for these individuals and families could be increased through federal vouchers, with the amount of the voucher determined by household income. The vouchers could be used to buy into the Federal Employees Health Benefits Program, which currently is open only to federal employees and their families and which offers subscribers a choice of 350 health plans. If uninsured people were allowed to buy into the federal employee program, they would have the risk-spreading advantages that people who work for large firms now enjoy. To prevent the inclusion of high-risk people from raising premiums for all federal employees (and thus arousing the antagonism of federal employees' unions), a separate risk pool could be created, with insurers bidding for the right to provide coverage to this group.

Allowing people to buy into the federal program would be a boon to early retirees—people in their 50s and early 60s—whose coverage has declined from 66 percent (among large employers) in 1988 to only 38 percent by 2003. Older adults are far more likely than younger people to report being in fair or poor health and to have a chronic illness such as heart disease, arthritis, or diabetes. Without the risk-spreading advantages of an employer plan, early retirees are forced into the individual insurance market, where they have a hard time purchasing coverage at any price because of aggressive screening by insurers.[21] Many are people like Bill, a former Kodak executive, who along with hundreds of other Kodak employees was downsized out of his job after 32 years with the company. It felt to Bill "like a mass burial. You expected to reach a top job level, say, from 50 to 62, where you'd make a significant contribution to the company. Instead the best thing they think we can contribute at 50 is to get out."[22] Like many older workers who were forced into early retirement, Bill had a generous pension package. But fewer and fewer of these packages include health insurance. In 2004 Sears Roebuck announced that it would no longer provide retiree health benefits for new hires or for current employees under age 40. Aetna cut its subsidy for retiree health benefits for all future retirees. Lucent made deep cuts in retiree health benefits and significantly raised retiree contributions.[23] Opening the federal plan to these people would help stem the erosion of retiree health benefits.

Permitting people to buy into the federal health plan has the added value of being able to reduce racial disparities in coverage, which are largely a by-product of employment patterns. The effectiveness of the federal health program in achieving this goal has already been proven. In 2002–3 nearly 60 percent of Hispanic nonelderly adults were uninsured for some time, compared to 43 percent of African Americans and 23 percent of whites.[24] Both African Americans and Hispanics are less likely than whites to be employed in the kind of companies that offer health benefits, but African Americans have a significant advantage over Hispanics because they are more likely to work for a state or the federal government.[25]

Another idea that merits consideration is to establish a stop-loss plan, also called a premium rebate pool. This idea, which was endorsed by presidential candidate John Kerry in the 2004 election, is actually a revival of the reinsurance concept that originated during the Eisenhower administration in the 1950s and was proposed by Senator Russell Long in the 1970s, with the backing of the insurance industry. Under Senator Kerry's proposal, the federal government would reimburse eligible health plans (including self-insured plans) for some percentage of their "catastrophic" cases—say, 75 percent of any costs that exceed $50,000.[26] A stop-loss program is already operating, in effect, with the Federal Emergency Management Agency (FEMA), which provides financial help to businesses and individuals that face catastrophic losses that their insurance policies do not cover.[27] Reinsurance is also working well in the Netherlands, where it covers the cost of catastrophic care and long-term care for the frail elderly and disabled. By eliminating the highest-cost cases, reinsurance there makes it possible for all other health insurance policies to cover basic health costs at predictable levels.[28]

The bulk of the problem today involves employees in small firms, a situation that has been gradually worsening. In 2004 nearly all large firms with 200 or more employees offered health coverage, but only 52 percent of the smallest companies (three to nine workers) did so.[29] If a federal stop-loss benefit was adopted in the United States, small employers would be able to offer the "bare bones" policy that many have advocated, and insurers could design basic plans, knowing that any excessively high expenses would be repaid through the premium rebate pool. Since most health care costs are incurred by a few individuals, insurers currently have pronounced incentives to use aggressive underwriting tactics to identify high-risk people. If the variation in costs across individuals could be significantly reduced through reinsurance, then insurers could offer reasonably priced coverage that would lower health care premiums for everyone. To be effective, certain conditions would have to be imposed. For example, employers that participate in the program would have to cover all workers in the firm and adopt various cost containment strategies such as disease management programs.[30] A side benefit would be to reduce the incentives employers have to discriminate against older workers and people with disabilities in their hiring decisions. To reduce start-up costs, stop-loss insurance could be phased in gradually, applying first only to small businesses that purchase health insurance in the small-group market (or would like to if costs could be kept under control). Later phases could include catastrophic long-term care costs for the elderly and then self-insured firms.

A less desirable option is to provide tax credits against the purchase of a private health insurance plan. Past experiments with tax credits have found them to be ineffective in extending coverage to the groups that need it most. In 1990 Congress gave tax incentives to low-income families to purchase coverage for their children. Children's health coverage failed to increase, because the tax credit was small, covering less than a quarter of average premiums. Many people were not even aware that their children were eligible, and there were widespread abuses by unscrupulous insurers. Three years later, Congress repealed the legislation.[31] Current tax credit proposals are equally meager. For example, in 2004 President George W. Bush proposed a tax credit of $1,000 per adult and $500 per child, with a $3,000 maximum, against the cost of health premiums. However, the average cost of a family policy in 2003 was $9,068. Further, tax credits would do little to help the 61 percent of people with incomes below the poverty level ($18,660 a year for a family of four) who were uninsured in 2003.[32] Nor would they help people with incomes up to 250 percent of the poverty level, who pay no income taxes anyway. The likely effect of a tax credit would be to reduce costs for already insured families but do nothing to extend coverage to the uninsured.

Every one of the options suggested above has been under consideration for more than half a century. The challenge is not in identifying feasible choices but in mustering the political will. What will it take to summon the political will to make significant progress toward universal coverage? We can look to the past to envision what might be possible in the future. At first glance, it might appear that opponents of health care reform were so often victorious because they had superior resources.[33] Yet closer scrutiny suggests that their success depended even more on their organizational strength. The AMA, the Health Insurance Association of America, the Federation of American Hospitals, the Chamber of Commerce, and the National Federation of Independent Business had in common a national leadership, state level organizations, and a local network—whether it consisted of physicians, hospital staff, small-business owners, or insurance agents—capable of marshaling a grassroots effort. In the notable instances when ordinary citizens defeated elite stakeholders, their success was predicated on their organizational capacity. Civil rights activists, trade unions, and senior citizens succeeded because they coordinated their efforts through organizations that mirrored the federated structure of American government.[34]

These events indicate that the best strategy for groups involved in health care reform is to forge a three-tiered coalition. At the top there must be a national leadership responsible for mapping out a grand plan to disseminate ideas, recruit members nationwide, and cultivate political insiders (influential congressional committee chairs and civil servants) who can introduce bills and devise ways to attach health care initiatives to less visible budget measures.[35] These activities could be coordinated by Washington insiders, those think tanks and policy institutes that have policy expertise but no grassroots force. At the middle level, the coalition must involve intermediate institutions such as state labor federations or senior citizens' clubs, whose leaders can coordinate activities, tap into indigenous social networks, and disseminate the organizations' models and ideas.[36] Recruitment could focus on organizations that represent employers and trade unions frustrated by rising health care costs (up 14 percent in 2004 alone), older people who fear losing their health coverage along with their jobs, as well as low-income uninsured people, especially those who live in districts of key members of Congress. Finally, the coalition needs local chapters that can funnel money to higher levels and mobilize grassroots activists to engage in social action to influence state and local politics. Such a structure ties leaders to one another, links local groups to larger issues, and affords opportunities for political leverage at the local, state, and national levels.

The challenge facing reformers in the current political climate is how to craft a message that can unify the various needy population groups that might form such a coalition. Current institutional arrangements have splintered the public into constituencies whose concerns vary according to the source and amount of their existing coverage. Privately insured families seek more secure benefits, the elderly want support for long-term care, and the uninsured want affordable coverage. Despite these differences, what unites these seemingly disparate groups is the shared risk of being uninsured that touches every family and every individual across the life course. That is the message that people understand. The public is willing. The time to act is now.

Notes

Introduction

1. Jamie Court and Francis Smith, *Making a Killing: HMOs and the Threat to Your Health* (Monroe, Me.: Common Courage Press, 1999), p. 1.
2. Personal interview, author's files.
3. Timothy Stoltzfus Jost, *Disentitlement? The Threats Facing Our Public Health Care Programs and a Rights-Based Response* (New York: Oxford University Press, 2003), p. 24.
4. Anna Dixon and Elias Mossialos, *Health Care Systems in Eight Countries: Trends and Challenges* (London: European Observatory on Health Care Systems, 2002), pp. 48, 65; Jon Ivar Elstad, *Recent Developments in the Norwegian Health Care System: Pointing in What Direction?* (Oslo: Norsk Institute for Forskning om Oppvekst, 1997).
5. Antonia Maioni, *Parting at the Crossroads: The Emergence of Health Insurance in the United States and Canada* (Princeton, N.J.: Princeton University Press, 1998).
6. Justin Keen, Donald Light, and Nicholas May, *Public-Private Relations in Health Care* (London: King's Fund Publishing, 2001), p. 33; Mary Ruggie, *Realignments in the Welfare State: Health Policy in the United States, Britain, and Canada* (New York: Columbia University Press, 1996), p. 193.
7. Dixon and Mossialos, *Health Care Systems in Eight Countries*, p. 18.
8. Donald Light, "The Practice and Ethics of Risk-Related Health Insurance," *Journal of the American Medical Association* 267, 18 (1992): 2503–4; see also Thomas Bodenheimer, "Should We Abolish the Private Health Insurance Industry?" *International Journal of Health Services* 20, 2 (1990): 213.
9. U.S. Census Bureau, *Health Insurance Coverage: 2003* (Washington, D.C.: Census Bureau, 2004).
10. Kathleen Stoll and Kim Jones, "One in Three: Non-Elderly Americans Without Health Insurance 2002–2003," Families USA Foundation, Washington, D.C., 2004, p. 3.
11. Ibid., p. 5.
12. John Broder, "Problem of Lost Health Benefits Is Reaching the Middle Class," *New York Times*, November 25, 2002, p. 1A.
13. "Second Class Medicine," *Consumer Reports*, September 2000, p. 50.
14. Mark Steinberg and Mark Merlis, "Working Without a Net: The Health Care Safety Net Still Leaves Millions of Low-Income Workers Uninsured," Families USA Foundation, Washington, D.C., 2004, p. 3.

15. "Second Class Medicine," p. 46.
16. Diane Rowland, "Health Care and the Uninsured," testimony before the House of Representatives, Ways and Means Committee, Washington, D.C., March 9, 2004; H. E. Freeman, L. H. Aiken, R. J. Blendon, and C. R. Corey, "Uninsured Working-Age Adults: Characteristics and Consequences," *Health Services Research* 24 (1990): 812–23; A. C. Monheit, M. M. Hagan, M. L. Berk, and P. J. Farley, "The Employed Uninsured and the Role of Public Policy," *Inquiry* 22 (1986): 348–64; Linda Bilheimer and David Colby, "Expanding Coverage: Reflections on Recent Efforts," *Health Affairs*, January/February 2001, p. 83; John Holahan and Niall Brennan, "Who Are the Adult Uninsured?" National Survey of America's Families, series B, no. B-14, Urban Institute, Washington, D.C., March 2000, p. 4; L. A. Faulkner and H. H. Schauffler, "The Effect of Health Insurance Coverage on the Appropriate Use of Recommended Clinical Preventive Services," *American Journal of Preventive Medicine* 13, 6 (1997): 453–58.
17. Peter Szilagyi, Jack Zwanger, Lance Rodewald, Jane Holl, Dana Mukamel, Sarah Trafton, Laura Shone, Andrew Dick, Lynne Jarrell and Ricard Raubertas, "Evaluation of a State Health Insurance Program for Low-Income Children," *Pediatrics* 105, 2 (2000): 363.
18. Institute of Medicine, *Insuring America's Health: Principles and Recommendations* (Washington, D.C.: Institute of Medicine, 2004), pp. 6–8.
19. "Cover the Uninsured Week, May 10–16, Kicks Off in Detroit," press release, PR Newswire, www.prnewswire.com, May 10, 2004.
20. Institute of Medicine, *Insuring America's Health*, pp. 6–8.
21. Hillary Rodham Clinton, *Living History* (New York: Simon and Schuster, 2003), p. 145.
22. Gerard F. Anderson, Uwe E. Reinhardt, Peter S. Hussey, and Varduhi Petrosyan, "It's the Prices, Stupid: Why the United States Is So Different from Other Countries," *Health Affairs* 22, 3 (2003): 89–105.
23. David Rothman, "A Century of Failure: Health Care Reform in America," *Journal of Health Policy Politics, Policy and Law* 18, 2 (1993): 273.
24. For a similar argument, see Colin Gordon, *Dead on Arrival: The Politics of Health Care in the Twentieth Century* (Princeton, N.J.: Princeton University Press, 2003).
25. Paul Starr, *The Social Transformation of American Medicine* (New York: Basic Books, 1982), p. 5.
26. Ibid., pp. 14–15.
27. Ibid., p. 168.
28. Beatrix Hoffman, *The Wages of Sickness: The Politics of Health Insurance in Progressive America* (Chapel Hill: University of North Carolina Press, 2001), p. 69.
29. Quoted in ibid., p. 81.
30. Edwin E. Witte, *The Development of the Social Security Act* (Madison: University of Wisconsin Press, 1962), pp. 174–81; Gordon, *Dead on Arrival*, pp. 16–18.
31. Gordon, *Dead on Arrival*, p. 15.
32. Statement on Truman Health Plan, *Journal of the American Medical Association* 146, 1 (1949): 114.
33. Starr, *The Social Transformation of American Medicine*, p. 231.
34. Hoffman, *The Wages of Sickness*, p. 69.

35. Florence Calvert Thorne, *Samuel Gompers, American Statesman* (New York: Philosophical Library, 1957), p. 63; Hoffman, *The Wages of Sickness*, pp. 115, 136.

36. Chamber of Commerce, *You and Socialized Medicine* (pamphlet), p. 3, Taft Papers, Library of Congress, Box 640, Legislative Files, File: Health Legislation, 1945.

37. Amie Forand Oral History, Columbia University Oral History Collection, p. 43.

38. Lawrence R. Jacobs, *The Health of Nations: Public Opinion and the Making of American and British Health Policy* (Ithaca, N.Y.: Cornell University Press, 1993), p. 52.

39. Edward Chase, "The Doctors' Bonanza," April 15, 1967, Anderson Papers, Library of Congress, Box 731, File: Finance Committee, Medicare.

40. Abraham Ribicoff, *The American Medical Machine* (New York: Saturday Review Press, 1972), p. 73.

41. Donald Light, "The Restructuring of the American Health Care System," in *Health Politics and Policy*, edited by Theodor J. Litman and Leonard S. Robins (Albany, N.Y.: Delmar, 1997), p. 51; Clark C. Havighurst, "Health Care as a (Big) Business: The Antitrust Response," *Journal of Health Politics, Policy and Law* 26, 5 (2001): 938–55; Donald Light, "Countervailing Powers: A Framework for Professions in Transition," in *Health Professions and the State in Europe*, edited by Terry Johnson, Gerry Larkin, and Mike Saks (London: Routledge, 1995), pp. 24–41.

42. Joseph Califano Jr., *America's Health Care Revolution: Who Lives? Who Dies? Who Pays?* (New York: Random House, 1986), p. 10.

43. Betty Leyerle, *Moving and Shaking American Medicine: The Structure of a Socioeconomic Transformation* (Westport, Conn.: Greenwood Press, 1984), p. 76.

44. Arnold Birenbaum, *Managed Care: Made in America* (Westport, Conn.: Praeger, 1997), p. 41.

45. Robert Schwartz, "How Law and Regulation Shape Managed Care," in *Managed Care: Financial, Legal, and Ethical Issues*, edited by David Bennahum (Cleveland: Pilgrim Press, 1999), p. 25; Birenbaum, *Managed Care*, p. 31.

46. "Clinton Health Plan Spells Change for Insurers," *Bestwire*, A. M. Best Co., September 20, 1993; "Lobbyism Axed Health Care Reform," *Houston Chronicle*, September 23, 1994, p. A18.

47. Seymour Martin Lipset, *American Exceptionalism: A Double-Edged Sword* (New York: W. W. Norton, 1996), p. 22; Seymour Martin Lipset and Gary Marks, *It Didn't Happen Here: Why Socialism Failed in America* (New York: W. W. Norton, 1999).

48. Lawrence R. Jacobs, "Health Reform Impasse: The Politics of American Ambivalence Toward Government," *Journal of Health Politics, Policy and Law* 18, 3 (1993): 630; Theodore Marmor, *The Politics of Medicare*, 2nd ed. (New York: Aldine de Gruyter, 2000), p. 101.

49. Roy Lubove, *The Struggle for Social Security, 1900–1935* (Pittsburgh: University of Pittsburgh Press, 1986), p. 2.

50. Jacobs, "Health Reform Impasse," p. 630.

51. Theda Skocpol, *Boomerang: Health Care Reform and the Turn Against Government in U.S. Politics* (New York: W. W. Norton, 1996), pp. 163–64, 171.

52. Theda Skocpol, *Protecting Soldiers and Mothers: The Political Origins of Social Policy in the United States* (Cambridge, Mass.: Harvard University Press, 1992), p. 16.

53. Vincente Navarro, "Why Some Countries Have National Health Insurance, Others Have National Health Services, and the U.S. Has Neither," *Social Science and Medicine* 28, 9 (1989): 887.

54. Skocpol, *Protecting Soldiers and Mothers*, p. 74; Lubove, *The Struggle for Social Security*, 41.

55. Nelson Lichtenstein, "Labor in the Truman Era: Origins of the Private Welfare State," in *The Truman Presidency*, edited by Michael J. Lacey (New York: Cambridge University Press, 1989), p. 131; Marie Gottschalk, *The Shadow Welfare State: Labor, Business, and the Politics of Health Care in the United States* (Ithaca, N.Y.: Cornell University Press, 2000), p. 167.

56. Jill Quadagno, *The Transformation of Old Age Security: Class and Politics in the American Welfare State* (Chicago: University of Chicago Press, 1988), p. 78.

57. Robert C. Lieberman, *Shifting the Color Line: Race and the American Welfare State* (Cambridge, Mass.: Harvard University Press, 1998).

58. Lee J. Alston and Joseph P. Ferrie, *Southern Paternalism and the American Welfare State: Economics, Politics, and Institutions in the South, 1865–1965* (New York: Cambridge University Press, 1999); Lieberman, *Shifting the Color Line*.

59. Kenneth Finegold and Theda Skocpol, *State and Party in America's New Deal* (Madison: University of Wisconsin Press, 1995); Edwin Amenta, *Bold Relief: Institutional Politics and the Origins of Modern American Social Policy* (Princeton, N.J.: Princeton University Press, 1998).

60. Jacob Hacker, "The Historical Logic of National Health Insurance: Structure and Sequence in the Development of British, Canadian and U.S. Medical Policy," *Studies in American Political Development* 12 (1998): 57–130; Lipset, *American Exceptionalism*, p. 6; Lipset and Marks, *It Didn't Happen Here*, p. 13; Louis Hartz, *The Liberal Tradition in America* (New York: Harcourt Brace, 1955), p. 147.

61. Hacker, "The Historical Logic of National Health Insurance," p. 59.

62. Maioni, *Parting at the Crossroads*, p. 23.

63. Daniel Beland and Jacob S. Hacker, "Ideas, Private Institutions, and American Welfare State 'Exceptionalism': The Case of Health and Old-Age Insurance, 1915–1965," *International Journal of Social Welfare* 13 (2004): 45.

64. Paul Pierson, "Increasing Returns: Path Dependence and the Study of Politics," *American Political Science Review* 94, 2 (2000): 252.

65. Jacob S. Hacker, *The Divided Welfare State: The Battle over Public and Private Social Benefits in the United States* (New York: Cambridge University Press, 2002), p. 26.

Chapter One

1. Ronald Radosh, *Debs* (Englewood Cliff, NJ: Prentice-Hall, 1971), p. 57, 59.

2. Ibid., 4; Robert Zieger, *John L. Lewis, Labor Leader* (Boston: Twayne, 1988), p. 16.

3. H. Wayne Morgan, *Eugene V. Debs, Socialist for President* (Syracuse, N.Y.: Syracuse University Press, 1962), p. 166.

4. John C. Farrell, *Beloved Lady: A History of Jane Addams' Ideas on Reform and Peace* (Baltimore, Md.: John Hopkins University Press, 1967), p. 126; Theda

Skocpol, *Protecting Soldiers and Mothers: The Political Origins of Social Policy in the United States* (Cambridge, Mass.: Harvard University Press, 1992), p. 265.

5. Beatrix Hoffman, *The Wages of Sickness: The Politics of Health Insurance in Progressive America* (Chapel Hill: University of North Carolina Press, 2001), p. 26.

6. Farrell, *Beloved Lady*, p. 59.

7. Florence Calvert Thorne, *Samuel Gompers, American Statesman* (New York: Philosophical Library, 1957), p. 12.

8. Hoffman, *The Wages of Sickness*, p. 69.

9. Colin Gordon, *Dead on Arrival: The Politics of Health Care in the Twentieth Century* (Princeton, N.J.: Princeton University Press, 2003), p. 213.

10. Paul Starr, *The Social Transformation of American Medicine* (New York: Basic Books, 1982), p. 253.

11. Hoffman, *The Wages of Sickness*, p. 37.

12. Quoted in ibid., p. 86.

13. Ibid., p. 105.

14. Quoted in ibid., p. 106.

15. Ibid., p. 2.

16. Ibid., pp. 115, 136.

17. Ibid., p. 113.

18. Isidore Falk Oral History, Columbia University Oral History Collection, p. 47.

19. Nelson Cruikshank Oral History, Columbia University Oral History Collection, p. 9; Gordon, *Dead on Arrival*, p. 15.

20. Falk Oral History, p. 55.

21. Albert Woodward, "The U.S. Health Insurance Industry: An Alternative View," *International Journal of Health Services* 8, 3 (1978): 493.

22. Donald Light, "The Restructuring of the American Health Care System," in *Health Politics and Policy*, edited by Theodor J. Litman and Leonard S. Robins (Albany, N.Y.: Delmar, 1997), p. 49.

23. Quoted in Michael B. Katz, *The Price of Citizenship: Redefining America's Welfare State* (New York: Henry Holt, 2001), p. 3. See Wilbur Cohen Oral History, Columbia University Oral History Collection, p. 55.

24. Quoted in Mark Peterson, "From Trust to Political Power: Interest Groups, Public Choice and Health Care," *Journal of Health Politics, Policy and Law* 26, 5 (2001): 1148; Starr, *Social Transformation of American Medicine*, p. 253.

25. Cited in Theodore Marmor, *The Politics of Medicare*, 2nd ed. (New York: Aldine de Gruyter, 2000), p. 6.

26. Oscar Ewing Oral History, August 26, 1966, Columbia University Oral History Collection, p. 7.

27. Alanson Willcox Oral History, Columbia University Oral History Collection, p. 5.

28. Cohen Oral History, p. 55.

29. Jill Quadagno, *The Transformation of Old Age Security: Class and Politics in the American Welfare State* (Chicago: University of Chicago Press, 1988), p. 42; Michael B. Katz, *The Price of Citizenship: Redefining America's Welfare State* (New York: Metropolitan Books, 2001), p. 10.

30. Woodward, "The U.S. Health Insurance Industry: An Alternative View," p. 494.

31. Sylvia A. Law, *Blue Cross: What Went Wrong* (New Haven, Conn.: Yale University Press, 1976), pp. 8–9.
32. Ibid., p. 10.
33. Ibid., pp. 8–9.
34. U.S. Congress, House Committee on Expenditures in Executive Departments, Investigation of the Participation of Federal Officials in the Formation and Operation of Health Workshops, Hearings Before the Subcommittee on Publicity and Propaganda, 80th Congress, 1st Session, May 28–June 18, 1947, p. 40.
35. Walter Reuther, "The Health Care Crisis: Where Do We Go from Here?" *American Journal of Public Health* 59, 1 (1969): 17.
36. Falk Oral History, p. 59.
37. Quoted in Gordon, *Dead on Arrival*, p. 216.
38. Rashi Fein, *Medical Care, Medical Costs: The Search for a Health Insurance Policy* (Cambridge, Mass.: Harvard University Press, 1986), p. 27.
39. Claude Denison Pepper with Hays Gorey, *Pepper: Eyewitness to a Century* (San Diego: Harcourt Brace Jovanovich, 1987), pp. xiii, 45.
40. Claude Pepper Oral History, Columbia University Oral History Collection, p. 17.
41. Ibid., p. 17.
42. Channing Frothingham, "Rx for National Health," *Social Progress*, November/December 1948, Pepper Library, Florida State University, Tallahassee, Series S201, Box 93, File 1.
43. Quoted in Starr, *Social Transformation of American Medicine*, p. 279.
44. Quoted in Bernard Asbell, *When F.D.R. Died* (London: Jonathan Cape, 1961), p. 164.
45. Sean J. Savage, *Truman and the Democratic Party* (Lexington: University Press of Kentucky, 1997), p. 8.
46. Ibid., p. 8.
47. Harry S. Truman, *Memoirs of Harry S. Truman*, vol. 2: *Years of Trial and Hope* (Garden City, N.Y.: Doubleday, 1956), p. 19.
48. Nelson Cruikshank Oral History, Columbia University Oral History Collection, p. 6.
49. Monty Poen, *Harry S. Truman Versus the Medical Lobby: The Genesis of Medicare* (Columbia: University of Missouri Press, 1979), pp. 60–61.
50. Arthur Herman, *Joseph McCarthy: Reexamining the Life and Legacy of America's Most Hated Senator* (New York: Free Press, 2000), p. 39; John E. Haynes, *Red Scare or Red Menace? American Communism and Anticommunism in the Cold War Era* (Chicago: Ivan Dee, 1996); Harvey Klehr, John E. Haynes, and Fridrikh I. Firsov, *The Secret World of American Communism* (New Haven, Conn.: Yale University Press, 1995).
51. Holly J. McCammon, Karen E. Campbell, Ellen M. Granberg, and Christine Mowery, "How Movements Win: Gendered Opportunity Structures and U.S. Women's Suffrage Movements, 1866 to 1919," *American Sociological Review* 66 (2001): 68.
52. Richard Gid Powers, *Not Without Honor: The History of American Anticommunism* (New Haven, Conn.: Yale University Press, 1998), p. 84.
53. Ibid., p. 86.
54. Haynes, *Red Scare or Red Menace*, p. 66.
55. Ibid., p. 68.

56. Iwan Morgan, *Nixon* (London: Oxford University Press, 2002), pp. 45–46.
57. *Message from the President of the United States, National Health and Disability Insurance Program, 80th Congress, 1st Session* (Washington, D.C.: U.S. Government Printing Office, 1947), p. 3.
58. Harry S. Truman to Watson B. Miller, March 19, 1946, Federal Security Administration, Administrator's Records, Harry S. Truman Presidential Library, Independence, Missouri, RG 235, Box 31, File 031.2.
59. Ewing Oral History, p. 35.
60. Frothingham, "Rx for National Health."
61. Oscar R. Ewing, *The Nation's Health: A Report to the President*, September 1948, Pepper Library, Series 201, File 92, Folder 10.
62. Louis L. Knowles and Kenneth Prewitt, eds., *Institutional Racism in America* (Englewood Cliffs, N.J.: Prentice-Hall, 1969); M. Meltsner, "Equality and Health," *Pennsylvania Law Review* 115, 1 (1966): 22–38.
63. Truman, *Memoirs*, p. 19.
64. Savage, *Truman and the Democratic Party*, p. 155.
65. "The Voluntary Way Is the American Way," 1949, Taft Papers, Box 643, Legislative Files 1924–53, File: Health—National Program for Medical Care (S. 1679–S. 1581).
66. Address of Representative Forest Harness Before the Conference of Executive Secretaries of the Indiana State Medical Association, February 15, 1948, National Archives, Washington, D.C., RG 233, Records of the U.S. House of Representatives, 80th Congress, Committee on Expenditures in Executive Departments, Box 462, File: Federal Security Agency: Correspondence, Hearings, Reports.
67. Lawrence Jacobs, *The Health of Nations* (Ithaca, N.Y.: Cornell University Press, 1993).
68. Harness Address, note 50.
69. Investigation of the Participation of Federal Officials in the Formation and Operation of Health Workshops, p. 10.
70. Forest A. Harness, "Our Most Dangerous Lobby," *Reader's Digest*, December 1947, RG 233, Records of the U.S. House of Representatives, National Archives, Washington, D.C., 80th Congress, Committee on Expenditures in Executive Departments, Box 447, File: AAA in Nebraska.
71. Notes on Conference—Miss Huffman and NM—8/4/47, National Archives, Washington, D.C., RG 233, Records of the U.S. House of Representatives, 80th Congress, Committee on Expenditures in Executive Departments, Box 462, File: Federal Security Agency: Correspondence, Hearings, Reports.
72. Executive Session—Confidential, RG 233, Records of the U.S. House of Representatives, 80th Congress, Committee on Expenditures in Executive Departments, Box 462, File: Federal Security Agency: Correspondence, Hearings, Reports.
73. Falk Oral History, p. 268.
74. Poen, *Harry S. Truman Versus the Medical Lobby*.
75. Testimony of Senator Robert A. Taft, National Health Program of 1949, May 24, 1949, U.S. Senate, Subcommittee on Health of the Committee on Labor and Public Welfare, Washington, D.C., p. 637.
76. Address of Robert Taft to Wayne County Medical Society, October 7, 1946, Taft Papers, Box 643, Legislative Files, 1924–53, File: Health—National Program for Medical Care (S. 1679–S. 1581).

77. Philip A. Klinkner and Rogers M. Smith, *The Unsteady March: The Rise and Decline of Racial Equality in America* (Chicago: University of Chicago Press, 1999), p. 222.
78. Nelson Cruikshank Oral History, p. 28.
79. "The President's Message and the Compulsory Health Insurance Bill," *Journal of the American Medical Association*, May 7, 1949, 111.
80. Robert C. Lieberman, *Shifting the Color Line: Race and the American Welfare State* (Cambridge, Mass.: Harvard University Press, 1998), p. 34; Jill Quadagno, *The Color of Welfare: How Racism Undermined the War on Poverty* (New York: Oxford University Press, 1994), p. 21.
81. Summary of the Voluntary Health Insurance Bill, Pepper Library, Series S201, Box 93, File 1.
82. Comparison of the Three Major Health Bills Before the 81st Congress, Pepper Library, Series S201, Box 93, File 1.
83. Daniel Mitchell, "Earl Warren's Lost Cause: How the United State Might Have Had Canadian-Style Health Insurance," *WorkingUSA*, summer 2002, pp. 19–20.
84. R. L. Sensenich, President's Address, Minutes of the Annual Session of the House of Delegates, American Medical Association, Atlantic City, June 6–10, 1949, reprinted in *Journal of the American Medical Association*, June 18, 1949, p. 613.
85. Address of Clem Whitaker, Minutes of the Annual Session of the House of Delegates, American Medical Association, Atlantic City, June 6–10, 1949, reprinted in *Journal of the American Medical Association*, June 18, 1949, p. 696.
86. Ibid.
87. John Flynn, *The Road Ahead: America's Creeping Revolution* (New York: Devin-Adair, 1949).
88. "Statement on Truman Health Plan," *Journal of the American Medical Association* 146, 1 (1949): 114.
89. Chamber of Commerce, *You and Socialized Medicine* (pamphlet), p. 3, Taft Papers, Box 640, Legislative Files, File: Health Legislation, 1945.
90. Marjorie Shearon, "Freedom of Choice Under the Wagner-Murray-Dingell Bill S. 1050," November 18, 1945, p. 7, Taft Papers, Box 640, File: Health Legislation.
91. "Socialized Medicine: A Medical OPA," p. 2, 1949, Taft Papers, Box 643, File: Health—National Program for Medical Care (S. 1679–S. 1581).
92. Caldwell Esselstyn Oral History, Columbia University Oral History Collection, p. 7.
93. Clem Whitaker and Leone Baxter, "A Simplified Blueprint of the Campaign Against Compulsory Health Insurance," 1949, National Education Campaign, American Medical Association, pp. 3–4, Taft Papers, Box 643, Legislative Files, File: National Program for Medical Care (S. 1679–S. 1581).
94. Ibid., pp. 4–12.
95. Letter from Marjorie Shearon to Senator Taft, January 9, 1945, Taft Papers, Box 643, File: Health: Social Security Legislation 1945–46.
96. "The Voluntary Way Is the American Way," Taft Papers, Box 643, File: Health—National Program for Medical Care (S. 1679–S. 1581), 1949.
97. Whitaker and Baxter, "A Simplified Blueprint," p. 2.
98. "Proposal for Action to Be Taken by Federal and State Governments and by Private Groups to Develop a National Health Program," February 6, 1946, Taft Papers, Box 643, File: Health—Social Security Legislation 1945–46.

99. Edward O'Connor, Statement Before the Senate Subcommittee on the Committee on Labor and Public Welfare, June 29, 1949, Pepper Library, Series S202E, Box 4, File 1.

100. Proposal for National Health Insurance in S. 1679, Statement of Ray D. Murphy, Vice President and Actuary of the Equitable Life Assurance Society to the United States before the Senate Committee on Labor and Public Welfare, June 1949, pp. 8–9, Pepper Library, Series S202E, Box 4, File 1.

101. Chamber of Commerce, *You and Socialized Medicine*.

102. "Socialized Medicine: A Medical OPA," p. 3.

103. Chamber of Commerce, *You and Socialized Medicine*.

104. Ibid.

105. Ewing Oral History, p. 41.

106. Michael Davis Oral History, Columbia University Oral History Collection, p. 49.

107. Ewing Oral History, p. 65.

108. Gallup Polls, *Public Opinion, 1935–71* (Bloomington, Ind.: Phi Delta Kappa, 1973), 2:801.

109. Letter from President Harry Truman to Ben Turoff, April 12, 1949, Truman Library, Correspondence Files, Textual Records, Series A.

110. Elmer Henderson, "A Fancy Package of Untruths," *Journal of the American Medical Association*, November 11, 1950, p. 11.

111. "11,000 Papers Get AMA Memo on Ad Payoff," *In Fact*, September 25, 1950, p. 2.

112. Bernard DeVoto, "Letter for a Family Doctor," *Harper's*, January 1951, p. 59, Pepper Library, Series S201, Box 92, Folder 10.

113. Esselstyn Oral History, p. 16.

114. Dr. Bernard Meyer, Physician's Forum, Testimony on Senate Bills 1456, 1581, and 1679, June, 22, 1949, Pepper Library, Series S202E, Box 4, Folder 1.

115. R. M. Cunningham Jr., "Can Political Means Gain Professional Ends?" *Modern Hospital* 77, 6 (1951): 51, Pepper Library, Series S201, Box 93, Folder 1.

116. "AMA Health Stand Scored by Ewing," 1949, Taft Papers, Box 643, File: Health—National Program for Medical Care (S. 1679–S. 1581).

117. Ewing Oral History, p. 57; Memo from Marjorie Shearon to Senator Robert Taft, January 17, 1946, Taft Papers, Box 643, File: Health—Social Security Legislation 1945–46.

118. Quotes from Address of Guy George Gabrielson, March 29, 1950, Pepper Library, Series S431C, Box 19, Folder 5.

119. Taft Papers, Box 643; Haynes, *Red Scare or Red Menace?*

120. Klehr, Haynes, and Firsov, *The Secret World of American Communism*, p. 49; Powers, *Not Without Honor*, p. 242.

121. Cunningham, "Can Political Means Gain Professional Ends?" pp. 53–54.

122. Ibid.

123. Stanley Kelley, *Professional Public Relations and Political Power* (Baltimore: Johns Hopkins University Press, 1956), chap. 3.

124. Letter from Louis Orr, M.D., to Dr. Arthur Schwartz, April 10, 1950, Pepper Library, Series S201, Box 93, File 1.

125. Cruikshank Oral History, p. 265.

126. Pepper Oral History, p. 52.

127. Ibid., p. 28.

128. Ibid., p. 52.

129. Pepper, *Pepper: Eyewitness to a Century*, pp. 193, 202.

130. Falk Oral History, p. 228.
131. The Medical Lobby's 1952 Platform, Bulletin 7, November, 1951, Committee for the Nation's Health, Pepper Library, Series S201, Box 93, Folder 1.
132. Sheri David, "Eisenhower and the American Medical Association: A Coalition Against the Elderly," in *Dwight D. Eisenhower: Soldier, President, Statesman,* edited by Joann Krieg (Westport, Conn.: Greenwood Press, 1987), p. 59.
133. Truman, *Memoirs,* p. 24.
134. Roswell Perkins Oral History, Columbia University Oral History Collection, p. 7.
135. Alan Pond Oral History, Columbia University Oral History Collection, pp. 11, 123.
136. Jacob S. Hacker, "Boundary Wars: The Political Struggle over Public and Private Social Benefits in the United States," doctoral dissertation, Yale University, 2000, p. 310.
137. Perkins Oral History, p. 36.
138. Ibid., p. 84.
139. Pond Oral History, p. 64.
140. Hacker, "Boundary Wars," p. 238; Pond Oral History, p. 3.
141. Perkins Oral History, pp. 36–37.
142. Pond Oral History, p. 9; Perkins Oral History, pp. 37, 42, 79.
143. Perkins Oral History, p. 43.
144. Ibid., pp. 44, 66.
145. Ibid., p. 58.
146. Ibid., p. 59.
147. Stephen Ambrose, *Eisenhower, the President* (New York: Simon and Schuster, 1984), p. 199.

Chapter Two

1. Melvyn Dubofsky and Warren Van Tine, *John L. Lewis: A Biography* (New York: Quadrangle/New York Times Book Company, 1977), p. 426.
2. Saul Alinsky, *John L. Lewis* (New York: G. P. Putnam's Sons, 1949), p. 344.
3. Ibid.
4. Robert Zieger, *John L. Lewis, Labor Leader* (Boston: Twayne, 1988), p. 153.
5. Alinsky, *John L. Lewis,* p. 329.
6. Ibid., p. 344.
7. Marie Gottschalk, *The Shadow Welfare State: Labor, Business, and the Politics of Health Care in the United States* (Ithaca, N.Y.: Cornell University Press, 2000), p. 46; Jennifer Klein, "The Business of Health Security: Employee Health Benefits, Commercial Insurers, and the Reconstruction of Welfare Capitalism, 1945–1960," *International Labor and Working Class History* 58 (2000): 198.
8. Health Insurance Plans in the United States, Report of the Committee on Labor and Public Welfare, U.S. Senate, Report No. 359, Part 1, 82nd Congress, 1st Session, May 28, 1951, p. 2.
9. Beth Stevens, "Blurring the Boundaries: How the Federal Government Has Influenced Welfare Benefits in the Private Sector," in *The Politics of Social Policy in the United States,* edited by Margaret Weir, Ann Shola Orloff, and Theda Skocpol (Princeton, N.J.: Princeton University Press, 1988), p. 125.

10. Archie Robinson, *George Meany and His Times: A Biography* (New York: Simon and Schuster, 1981), p. 18.
11. Jennifer Klein, *For All These Rights: Business, Labor and the Shaping of America's Public-Private Welfare State* (Princeton, N.J.: Princeton University Press, 2003), p. 177.
12. Ibid., p. 178.
13. Klein, "The Business of Health Security," p. 295; Louis Reed, "Private Health Insurance: Coverage and Financial Experience," *Social Security Bulletin* 30 (1967): 3–22; Stevens, "Blurring the Boundaries," pp. 133–34.
14. Stevens, "Blurring the Boundaries," p. 133.
15. Klein, "The Business of Health Security," 295.
16. Elizabeth Fones-Wolf, *Selling Free Enterprise: The Business Assault on Labor and Liberalism, 1945–60* (Urbana: University of Illinois Press, 1994).
17. Klein, "The Business of Health Security," p. 299.
18. Nelson Lichtenstein, "Labor in the Truman Era: Origins of the Private Welfare State," in *The Truman Presidency*, edited by Michael J. Lacey (New York: Cambridge University Press, 1989), p. 129.
19. Nelson Cruikshank Oral History, Columbia University Oral History Collection, p. 50.
20. U.S. Congress, House Committee on Expenditures in Executive Departments, Investigation of the Participation of Federal Officials in the Formation and Operation of Health Workshops, Hearings before the Subcommittee on Publicity and Propaganda, 80th Congress, 1st Session, May 28–June 18, 1947, p. 40.
21. Alan Derrickson, "Health Security for All?" *Journal of American History* 80 (1994): p. 1358; Lichtenstein, "Labor in the Truman Era," p. 139.
22. Gottschalk, *The Shadow Welfare State*, p. 52; Nelson Lichtenstein, "From Corporatism to Collective Bargaining: Organized Labor and the Eclipse of Social Democracy in the Postwar Era," in *The Rise and Fall of the New Deal Order, 1930–1980*, edited by Steve Fraser and Gary Gerstle (Princeton, N.J.: Princeton University Press, 1989), pp. 122–52.
23. Judith Stepan-Norris and Maurice Zeitlin, "Union Democracy, Radical Leadership, and the Hegemony of Capital," *American Sociological Review* 60 (1995): 829–50; Judith Stepan-Norris and Maurice Zeitlin, *Left Out: Reds and America's Industrial Unions* (Cambridge: Cambridge University Press, 2002).
24. Stevens, "Blurring the Boundaries," p. 141.
25. Michael Brown, "Bargaining for Social Rights: Unions and the Reemergence of Welfare Capitalism," *Political Science Quarterly* 112, 4 (1997–98): 653.
26. Stevens, "Blurring the Boundaries," p. 141.
27. Alan Derickson, "Health Security For All?" *Journal of American History* 80 (1994): 1351.
28. Cruikshank Oral History, p. 9.
29. Colin Gordon, "Why No National Health Insurance in the U.S.: The Limits of Social Provision in War and Peace, 1941–1948," *Journal of Policy History* 9, 3 (1997): 277–310.
30. Quoted in Lichtenstein, "Labor in the Truman Era," p. 138.
31. Frank Cormier and William J. Eaton, *Reuther* (Englewood Cliffs, N.J.: Prentice-Hall, 1970), p. 321.
32. Edward D. Berkowitz, *Mr. Social Security: The Life of Wilbur Cohen* (Lawrence: University Press of Kansas, 1995), p. 55.

33. Kathryn Ellickson Oral History, Columbia University Oral History Collection, p. 72.
34. Cruikshank Oral History, p. 56.
35. Arthur Hess Oral History, Columbia University Oral History Collection, p. 88; M. G. Gluck and Virginia Reno, eds., *Reflections on Implementing Medicare: Implementation Aspects of National Health Care Reform* (Washington, D.C.: National Academy of Social Insurance, 2001), p. 20.
36. Hess Oral History, p. 36.
37. Ibid., p. 39.
38. Isidore S. Falk Oral History, Columbia University Oral History Collection, p. 193.
39. Ibid., p. 88; Gluck and Reno, *Reflections on Implementing Medicare*, p. 20.
40. E. H. O'Connor, "The Doctors' Case Against Compulsory Disability Insurance," Conference of Medical Service, Chicago, February 11, 1951, pp. 1–2, 8, Pepper Library, S201, Box 93, File 1.
41. Cruikshank Oral History, p. 44.
42. Edward Berkowitz, "Disability Insurance and the Limits of American History," *Public Historian* 8, 2 (1986): 65–82.
43. Cruikshank Oral History, p. 56.
44. Oscar Ewing Oral History, Columbia University Oral History Collection, p. 77.
45. Sylvia A. Law, *Blue Cross: What Went Wrong* (New Haven, Conn.: Yale University Press, 1976), p. 12.
46. Ewing Oral History, p. 77.
47. Elizabeth Wickenden Oral History, Columbia University Oral History Collection, p. 162. The Social Security Board was now called the Social Security Administration.
48. Joseph Stetler Oral History, Columbia University Oral History Collection, p. 17.
49. Leonard Woodcock Oral History, Columbia University Oral History Collection, p. 2.
50. Ibid., p. 3.
51. Gottschalk, *The Shadow Welfare State*, p. 58.
52. Cruikshank Oral History, p. 75.
53. Ellickson Oral History, p. 277.
54. Ibid., p. 124.
55. Ibid., p. 122.
56. Ibid., p. 128.
57. Amendments to Title II of the Social Security Act; Ellickson Oral History.
58. Ellickson Oral History, p. 45.
59. Nelson H. Cruikshank, *The Cruikshank Chronicles: Anecdotes, Stories, and Memoirs of a New Deal Liberal*, edited by Alice Hoffman and Howard Hoffman (Hamden, Conn.: Archon Books, 1989), p. 157.
60. Amie Forand Oral History, Columbia University Oral History Collection, p. 20.
61. Lisbeth Bamberger Schorr and Leonard Lesser Oral History, Columbia University Oral History Collection, p. 70.
62. *Congressional Quarterly Almanac, 1960* (Washington, D.C.: Government Printing Office, 1960), p. 154.
63. Schorr and Lesser Oral History, p. 18.
64. Ibid., pp. 66, 3.

65. Gallup *Poll Reports, 1935–68* (Princeton, New Jersey: American Institute of Public Opinion, 1969), p. 337.
66. Ivan Nestingen Oral History, Columbia University Oral History Collection, pp. 69–70.
67. Cruikshank, *The Cruikshank Chronicles*, p. 155.
68. Stetler Oral History, p. 27, 30.
69. Perkins Oral History, p. 81.
70. Walter McNerney Oral History, Columbia University Oral History Collection, p. 15.
71. David Sheri, "Eisenhower and the American Medical Association: A Coalition Against the Elderly," in *Dwight D. Eisenhower: Soldier, President, Statesman,* edited by Joanne P. Krieg (Westport, Conn.: Greenwood Press, 1987), p. 61.
72. Dora L. Costa, *The Evolution of Retirement: An American Economic History, 1880–1990* (Chicago: University of Chicago Press, 1998).
73. Robert Myers Oral History, Columbia University Oral History Collection, pp. 36, 40.
74. Stetler Oral History, p. 43.
75. The AMA accused the AFL-CIO of fighting Kerr-Mills in the states, an accusation union leaders did not entirely deny. According to Ellickson, the AFL-CIO did not fight it but did compile material to show that it was inadequate. They provided cost estimates and when the insurance companies attacked their estimates, they tried "to find out how the insurance industry had developed their cost estimates" (Ellickson Oral History, p. 62).
76. Letter from Clinton P. Anderson to Mrs. Leslie Hines, November 23, 1964, Anderson Papers, Library of Congress, Box 680, File: Finance, Social Security, Medical Care for the Aged.
77. *Medical Assistance for the Aged, the Kerr-Mills Program 1960–1963, Report by the Subcommittee on Health of the Elderly to the Special Committee on Aging, U.S. Senate* (Washington, D.C.: Government Printing Office, October 1963), p. 6.
78. Ibid., p. 4.
79. Ibid., p. 4.
80. Cohen Oral History, p. 27.
81. Ellickson Oral History, p. 61.
82. *Blue Cross and Private Health Insurance Coverage of Older Americans, A Report by the Subcommittee on Health of the Elderly, Senate Special Committee on Aging, July 1964* (Washington, D.C.: Government Printing Office, 1964), p. 22.
83. Ibid., p. 42.
84. *Blue Cross and Private Health Insurance Coverage,* p. 33.
85. Ellickson Oral History, p. 246.
86. Cruikshank Oral History, p. 320.
87. Letter from Martha Botts to Clinton Anderson, September 26, 1964, Anderson Papers, Box 681, File: Finance, Social Security, Medicare—Con.
88. Letter from Ned Flightner to Clinton Anderson, September 17, 1964, Anderson Papers, Box 681, File: Finance, Social Security, Medicare—Con. See also letter from L. W. Dempsey, who complained, "This is the very best and first Socialistic peace of legislation ever considered by an elected congress under a Republic. These men who are interested in this for political gain in office have shed there [sic] oath of office. To protect that Republic. And our United States Constitution. From socialism."

89. Letter from Mrs. J. L. Flinchum to Clinton Anderson, November 13, 1964, Anderson Papers, Box 681, File: Finance, Social Security, Medicare—Con.

90. Letter from Clinton Anderson to Mrs. Andrew F. Bott, October 21, 1964, Anderson Papers, Box 681, File: Finance, Social Security, Medicare—Con.

91. Esselstyn Oral History, p. 4–5.

92. Ibid., p. 6.

93. Schorr and Lesser Oral History, p. 103.

94. Esselstyn Oral History, p. 25.

95. Ibid., p. 39.

96. Schorr and Lesser Oral History, p. 103.

97. Peter Corning, *The Evolution of Medicare: From Idea to Law*, Social Security Administration, Office of Research and Statistics, Research Report 29 (Washington, D.C.: U.S. Department of Health, Education and Welfare, 1969), p. 91.

98. Esselstyn Oral History, p. 35.

99. Cruikshank Oral History, p. 321.

100. Gerald Markowitz and David Rosner, "Seeing Common Ground: A History of Labor and Blue Cross," *Journal of Health Politics, Policy and Law* 16, 4 (1991): 700.

101. Wickenden Oral History, p. 134.

102. Blue Carstenson Oral History, Columbia University Oral History collection, pp. 213, 212.

103. Ibid., pp. 76–79.

104. Letter from F. L. Chatham to Clinton P. Anderson, December 15, 1964, Anderson Papers, Box 680, File: Finance, Social Security, Medical Care for the Aged.

105. Stetler Oral History, p. 52.

106. Carstenson Oral History, p. 97.

107. Ibid., p. 204.

108. Ibid., pp. 163–66.

109. Statement by AFL-CIO Executive Council on Hospital Insurance for the Aged, February 23, 1965, RG 233, Records of the House of Representatives, 89th Congress, Committee on Ways and Means, Legislative Files, Box 22, File: HR 6675—8 of 94.

110. Corning, *The Evolution of Medicare*, p. 93.

111. Carstenson Oral History, p. 47.

112. Cohen Oral History, p. 27.

113. Irving Bernstein, *Guns or Butter: The Presidency of Lyndon Johnson* (New York: Oxford University Press, 1996).

114. Theodore Marmor, *The Politics of Medicare*, 2nd edition (New York: Aldine de Gruyter, 2000), p. 38.

115. Richard Harris, *A Sacred Trust* (New York: New American Library, 1966), p. 39.

116. Carstenson Oral History, p. 185.

117. Forand Oral History, p. 43.

118. Wickenden Oral History, p. 169.

119. "Washington News," *Journal of the American Medical Association* 186, 9 (1963): 16–17.

120. "Washington News," *Journal of the American Medical Association* 187, 3 (1964): 17.

121. Stetler Oral History, p. 49.

122. Carstenson Oral History, p. 14.
123. Ewing Oral History, p. 66.
124. Ellickson Oral History, p. 71.
125. Robert Dallek, *Flawed Giant: Lyndon Johnson and His Times, 1961–1973* (New York: Oxford University Press, 1998), p. 49.
126. Joseph Califano Jr., *The Triumph and Tragedy of Lyndon Johnson* (New York: Simon and Schuster, 1991), p. 9.
127. "Washington News," *Journal of the American Medical Association* 187, 7 (1964): 17.
128. *Blue Cross and Private Health Insurance Coverage,* note 50, p. 29.
129. Ibid., pp. 10–11.
130. Irwin Unger, *The Best of Intentions: The Triumphs and Failures of the Great Society Under Kennedy, Johnson, and Nixon* (New York: Doubleday, 1996).
131. Carstenson Oral History, p. 52.
132. Ibid., p. 55.
133. Cruikshank Oral History, p. 79.
134. Wickenden Oral History, p. 148.
135. Julian Zelizer, *Taxing America: Wilbur Mills, Congress, and the State, 1974–1975* (Cambridge: Cambridge University Press, 1998).
136. Carstenson Oral History, p. 57.
137. Robert Myers with Richard Vernaci, *Within the System: My Half Century in Social Security* (Winsted, Conn.: ACTEX, 1992), p. 161.
138. Berkowitz, "Disability Insurance," p. 192.
139. Alanson Willcox Oral History, Columbia University Oral History Collection, p. 43.
140. Ibid., p. 67.
141. Cohen Oral History, p. 32.
142. McNerney Oral History, p. 24.
143. Law, *Blue Cross.*
144. Wickenden Oral History, p. 52.
145. "After Medicare, What?" editorial comment, *National Underwriter,* January 9, 1961, p. 22.
146. Corning, *The Evolution of Medicare,* p. 102.
147. Eldercare Act of 1965, AFL-CIO Department of Social Security, March 1, 1965, RG 233, Records of the House of Representatives, 89th Congress, Committee on Ways and Means, Legislative Files, Box 21, File: HR 6675—3 of 94.
148. "Eldercare Branded Empty Propaganda," *AFL-CIO News,* February 20, 1965, RG 233, Records of the House of Representatives, 89th Congress, Committee on Ways and Means, Legislative Files, Box 21, File: HR 6675–3 of 94.
149. Wickenden Oral History, p. 169.
150. Letter from Leo H. Irwin, Chief Counsel, U.S. House of Representatives, to John Slack, June 18, 1965, RG 233, Records of the House of Representatives, 89th Congress, Committee on Ways and Means, Legislative Files, Box 21, File: HR 6675–4 of 94.
151. Bernstein, *Guns or Butter,* p. 171.
152. Quoted in Berkowitz, "Disability Insurance," p. 196.
153. Gluck and Reno, *Reflections on Implementing Medicare,* p. 2.
154. Lawrence R. Jacobs, *The Health of Nations: Public Opinion and the Making of American and British Health Policy* (Ithaca, N.Y.: Cornell University Press, 1993).

155. Schorr and Lesser Oral History, p. 26.
156. McNerney Oral History, p. 34.
157. Schorr and Lesser Oral History, p. 30.
158. Ibid., p. 74.
159. Ellickson Oral History, p. 64.
160. Schorr and Lesser Oral History, p. 75.
161. Ibid., p. 27.
162. Bernstein, *Guns or Butter*, p. 176.
163. Letter from Irwin to Slack, June 18, 1965.
164. Cruikshank Oral History, pp. 371–72.
165. Cruikshank, *The Cruikshank Chronicles*, p. 170.
166. Stetler Oral History, p. 8.
167. Cohen Oral History, p. 27.
168. Stetler Oral History, p. 14.

Chapter Three

1. Hugh Davis Graham, *The Civil Rights Era: Origins and Development of National Policy* (New York: Oxford University Press, 1990), pp. 3–5.
2. Quoted in Howard Schuman, Charlotte Steeh, Lawrence Bobo, and Maria Krysan, *Racial Attitudes in America* (Cambridge, Mass.: Harvard University Press, 1997), p. 10.
3. David R. James, "The Transformation of the Southern Racial State: Class and Race Determinants of Local-State Structures," *American Sociological Review* 53 (1988): 193.
4. Memo from Alanson Willcox to the Secretary, March 4, 1964, National Archives, College Park, Maryland, MRG 235, Box 7: Hospital Construction, File: Segregation and Discrimination.
5. Isidore Falk Oral History, Columbia University Oral History Collection, p. 279.
6. Ibid., p. 279.
7. Rufus Miles Jr., *The Department of Health, Education and Welfare* (New York: Praeger, 1974), p. 112.
8. Karen Kruse Thomas, "The Blueprint of Segregation: The Influence of Southern State Health Policy on the Federal Hill-Burton Hospital Construction Program, 1939–54," paper presented to the Southern Historical Association, Baltimore, November 9, 2002, p. 10.
9. Memo from Harrison to Siegel, January 18, 1954, note 45, National Archives, College Park, Maryland, RG 235, Box 7, File: Segregation and Discrimination.
10. Letter from Dr. Hubert Eaton to Dr. Boisfeuillet Jones, October 13, 1962; letter from Boisfeuillet Jones, Special Assistant to the Secretary, to Dr. Hubert Eaton, November 13, 1962, National Archives, College Park, Maryland, RG 235, Box 7, File: Segregation and Discrimination.
11. Thomas, "The Blueprint of Segregation," p. 2; Memo from Alanson Willcox to the Secretary, March 4, 1964, National Archives, College Park, Maryland, RG 235, Box 7, File: Segregation and Discrimination.
12. Malvin Schechter, "Segregated Blood: A Backlash Backfires," *Hospital Practice*, July 1969, p. 21.

13. David Barton Smith, "Addressing Racial Inequities In Health Care: Civil Rights Monitoring and Report Cards," *Journal of Health Politics, Policy and Law* 23, 1 (1998): 75-105.

14. Thomas, "The Blueprint of Segregation," p. 9.

15. Ibid., p. 17.

16. Quoted in Schuman, Steeh, Bobo, and Krysan, *Racial Attitudes in America*, p. 20.

17. Memo from Darrell Lane to Parke Banta, June 10, 1954; memo: Hospital Survey and Construction—Nondiscrimination Requirements Under Present Statute, January 31, 1956, National Archives, College Park, Maryland, RG 235, Box 7, File: Segregation and Discrimination.

18. Memo from Edward Rourke, October 11, 1961, National Archives, College Park, Maryland, RG 235, Box 7, File: Segregation and Discrimination.

19. Hospital Construction Program—Nondiscrimination—Constitutional Question, November 16, 1956, National Archives, College Park, Maryland, RG 235, Box 7, File: Segregation and Discrimination.

20. Memo from Gladys Harrison to Parke Banta, January 31, 1956, National Archives, College Park, Maryland, RG 235, Box 7, File: Segregation and Discrimination.

21. Memo from Alanson Willcox to Jack Haldeman, February 12, 1963, National Archives, College Park, Maryland, RG 235, Box 7, File: Segregation and Discrimination.

22. Karen Kruse Thomas, "The Wound of My People: Segregation and the Modernization of Health Care in North Carolina, 1935–1975," doctoral dissertation, University of North Carolina, 1999, p. 10.

23. Augustus K. Jones Jr., *Law, Bureaucracy, and Politics: The Implementation of Title VI of the Civil Rights Act of 1964* (Washington, D.C.: University Press of America, 1982).

24. Aldon D. Morris, *The Origins of the Civil Rights Movement: The Implementation of Title VI of the Civil Rights Act of 1964* (New York: Free Press, 1986).

25. Correspondence Between Catherine Patterson, Burke Marshall, and Alanson Willcox, October 4, October 23, October 25, 1963, National Archives, College Park, Maryland, RG 235, Box 1, File: Alabama.

26. Letter from Horace Reed to T. Fletcher Little, May 2, 1962, National Archives, College Park, Maryland, RG 235, HEW, Box 7, Hospital construction, File: Segregation and Discrimination.

27. David Barton Smith, *Health Care Divided: Race and Healing a Nation* (Ann Arbor: University of Michigan Press, 1999), pp. 75–76.

28. Letter from Reginald Hawkins to Alanson Willcox, July 27, 1963, National Archives, College Park, Maryland, RG 235, Box 7, File: Segregation and Discrimination.

29. Schuman, Steeh, Bobo, and Krysan, *Racial Attitudes in America*, pp. 25–26.

30. Smith, "Addressing Racial Inequities in Health Care," p. 81.

31. Memo from Office of General Counsel to Carl Harper, Regional Attorney, December 31, 1959, National Archives, College Park, Maryland, RG 235, Box 7, File: Segregation and Discrimination.

32. Memo from Carl Harper to Edward Rourke, Assistant General Counsel, Office of General Counsel, May 4, 1962, National Archives, College Park, Maryland, RG 235, Box 7, File: Segregation and Discrimination.

33. Letter from James S. Carr, Deputy Regional Attorney to Edward Burke, Assistant General Counsel to HEW, October 16, 1962, National Archives, College Park, Maryland, RG 235, Box 7, File: Segregation and Discrimination.

34. "Negroes' Suit Demands Full Grady Hospital Integration," *Atlanta Constitution*, September 25, 1962, p. 1, National Archives, College Park, Maryland, RG 235, Box 7, File: Segregation and Discrimination.

35. Letter from James S. Carr, Deputy Regional Attorney to Edward Burke, Assistant General Counsel to HEW, October 16, 1962, National Archives, College Park, Maryland, RG 235, Box 7, File: Segregation and Discrimination.

36. Memo from General Counsel to Marion E. Gardner, *Wood v. Hogan*, Lynchburg General Hospital, June 25, 1962, National Archives, College Park, Maryland, RG 235, Box 7, File: Segregation and Discrimination.

37. Letter from Virgil A. Wood to Robert F. Kennedy, June 8, 1962, National Archives, College Park, Maryland, RG 235, Box 7, File: Segregation and Discrimination.

38. Adam Clayton Powell, "Hospital Integration and Job Opportunity: Equality Goals for 1963," *Journal of the National Medical Association*, July 1963, pp. 338–41.

39. Memo from Edward Rourke to Luther Terry, April 6, 1964, National Archives, College Park, Maryland, RG 235, Box 7, File: Segregation and Discrimination.

40. Kenneth Wing, "Title VI and Health Facilities: Forms Without Substance," *Hastings Law Journal* 30 (1978): 138.

41. Letter from Alanson Willcox to Reginald Hawkins, August 20, 1964, National Archives, College Park, Maryland, RG 235, Box 7, File: Segregation and Discrimination.

42. Memo from Alanson Willcox to Wilbur Cohen, August 14, 1963, National Archives, College Park, Maryland, RG 235, Box 7, File: Segregation and Discrimination.

43. Conduct Required Under State Statutes Which Is Inconsistent with the Nondiscrimination Assurances in the Hill-Burton, Mental Retardation Facilities and Community Mental Health Centers Construction Programs, June 26, 1964, National Archives, College Park, Maryland, RG 235, Box 7, File: Segregation and Discrimination.

44. Memo from Gladys Harrison to Parke Banta, January 31, 1956, Appendix I, State Statutes, National Archives, College Park, Maryland, RG 235, Box 7, File: Segregation and Discrimination.

45. Conduct Required Under State Statutes Which Is Inconsistent with the Nondiscrimination Assurances in the Hill-Burton, Mental Retardation Facilities and Community Mental Health Centers Construction Programs, June 26, 1964, National Archives, College Park, Maryland, RG 235, Box 7, File: Segregation and Discrimination.

46. Letter from Senator Harrison Williams to Jack Haldeman, February 4, 1963, National Archives, College Park, Maryland, RG 235, Box 7, File: Segregation and Discrimination.

47. Memo from Lisle Carter to Alanson Wilcox, June 18, 1962, National Archives, College Park, Maryland, RG 235, Box 7, File: Segregation and Discrimination.

48. Memo from James Quigley to Alanson Wilcox, July 10, 1963, National Archives, College Park, Maryland, RG 235, Box 7, File: Segregation and Discrimination.
49. *Congressional Record*, April 3, 1957, pp. 4480–82.
50. Smith, "The Racial Integration of Health Facilities," p. 858.
51. Title VI of the Civil Rights Act, December 14, 1965, National Archives, College Park, Maryland, RG 47, Box 300. File: PA 16 Title VI Compliance.
52. Jeremy Rabkin, "Office for Civil Rights," in *The Politics of Regulation*, edited by James Q. Wilson (New York: Basic Books, 1980), p. 310.
53. Jones, *Law, Bureaucracy, and Politics*, p. 122.
54. Memo from Robert Nash to James Murray, Medicare and Civil Rights, March 19, 1966, National Archives, College Park, Maryland, RG 47, Box 300, File: PA 16 Title VI Compliance.
55. Miles, *The Department of Health, Education, and Welfare*, p. 64.
56. M. G. Gluck and Virginia Reno, eds., *Reflections on Implementing Medicare: Implementation Aspects of National Health Care Reform* (Washington, D.C.: National Academy of Social Insurance, 2001), p. 7.
57. Title VI of Civil Rights Act of 1965, National Archives, College Park, Maryland, RG 47, Box 300, File: PA 16, Title VI Compliance, p. 1.
58. Robert C. Lieberman, *Shifting the Color Line: Race and the American Welfare State* (Cambridge, Mass.: Harvard University Press, 1998), p. 71.
59. Commissioner's Bulletin, National Archives, College Park, Maryland, RG 47, Box 300, File: PA 16, Title VI Compliance.
60. Telephone interview with Dr. Richard Smith, career service officer in the Public Health Service and Special Projects officer, February 17, 1999.
61. Letter from Robert Ball to the Secretary, Nov. 1, 1965, National Archives, College Park, Maryland, RG 47, Box 330, File: PA Title VI Compliance.
62. Memo from Robert Ball to the Under Secretary, October 13, 1965, National Archives, College Park, Maryland, RG 47, Box 300, File: PA 16, Title VI Compliance.
63. Memo from Robert Ball to the Secretary, March 14, 1966, National Archives, College Park, Maryland, RG 47, Box 300, File: PA 16, Title VI Compliance.
64. Telephone interview with Carlton Spitzer, April 11, 2003; Carlton E. Spitzer, "A Crusader for Civil Rights and Racial Equality," Special to the *Star-Democrat*. Spitzer Files, manuscript sent to author.
65. Hospital Application for Participation; Guidelines for Compliance with Title VI, National Archives, College Park, Maryland, RG 47, Box 300, File: PA 16, Title VI Compliance.
66. Letter from James Murray to Robert Ball, February 15, 1966, National Archives, College Park, Maryland, RG 47, Box 300, File PA 16, Title VI Compliance.
67. Memoirs of Morton Lebow, Public Information Office, Office of Equal Health Opportunity, prepared for the author, p. 2.
68. Letter from Roy Swift to Robert Ball, undated, National Archives, College Park, Maryland, RG 47, Box 298, File: PA Title VI Compliance.
69. Memo from Louis Zawatzky to Jack Futterman, January 18, 1966, National Archives, College Park, Maryland, RG 47, Box 300, File: PA 16, Title VI Compliance.
70. Note from Robert Ball to Irv Wolkstein, July 2, 1966, National Archives, College Park, Maryland, RG 47, Box 300, File: PA 16, Title VI Compliance.

71. "AMA Head Urges Doctors Not to Thwart Medicare Program That Starts Friday," *Wall Street Journal*, June 27, 1966, Anderson Papers, Library of Congress, Box 702, File: Finance Committee, Medicare—General.
72. Edward Berkowitz, *Mr. Social Security: The Life of Wilbur J. Cohen* (Lawrence: University Press of Kansas, 1995).
73. Lebow Memoirs, p. 1; memo from Roy Swift, Corrected Number of Southern Counties with No Medicare Hospitals, July 25, 1966, National Archives, College Park, Maryland, RG 47, Box 298, File: PA 16 Hospital Compliance Report; Title VI Compliance Problems, RG 47, Box 298, File: PA 16 Hospital Compliance Report.
74. Robert Nash, "Compliance of Hospitals and Health Agencies with Title VI of the Civil Rights Act," *American Journal of Public Health* 58 (1968): 246–51.
75. Lebow Memoirs.
76. Telephone interview with Dr. Richard Smith, career service officer in the Public Health Service and Special Projects officer, February 17, 1999.
77. Memo from Roy Swift to Robert Ball, May 27, 1966, Observations on Title VI Compliance Efforts, National Archives, College Park, Maryland, RG 47, Box 298, File: PA 16 Hospital Compliance Report.
78. Letter from Robert Nash to James Murray, March 10, 1966, National Archives, College Park, Maryland, RG 47, Box 300, File: Title VI Compliance.
79. Memo from James Murray to Robert Ball, Medicare and civil rights, February 15, 1966, National Archives, College Park, Maryland, RG 47, Box 300, File: PA 16, Title VI Compliance.
80. Telephone interview with Dr. Richard Smith, career service officer in the Public Health Service and Special Projects officer, February 17, 1999.
81. "Federal Compliance Complaint Is Puzzle for Officials of Two Hospitals in Lincoln," *Elk Valley Times*, June 29, 1966, National Archives, College Park, Maryland, RG 47, Box 298, File: PA 16 Hospital Compliance Report.
82. Taborian Hospital, National Archives, College Park, Maryland, RG 47, Box 298, File: PA 16 Hospital Compliance Report.
83. Report of Title VI Issues, Natchez, Mississippi, July 15, 1966, National Archives, College Park, Maryland, RG 47, Box 298, File: PA Title VI Compliance.
84. Letter from Roy Swift to Robert Ball, undated, National Archives, College Park, Maryland, RG 47, Box 298, File: PA Title VI Compliance.
85. Berkowitz, *Mr. Social Security*.
86. Malvin Schechter, "Medicare and Desegregation," *Hospital Practice*, January 1967, p. 14.
87. Determination of Inability to Secure Compliance by Voluntary Means, December 30, 1966, National Archives, College Park, Maryland, RG 47, Box 298, File: PA 16 Hospital Compliance Report.
88. Malvin Schechter, "Emergency Medicare and Desegregation: A Special Report," *Hospital Practice*, July 1968, pp. 14–15; Malvin Schechter, "Emergency Medicare and Desegregation: Subterfuge Ends," *Hospital Practice*, January 1970, p. 17; memo from Peter Libassi to Robert Ball, July 25, 1966, National Archives, College Park, Maryland, RG 47, Box 298, File: PA 16 Hospital Compliance Report; Interview with Robert Ball, October 24, 1997.

Chapter Four

1. Joseph A. Califano Jr., *The Triumph and Tragedy of Lyndon Johnson: The White House Years* (New York: Simon and Schuster, 1991), pp. 9–10.

2. Robert Dallek, *Flawed Giant: Lyndon Johnson and His Times, 1961–1973* (New York: Oxford University Press, 1998), p. 210.
3. Marilyn Moon, *Medicare Now and in the Future* (Washington, D.C.: Urban Institute Press, 1993), p. 30.
4. Claude Pepper Oral History, Columbia University Oral History Collection, p. 45.
5. M. G. Gluck and Virginia Reno, eds., *Reflections on Implementing Medicare: Implementation Aspects of National Health Care Reform* (Washington, D.C.: National Academy of Social Insurance, 2001), pp. 35–37.
6. Telephone conversation between Art Fogleson and Martin Cohen of HIP, New York. August 9, 1966, National Archives, College Park, Maryland, RG 47, Office of the Commissioner, Box 298, File: PA 16, Enrollment April through December 1966.
7. Memo from Roy Swift to Bob Ball, September 12, 1966, National Archives, College Park, Maryland, RG 47, Office of the Commissioner, Box 298, File: PA 16, Enrollment April through December 1966.
8. Edward Berkowitz, "Disability Insurance and the Limits of American History," *Public Historian* 8, 2 (1986): 210.
9. Beneficiary Notice to John Sterusky, National Archives, College Park, Maryland, RG 47, Office of the Commissioner, Box 298, File: PA 16 Enrollment April through December 1966.
10. Robert Stevens and Rosemary Stevens, *Welfare Medicine in America* (New York: Free Press, 1974), p. 50; Letter from Leo H. Irwin, Chief Counsel, U.S. House of Representatives, to John Slack, June 18, 1965, National Archives, Washington, D.C., RG 233, Records of the House of Representatives, 89th Congress, Committee on Ways and Means, Legislative Files, Box 21, File: HR 6675–4 of 94; Lawrence R. Jacobs, *The Health of Nations: Public Opinion and the Making of American and British Health Policy* (Ithaca, N.Y.: Cornell University Press, 1993).
11. Quoted in Berkowitz, "Disability Insurance," 203.
12. Quoted in Jonathan Oberlander, *The Political Life of Medicare* (Chicago: University of Chicago Press, 2003), p. 109.
13. Letter from Robert Ball to Bowman Doss, President, Nationwide Mutual Insurance Company, February 11, 1966, National Archives, College Park, Maryland, RG 47, Office of the Commissioner, Box 298, File: PA 16 Contracts. Agreements for Carrying Out Title XVII of the Social Security Act, 1966; Robert Ball, Report to Social Security Administration Staff on the Implementation of the Social Security Amendments of 1965, November 15, 1965, in Gluck and Reno, *Reflections on Implementing Medicare*, p. 39.
14. Memo from Jay Constantine to Senator Anderson, April 14, 1966, Anderson Papers, Library of Congress, Box 702, File: Finance Committee, Medicare—General.
15. Memo from Arthur Hess to Robert Ball, May 18, 1966, National Archives, College Park, Maryland, RG 47, Office of the Commissioner, Box 298, File: PA 16 Contracts, Agreements for Carrying Out Title XVII of the Social Security Act, 1966. Although most of the planning involved the SSA and the BCA, some commercial insurers also participated.
16. Letter from Robert Ball to Bowman Doss, President, Nationwide Mutual Insurance Company, February 11, 1966, National Archives, College Park, Maryland, RG 47, Office of the Commissioner, Box 298, File: PA 16 Contracts, Agreements for Carrying Out Title XVII of the Social Security Act, 1966.

17. *Congressional Record,* July 8, 1965, pp. 159, 70–71.
18. Memo to Senator Anderson, February 9, 1966, Anderson Papers, Box 702, File: Finance Committee, Medicare—Correspondence.
19. Memo from Robert Myers to Robert Ball, February 10, 1966, Anderson Papers, Box 702, File: Finance Committee, Medicare—General.
20. Sylvia A. Law, *Blue Cross: What Went Wrong?* (New Haven, Conn.: Yale University Press, 1976), pp. 72–73. One scandal came to light in 1971 when memos were published from Blue Cross officials describing a task force aimed at persuading key members of Congress that BCA should have a prominent role in any national health insurance program that might be enacted. Medicare tax dollars were being used to fund a campaign against proposals by some members of Congress.
21. Law, *Blue Cross: What Went Wrong,* pp. 63–64.
22. "Nursing Home Costs Will Soar Highly," undated newspaper clipping, Anderson Papers, Box 732, File: Finance Committee, Medicare—Correspondence.
23. "Hospitals to Demand Profit-Return Parity," *Washington Post,* August 30, 1966, Anderson Papers, Box 701, File: Finance Committee, Medicare—Title 19.
24. Alanson Willcox Oral History, Columbia University Oral History Collection, p. 96.
25. Elizabeth Wickenden Oral History, Columbia University Oral History Collection, p. 144.
26. Joseph Califano Jr., *America's Health Care Revolution: Who Lives? Who Dies? Who Pays?* (New York: Random House, 1986), pp. 98–100.
27. Letter from C. J. Jannings to Clinton Anderson, September 29, 1964, Anderson Papers, Box 681, File: Social Security, Medicare—Con.
28. "Physicians Rebel Against Medicare Forms in Ohio; Revolt Soon May Hit Other States," *Wall Street Journal,* undated, Anderson Papers, Box 702, File: Finance Committee, Medicare—General.
29. Law, *Blue Cross: What Went Wrong,* p. 91.
30. Thomas Bodenheimer, "Should We Abolish the Private Health Insurance Industry?" *International Journal of Health Services* 20, 2 (1990): 211.
31. Law, *Blue Cross: What Went Wrong,* p. 89.
32. Memo from Jay Constantine to Senator Anderson, March 2, 1966, Anderson Papers, Box 702, File: Finance Committee, Medicare—General.
33. Paul Starr, *The Social Transformation of American Medicine* (New York: Basic Books, 1982), p. 375.
34. Berkowitz, "Disability Insurance," p. 216.
35. Memo to Wilbur Cohen and Robert Ball, status of definitive contracts, June 28, 1966, National Archives, College Park, Maryland, RG 47, Box 298, File: PA 16 Contracts, Agreements for Carrying Out Title XVII of the Social Security Act, 1966.
36. Visit to headquarters of Mississippi State Medical Society, National Archives, College Park, Maryland, RG 47, Office of the Commissioner, Box 298, File: Contracts, Agreements for Carrying Out Title XVII of the Social Security Act, 1966.
37. Oberlander, *The Political Life of Medicare,* p. 110.
38. Visit to Headquarters of Traveler's Life Insurance Company's Medicare Center, National Archives, College Park, Maryland, RG 47, Office of the

Commissioner, Box 298, File: Contracts, Agreements for Carrying Out Title XVII of the Social Security Act, 1966.

39. Re: Part B of Medicare, Memo from Jay Constantine to Senator Anderson, October 4, 1968, Anderson Papers, Box 732, File: Finance Committee, Medicare—Correspondence.

40. Re: Part B of Medicare, Memo from Jay Constantine to Senator Anderson, October 4, 1968, Anderson Papers, Box 732, File: Finance Committee, Medicare—Correspondence.

41. Letter from Brendan Mylans to Senator Anderson, January 5, 1968. Anderson Papers, Box 732, File: Finance Committee, Medicare—Correspondence.

42. Edward Berkowitz, *Robert Ball and the Politics of Social Security* (Madison: University of Wisconsin Press, 2004), p. 225.

43. Memo from Howard to Senator Anderson, February 9, 1966, Anderson Papers, Box 702, File: Finance Committee, Medicare—Correspondence.

44. "AMA Urges Doctors to Choose Alternative of Billing Patients Directly for Medicare," *Wall Street Journal*, June 30, 1966, Anderson Papers, Box 702, File: Finance Committee, Medicare—Correspondence.

45. "Payments Plague Medicare," newspaper clipping, Anderson Papers, Box 732, File: Finance Committee, Medicare—Correspondence.

46. Edward Chase, "The Doctors' Bonanza," April 15, 1967, Anderson Papers, Box 731, File: Finance Committee, Medicare.

47. William A. Nolen, M.D., "Are Doctors Profiteering on Medicare?" *Medical Economics*, 1967, p. 98, Anderson Papers, Box 702, File: Finance Committee, Medicare—General.

48. Starr, *The Social Transformation of American Medicine*, p. 381.

49. Letter from Clinton P. Anderson to Russell Long, December 6, 1965, Anderson Papers, Box 702, File: Finance Committee, Medicare—Correspondence.

50. Memo from Jay Constantine to Senator Anderson, January 29, 1966, Anderson Papers, Box 702, File: Finance Committee, Medicare—Correspondence.

51. Quoted in Berkowitz, "Disability Insurance," p. 226.

52. Stevens and Stevens, *Welfare Medicine in America*, p. 66.

53. Law, *Blue Cross: What Went Wrong*, p. 46.

54. Memo from George Rawson to Arthur Hess, April 11, 1966, National Archives, College Park, Maryland, RG 47, Office of the Commissioner, Box 298, File: PA 16 Enrollment April through December, 1966. Once again the South was the laggard. The only southern state participating in Medicaid was Arkansas.

55. Starr, *The Social Transformation of American Medicine*, p. 372.

56. Memo from George Rawson to Arthur Hess, April 11, 1966, National Archives, College Park, Maryland, RG 47, Box 298, File: PA 16 Enrollment April through December, 1966.

57. Law, *Blue Cross: What Went Wrong*, p. 48.

58. Colleen Grogan and Eric Patashnik, "Between Welfare Medicine and Mainstream Entitlement: Medicaid at the Political Crossroads," *Journal of Health Politics, Policy and Law* 28, 5 (2003): 841.

59. Ibid., p. 242.

60. Law, *Blue Cross: What Went Wrong*, p. 102.

61. Julian E. Zelizer, *Taxing America: Wilbur Mills, Congress, and the State, 1945–1975* (Cambridge: Cambridge University Press, 1998), p. 262.
62. Reported in Abraham Ribicoff, *The American Medical Machine* (New York: Saturday Review Press, 1972), p. 93.
63. Quoted in Democratic Advisory Council of Elected Officials, Domestic Affairs Task Force Summary, Health Security, p. 9, files of Rashi Fein, Department of Social Medicine, Harvard Medical School, Cambridge, Massachusetts.
64. "Hospital Costs to Climb Again This Year Blue Cross President Tells House Panel," *Wall Street Journal*, March 6, 1967, p. 1.
65. Ribicoff, *The American Medical Machine*, p. 98.
66. Rowen, *Self-Inflicted Wounds*, pp. 72–73.
67. Memo from George Crawford to Peter Flanigan, September 23, 1971, Nixon Presidential Materials, National Archives, College Park, Maryland, Subject File IS, Box 2, File 6/1/72–8/9/74.
68. Memo from George Crawford to Peggy Harlow, October 7, 1971, Nixon Presidential Materials, Subject File IS, Box 2, File 6/1/72–8/9/74.
69. Rowen, *Self-Inflicted Wounds*, pp. 81–83.
70. "Hospital Costs to Climb Again This Year," p. 1.
71. Law, *What Went Wrong*? p. 130.
72. Oberlander, *The Politics of Medicare*, p. 116.
73. Oberlander, *The Politics of Medicare*, p. 117.
74. Julian Zelizer, *Taxing America: Wilbur D. Mills, Congress and the State, 1945–1075* (Cambridge, England: Cambridge University Press, 1998), p. 342.
75. Oberlander, *The Politics of Medicare*, pp. 118–19.
76. Kant Patel and Mark Rushefsky, *Health Care Politics and Policy in America* (Armonk, N.Y.: M. E. Sharpe, 1999), p. 400; Starr, *The Social Transformation of American Medicine*, p. 400.
77. Issue Report No. 1, The Health Crisis, July 18, 1974, Democratic Study Group, U.S. House of Representatives, files of Rashi Fein, Department of Social Medicine, Harvard Medical School, Boston.
78. Starr, *The Social Transformation of American Medicine*, p. 407.
79. Carolyn Tuohy, *Accidental Logics: The Dynamics of Change in the Health Care Arena in the United States, Britain, and Canada* (New York: Oxford University Press, 1999), p. 131; Law, *Blue Cross: What Went Wrong*, p. 122.
80. Russell B. Roth, M.D., "A Bankrupt Law," *American Medical News*, November 22, 1976, p. 10; Hacker, *The Divided Welfare State*, p. 253.
81. Ribicoff, *The American Medical Machine*, p. 14.
82. Democratic Advisory Council of Elected Officials, Domestic Affairs Task Force Summary, Health Security, p. 7, files of Rashi Fein, Department of Social Medicine, Harvard Medical School, Boston.

Chapter Five

1. Stephen E. Ambrose, *Nixon: The Triumph of a Politician, 1962–1972* (New York: Simon and Schuster, 1989), p. 220.
2. Jill Quadagno, *The Color of Welfare: How Racism Undermined the War on Poverty* (New York: Oxford University Press, 1994), Chapter 6.
3. Disabled SSI recipients who return to work but continue to be medically disabled may remain eligible for Medicaid. States have three options as

to how to treat SSI recipients in regard to Medicaid eligibility. They may cover all SSI recipients under Medicaid, they may provide Medicaid to SSI recipients only if the recipient completes a separate application with the state agency that administers Medicaid. or they may impose more rigid eligibility criteria for Medicaid than for SSI. Thus access to health insurance for the disabled partly depends on residence.

4. Oscar Ewing Oral History, Columbia University Oral History Collection, p. 59.
5. Isidore S. Falk, "Beyond Medicare," *American Journal of Public Health* 59, 3 (1969): 619.
6. A Grid to Evaluate the Mounting Debate About National Health Insurance, p. 5, files of Rashi Fein, Department of Social Medicine, Harvard Medical School, Boston.
7. Walter P. Reuther, "The Health Care Crisis: Where Do We Go From Here?" *American Journal of Public Health* 59, 1 (1969): 14.
8. National Health Insurance, interview with Walter P. Reuther, Chairman, Committee of One-Hundred for National Health Insurance, pp. 7–8, files of Rashi Fein.
9. Statement by AFL-CIO Executive Council on National Health Insurance, February 17, 1970, p. 1, files of Rashi Fein.
10. Nelson Lichtenstein, *The Most Dangerous Man in Detroit: Walter Reuther and the State of American Labor* (New York: Basic Books, 1995), p. 297.
11. John Barnard, *Walter Reuther and the Rise of the Auto Workers* (Boston: Little, Brown, 1983), p. 182.
12. Ibid., pp. 78–79.
13. Lichtenstein, *The Most Dangerous Man in Detroit*, pp. 430–33; Frank Cormier and William Eaton, *Reuther* (Englewood Cliffs, N.J.: Prentice-Hall, 1970), p. 419.
14. Theo Lippman Jr., *Senator Ted Kennedy* (New York: W. W. Norton, 1976), p. 236.
15. National Health Insurance, interview with Walter P. Reuther, Chairman, Committee of One-Hundred for National Health Insurance, p. 4, files of Rashi Fein.
16. Memo from Carry to Rashi Fein, July 6, 1970, files of Rashi Fein.
17. "Health Security for America," *Congressional Record*, Proceedings and Debates of the 92nd Congress, First Session, p. 1.
18. William H. Honan, *Ted Kennedy: Profile of the Survivor* (New York: Quadrangle Books, 1972), p. 105.
19. Anthony Summers, *The Arrogance of Power: The Secret World of Richard Nixon* (New York: Viking, 2000), p. 379.
20. Letter from Dr. Robert Heidt to President Nixon, July 13, 1970. White House Central Files, Subject Files, (HE) Health, Box 4, File: (GEN) HE 7/1/70–12/31/70, National Archives, Nixon Presidential Materials Staff, College Park, Maryland.
21. Richard Lyons, "Nixon National Health Insurance Program," *New York Times*, January 9, 1974, p. 1.
22. Quadagno, *The Color of Welfare*.
23. Design and Cost Estimates of a Tax Credit System to Finance Medical Care, May 16, 1969, American Medical Association, Washington, D.C., p. 4, files of Rashi Fein, Department of Social Medicine, Harvard Medical School, Boston.

24. A Grid to Evaluate the Mounting Debate, p. 2.

25. Income Tax Credits to Assist in the Purchase of Voluntary Health Insurance, File: Tax Credit for Health Insurance (Nixon Task Force), files of Rashi Fein.

26. A Grid to Evaluate the Mounting Debate, p. 4.

27. Iwan W. Morgan, *Nixon* (London: Arnold, 2002), p. 71.

28. Cited in Norbert Israel Goldfield, *National Health Reform American Style: Lessons from the Past: A Twentieth Century Journey* (Tampa, Fla.: American College of Physician Executives, 2000), p. 109.

29. Statement of Senator Edward M. Kennedy on the President's Health Message, February 18, 1971, files of Rashi Fein.

30. Paul Starr, "Transformation in Defeat: The Changing Objectives of National Health Insurance, 1915–1980," *American Journal of Public Health* 72, 19 (1982): 85.

31. "Health Maintenance Organizations Promoted by Nixon," *New York Times*, October 10, 1972, p. 1A; Paul Starr, *The Social Transformation of American Medicine* (New York: Basic Books, 1982), p. 396.

32. Quoted in Lawrence D. Brown, *Politics and Health Care Organization: HMOs as Federal Policy* (Washington, D.C.: Brookings Institution, 1983), p. 206.

33. David Bennahum, "The Crisis Called Managed Care," in *Managed Care: Financial, Legal, and Ethical Issues,* edited by David Bennahum (Cleveland: Pilgrim Press, 1999), p. 3; Jake Spidle, "The Historical Roots of Managed Care," in *Managed Care: Financial, Legal, and Ethical Issues,* edited by David Bennahum (Cleveland: Pilgrim Press, 1999), p. 16.

34. Brown, *Politics and Health Care Organization*, p. 219. Lippman, *Senator Ted Kennedy*, p. 233.

35. National Health Insurance, American Hospital Association, files of Rashi Fein.

36. "National Council of Senior Citizens Says False Claims Being Made," *New York Times*, November 7, 1972, p. 21.

37. Don Wenger, chairman of the board, Ironside Corporation, "J'Accuse: Health Field Fiscal Foolishness," January 5, 1972, HE, Box 2, File: EX HE 1/1/72–1/31/72, Nixon Presidential Materials, National Archives, College Park, Maryland.

38. Lichtenstein, *The Most Dangerous Man in Detroit*, p. 437.

39. Archie Robinson, *George Meany and His Times: A Biography* (New York: Simon and Schuster, 1981), p. 283.

40. Letter from David S. Turner to Members of the U.S. Congress, October 5, 1970, Pepper Library, Florida State University, Tallahassee, Series 3098, Box 52, File 1; AFL-CIO Executive Council Statement, February 17, 1970, p. 1 (note 22); Katherine Ellickson Oral History, Columbia University Oral History Collection, p. 135; Goldfield, *National Health Reform American Style*, p. 114.

41. Minutes of Meeting of Technical Committee of Committee for National Health Insurance, August 31, 1972, files of Rashi Fein.

42. Minutes of Meeting of Technical Committee of Committee for National Health Insurance, August 31, 1972, files of Rashi Fein.

43. Brown, *Politics and Health Care Organization*, p. 257.

44. Kennedy HMO Proposal, HE, Box 2, File: EX HE 3/1/72–3/31/72, Nixon Presidential Materials.

45. Memo from Minority Staff of the Subcommittee on Health and Long-Term Care, Hearing on Medicare HMOs, April 24, 1985, Pepper Library, Series S302A, Box 25, File 1; Lawrence David Weiss, *Private Medicine and Public Health: Profit, Politics, and Prejudice in the American Health Care Enterprise* (Boulder, Colo.: Westview Press, 1997), p. 90.

46. Summers, *The Arrogance of Power*, p. 380.

47. Julian Zelizer, *Taxing America: Wilbur D. Mills, Congress and the State, 1945–1975* (Cambridge: Cambridge University Press, 1998), p. 331.

48. Lippman, *Senator Ted Kennedy*, p. 238.

49. Memo from Ken Cole to Dick Nathan, July 29, 1971, IS, Box 2, File 6/1/72–8/9/74, Nixon Presidential Materials.

50. News Media, HE, Box 2, File 5/1/72, Nixon Presidential Materials.

51. Memo from Ray Waldman, September 7, 1972, Re: Human Resources Committee of the National Governors' Conference, HE, Box 2, File 5/1/72, Nixon Presidential Materials; see also memo from Jim Cavanaugh to Ken Cole, September 22, 1972.

52. Memo from David Parker to H. R. Haldeman, October 10, 1972, HE, Box 2, File 5/1/72, Nixon Presidential Materials.

53. Memo from Dave Gergen to Tod Hullin, Proposed President's Statement, October 29, 1972, HE, Box 2, File 5/1/72, Nixon Presidential Materials.

54. President Nixon's Rx: Health Care: With Government Help—But Without Government Takeover, Staff Member and Office Files, Patrick J. Buchanan, Box 11, File: Health Care, Nixon Presidential Materials.

55. Zelizer, *Taxing America*, p. 319.

56. Ambrose, *Nixon*, p. 554.

57. Joint Statement of Representative Wilbur D. Mills and Senator Edward M. Kennedy Before the Democratic Platform Committee, June 17, 1972, HE, Box 2, File 5/1/72, Nixon Presidential Materials; Barnard, *Walter Reuther and the Rise of the Auto Workers*, pp. 41–43.

58. Ambrose, *Nixon*, p. 584.

59. Schedule proposal, Greeting: Dr. Malcolm Todd, August 6, 1973, HE, Box 2, File 8/1/73, Nixon Presidential Materials.

60. Summers, *The Arrogance of Power*, p. 459.

61. Richard Madden, "93rd Congress' 2nd Session Set for Jan. 21," *New York Times*, January 21, 1974, p. 16.

62. Quoted in Flint Wainess, "The Ways and Means of National Health Care, 1974 and Beyond," *Journal of Health Politics, Policy and Law* 24, 2 (1999): 313.

63. Memo for the President from Caspar Weinberger, November 2, 1973, White House Central Files, Subject Files, HE (Health) Box 2, File: EX HE 8/1/73, Nixon Presidential Materials.

64. Quoted in Wainess, "The Ways and Means of National Health Care," p. 315.

65. Game Plan on the Health Issue, HE, Box 3, File 1/1/73–5/31/74, Nixon Presidential Materials.

66. Harold M. Schnaeck Jr., "Pres. Nixon Sends to Congress His National Health Insurance Proposal," *New York Times*, February 7, 1974, p. 34.

67. Isadore S. Falk, A Modification of the Health Security Program (S. 3; H.R. 22) to Provide for Functional Participation by the Insurance Industry, July 13, 1972, files of Rashi Fein.

68. David Dranove, *The Economic Evolution of American Health Care: From Marcus Welby to Managed Care* (Princeton, N.J.: Princeton University Press, 2000), p. 30.

69. Quoted in Cathie Jo Martin, "Together Again: Business, Government and the Quest for Cost Control," *Journal of Health Politics, Policy and Law* 18, 2 (1993): 369.

70. Author's interview with Rashi Fein, Boston, March 7, 2001.

71. "Kennedy's Collapse: Health Professionals for Political Action," *Notes on Health Politics* 2, 7 (1974), files of Rashi Fein.

72. John Herbers, "Weinberger Says Democrats Failed to Move on Health Insurance Issue," *New York Times*, February 27, 1974, p. 1.

73. Memo from Frank Carlucci to the President, received August 29, 1974, IS, Box 2, File 6/1/72–8/9/74, Nixon Presidential Materials.

74. Wainess, "The Ways and Means of National Health Care," p. 307.

75. "The Health Insurance Debate," *Washington Post*, May 26, 1974, p. C6.

76. Remarks by Charles M. Boteler Jr., President of the National Association of Mutual Insurance Agents, IS, Box 2, File 6/1/72–8/9/74, Nixon Presidential Materials.

77. "Chances of NHI Passage Rise as Ford Takes Over," *American Medical News*, August 19, 1974, p. 1, Pepper Library, S303A, Box 1, File 15.

78. Wainess, "The Ways and Means of National Health Care," p. 326.

79. Howard Wolinsky and Tom Brune, *The Serpent on the Staff: The Unhealthy Politics of the American Medical Association* (New York: Putnam, 1994), p. 31.

80. "Rep. Mills' NHI Plan Is Shelved," *American Medical News*, August 26, 1974, p. 1, Pepper Library, S303A, Box 1, File 15.

81. A Digest of Congressional Activities Relating to the Topic of National Health Insurance, Pepper Library, Series 301, Box 286, File 8.

82. Zelizer, *Taxing America*, pp. 351–52.

83. Rashi Fein, *Medical Care, Medical Costs: The Search for a Health Insurance Policy*. (Cambridge, Mass.: Harvard University Press, 1986), p. 150.

84. Memo from Max W. Fine to Leonard Woodcock, August 28, 1974, Subject: An Alternative Bill, files of Rashi Fein.

85. Memo from Dick Shoemaker to Bert Seidman, November 21, 1974, Subject: Hip Pocket NHI Program, files of Rashi Fein.

86. Hobart Rowen, *Self-Inflicted Wounds: From LBJ's Guns and Butter to Reagan's Voodoo Economics* (New York: Times Books, 1994), pp. 169, 196.

87. Burton Hersh, *The Shadow President: Ted Kennedy in Opposition* (South Royalton, Vt.: Steerforth Press, 1997), p. 25.

88. Taylor Dark, "Organized Labor and the Carter Administration: The Origins of Conflict," in *The Presidency and Domestic Policies of Jimmy Carter*, edited by Herbert Rosenbaum and Alexej Ugrinsky (Westport, Conn.: Greenwood Press, 1994), p. 766.

89. Joseph Califano Jr., *Governing America: An Insider's Report from the White House and Cabinet* (New York: Simon and Schuster, 1981), p. 89; Gary M. Fink, "Fragile Alliance: Jimmy Carter and the American Labor Movement," in *The Presidency and Domestic Policies of Jimmy Carter*, edited by Herbert Rosenbaum and Alexej Ugrinsky (Westport, Conn.: Greenwood Press, 1994), p. 794.

90. Califano, *Governing America*, p. 89.

91. Author's interview with Rashi Fein, Boston, March 7, 2001.

92. Ibid.
93. Hospital Cost Containment Nearing a Vote, Background Report by Office of Medical Liaison, White House Press Office, October 29, 1979, p. 3, Carter Library, Atlanta, Records of Chief of Staff Landon Butler, Box 101, File: Hospital Cost Containment, 1/24/79–10/29/79.
94. Califano, *America's Health Care Revolution*, p. 10; Michael G. Krukones, "Campaigner and President: Jimmy Carter's Campaign Promises and Presidential Performance," in *The Presidency and Domestic Policies of Jimmy Carter*, edited by Herbert Rosenbaum and Alexej Ugrinsky (Westport, Conn.: Greenwood Press, 1994), p. 133.
95. John Inglehart, "The Hospital Lobby Is Suffering from Self-Inflicted Wounds," *National Journal*, October 1, 1977, p. 1526, Carter Library, Records of Chief of Staff Landon Butler, Box 101, File: Hospital Cost Containment, 1/24/79–10/29/79.
96. Ibid., p. 1528.
97. "The Voluntary Effort," American Hospital Association, American Medical Association, Federation of American Hospitals, January 30, 1978, Carter Library, Staff Offices, Peter Bourne, Special Assistant to the President, Box 33, File: Hospital Cost Containment 10/1/77–2/2/78.
98. Inglehart, "The Hospital Lobby," p. 1526.
99. Letter from John Alexander McMahon, James Sammons, and Michael Bromberg, American Hospital Association, to the President, February 2, 1978, Carter Library, Staff Offices, Peter Bourne, Special Assistant to the President, Box 33, File: Hospital Cost Containment 10/1/77–2/2/78.
100. Author's interview with anonymous hospital administrator, May 2, 2003.
101. Inglehart, "The Hospital Lobby," p. 1527.
102. Letter from Stuart Eisenstadt to Walter Wristo, Citibank, May 22, 1979, Carter Library, Office of the Deputy of the Chief of Staff, Stephen Selig's Subject File, 1979–1981, Box 175, File: Hospital Cost Containment, 3/21/79–9/28/79.
103. Note to Stuart Eisenstadt, Ann Wexler, and Landon Butler from Dick Warden, September 11, 1978, Carter Library, Records of Chief of Staff Landon Butler, Box 100, File: Hospital Cost Containment, 9/12/78–10/15/78.
104. Memo from Landon Butler to Steve Selig, September 21, 1978, Carter Library, Records of Chief of Staff Landon Butler, Box 100, File: Hospital Cost Containment, 9/12/78–10/15/78.
105. Excessive Hospital Bills: Letters from the Public, Carter Library, White House Press Office, White House Office Subject File, Box 61, File: Hospital Cost Containment 7/78.
106. "A GOP View on Hospital Costs," *National Journal*, October 1, 1977, p. 1528, Carter Library, Records of Chief of Staff Landon Butler, Box 101, File: Hospital Cost Containment, 1/24/79–10/29/79.
107. Memo from Zachary Dyckman to Alfred Karn, Special Assistant to the President on Inflation, Carter Library, Domestic Policy Staff Files, Subject File, 1976–1981, Box 216, File: Hospital Cost Containment.
108. State of the Union Address, 1979, Carter Library. See also Hospital Cost Containment Nearing a Vote, Background Report by Office of Medical Liaison, White House Press Office, October 29, 1979, p. 3, Carter Library, Records of Chief of Staff Landon Butler, Box 101, File: Hospital Cost Containment, 1/24/79–10/29/79.

109. Hospital Cost Containment/Business Strategy, Memo from Richard Reiman to Richard Moe, February 9, 1979, Carter Library, Office of the Deputy of the Chief of Staff, Stephen Selig's Subject File, 1979–1981, Box 175, File: Hospital Cost Containment, 5/12/78–2/13–79.

110. Outreach Strategy—Hospital Cost Containment, Memo from Anne Wexler to Dick Moe, February 2, 1979, Carter Library, Records of Chief of Staff Landon Butler, Box 101, File: Hospital Cost Containment, 1/24/79–10/29/79.

111. Author's telephone interview with anonymous American Hospital Association officer, September 3, 2003.

112. Background Report, AFL-CIO Executive Council on Hospital Cost Containment, Bal Harbour, Florida, February, 1979, Carter Library, Records of Chief of Staff Landon Butler, Box 101, File: Hospital Cost Containment, 2/24/79–6/15/79.

113. Update—Hospital Cost Containment, Memo from Steve Selig to Anne Wexler, March 28, 1979, Carter Library, Office of the Deputy of the Chief of Staff, Stephen Selig's Subject File, 1979–1981, Box 175, File: Hospital Cost Containment, 3/21/79–9/28/79.

114. "Administration Launches Last-Ditch Fight to Get Hospital Cost Control," *Congressional Quarterly*, September 16, 1978, p. 2480.

115. "Hospital Cost Control Legislation Dies," *Congressional Quarterly*, October 21, 1978, p. 3074.

116. President's Daily Diary, February 13, April 11, April 24, May 7, 1979; May 23, 1979, Carter Library.

117. Califano, *Governing America*, p. 147.

118. Exit interview with Bill Cable, congressional liaison during the Carter administration, February 21, 1981, Carter Library.

119. Califano, *America's Health Care Revolution*, p. 147.

120. Ibid., pp. 127–28.

121. Health Cost Containment Task Force—Proposed Strategy, Memo from Richard Moe from Hamilton Jordan, Frank Moore, March 1, 1979, Carter Library, Office of the Chief of Staff, Subject File, 1977–1980, Box 46, File: Health/Hospital Costs.

122. Califano, *Governing America*, p. 98.

123. Hersh, *The Shadow President*, p. 25.

124. Califano, *Governing America*, pp. 98–99.

125. Ibid., pp. 92–93.

126. Fink, "Fragile Alliance," p. 795.

127. National Health Insurance, Memo from Landon Butler to Hamilton Jordan, September 6, 1979, Carter Library, Office of the Chief of Staff, Subject File, 1977–1980, Box 46, File: Health/Hospital Costs.

128. Stuart Eisenstadt, "President Carter, the Democratic Party, and the Making of Domestic Policy," in *The Presidency and Domestic Policies of Jimmy Carter*, edited by Herbert Rosenbaum and Alexej Ugrinsky (Westport, Conn.: Greenwood Press, 1994), p. 13.

129. Fink, "Fragile Alliance," p. 796.

130. Statement of Senator Edward Kennedy on Introduction of a New National Health Insurance Outline, October 2, 1978, files of Rashi Fein.

131. Health Care for All Americans Act of 1979; see also Press Release, Committee for National Health Insurance, August 18, 1980, files of Rashi Fein; see also Memo from Douglas Fraser to Members of the Committee for

National Health Insurance Committee of One Hundred, October 4, 1979, files of Rashi Fein.

132. Executive Committee Meeting, Committee for National Health Insurance, March 20, 1978, files of Rashi Fein, folder: Committee for National Health Insurance, Kennedy-Carter Discussions; see also Public Papers of the Presidents of the United States, Jimmy Carter, Book 1—January 1 to June 22, 1979 (Washington, D.C.: Government Printing Office, 1980), pp. 1029–30.

133. Letter from I. S. Falk to Senator Edward Kennedy, August 9, 1979, files of Rashi Fein.

134. Confidential memo, April 4, 1978, Proposed basic principles for a White House National Health Insurance proposal, files of Rashi Fein, Department of Social Medicine, Harvard Medical School, Boston, folder: Committee for National Health Insurance, Kennedy-Carter Discussions.

135. Betty Glad, Jimmy Carter, in Search of the Great White House (New York: W. W. Norton, 1980), pp. 447–48.

136. "Iran Outlines Demands for Hostages Release," Washington Post, November 14, 1979, p. A1.

137. E. J. Dionne, Jr., Why Americans Hate Politics (New York: Simon and Schuster, 1991), p. 132.

138. "Significant Dates in the Hostage Crisis," New York Times, January 21, 1981, p. A7.

139. "Reagan Takes Oath as 40th President," New York Times, January 20, 1980, p. A1.

140. Author's interview with Rashi Fein, Boston, March 7, 2001.

141. "Reagan Takes Oath as 40th President."

142. Rowen, Self-Inflicted Wounds, p. 208.

143. Jill Quadagno, "Generational Equity and the Politics of the Welfare State," Politics and Society 17 (1989): 356.

144. Gordon, Dead on Arrival, p. 38.

145. Helen Slessarev, "Racial Tensions and Institutional Support: Social Programs During a Period of Retrenchment," in The Politics of Social Policy in the United States, edited by Margaret Weir, Ann Shola Orloff, and Theda Skocpol (Princeton, N.J.: Princeton University Press, 1988), p. 360.

146. Califano, America's Health Care Revolution, p. 148.

147. Charlene Harrington, "Social Security and Medicare: Policy Shifts in the 1980s," in Fiscal Austerity and Aging: Shifting Government Responsibility for the Elderly, edited by Carroll Estes, Robert Newcomer, and Associates (Beverly Hills, Calif.: Sage, 1983), pp. 92–93.

148. Linda Demkovich, "On Health Issues, This Business Group Is a Leader, But Is Anyone Following?" National Journal, June 18, 1983, pp. 1278–80.

149. Jonathan Oberlander, The Political Life of Medicare (Chicago: University of Chicago Press, 2003), p. 119.

150. In 1977 Congress raised payroll taxes, the second increase in six years, and enacted modest, less visible cuts by changing the formula for calculating benefits. Edward Berkowitz, America's Welfare State: From Roosevelt to Reagan (Baltimore, Johns Hopkins University Press, 1991), p. 72.

151. Paul Charles Light, Artful Work: The Politics of Social Security Reform (New York: Random House, 1985), p. 122.

152. Lawrence Alfred Powell, Kenneth J. Branco, and John B. Williamson, The Senior Rights Movement: Framing the Policy Debate in America (New York: Twayne, 1996), p. 160.

153. Minutes of the Board of Directors, Committee for National Health Insurance, June 21, 1982, files of Rashi Fein.
154. Light, *Artful Work*, p. 124.
155. Carolyn Rinkus Thompson, "The Political Evolution of the Medicare Catastrophic Health Care Act of 1988," doctoral dissertation, Johns Hopkins University, 1990, pp. 66–67.
156. Light, *Artful Work*, pp. 180–83.
157. Paul Pierson, *Dismantling the Welfare State: Reagan, Thatcher, and the Politics of Retrenchment* (Cambridge: Cambridge University Press, 1994), p. 67; Light, *Artful Work*, p. 119.
158. Light, *Artful Work*, p. 189.
159. Dranove, *The Economic Evolution of American Health Care*, p. 50.
160. James Morone and Andrew Dunham, "Slouching Towards National Health Insurance: The Unanticipated Politics of DRGs," *Bulletin of the New York Academy of Medicine* 62, 6 (1986): 264; Donald Light, "The Restructuring of the American Health Care System," in *Health Politics and Policy*, edited by Theodor J. Litman and Leonard S. Robins (Albany, N.Y.: Delmar, 1997), p. 55.
161. The hospital cost containment program, which had begun as an experiment in New Jersey, was now applied to the entire Medicare program; see Chapter 4.
162. Author's telephone interview with anonymous American Hospital Association officer, September 3, 2003.
163. Betty Leyerle, *Moving and Shaking American Medicine: The Structure of a Socioeconomic Transformation* (Westport, Conn.: Greenwood Press, 1984), p. 38; Linda Bergthold, *Purchasing Power in Health: Business, the State, and Health Care Politics* (New Brunswick, N.J.: Rutgers University Press, 1990), pp. 42–44.
164. Jeff Goldsmith, "Death of a Paradigm: The Challenge of Competition," *Health Affairs* 3, 3 (1984): 7.
165. Author's interview with anonymous hospital administrator, May 2, 2003.
166. Califano, *America's Health Care Revolution*, p. 119.
167. Ibid., p. 120.
168. Goldsmith, "Death of a Paradigm," p. 8.
169. Testimony of John Motley III, Director of Federal Governmental Relations, National Federation of Independent Business before the U.S. Bipartisan Commission on Comprehensive Health Care (Pepper Commission), October 24, 1989, p. 177, Pepper Library, Series 302, Box 63, File 8.
170. "Holding Down Medicare Costs," *Chicago Tribune*, January 21, 1985, Section 1, p. 10.
171. Miriam Laugesen and Thomas Rice, "Is the Doctor In? The Evolving Role of Organized Medicine in Health Policy," *Journal of Health Policy, Politics and Law* 28, 2–3 (2003): 306.
172. Kant Patel and Mark Rushefsky, *Health Care Politics and Policy in America* (Armonk, N.Y.: M. E. Sharpe, 1999), pp. 115–16.
173. Oberlander, *The Political Life of Medicare*, p. 124.

Chapter Six

1. Alain C. Enthoven, *Health Plan: The Only Practical Solution to the Soaring Cost of Medical Care* (Reading, Mass.: Addison-Wesley, 1980), p. xvii.

2. Joseph Califano Jr., *America's Health Care Revolution: Who Lives? Who Dies? Who Pays?* (New York: Random House, 1986), p. 5.

3. Linda Bergthold, *Purchasing Power in Health: Business, the State, and Health Care Politics* (New Brunswick, N.J.: Rutgers University Press, 1990), p. 4; Betty Leyerle, *Moving and Shaking American Medicine: The Structure of a Socioeconomic Transformation* (Westport, Conn.: Greenwood Press, 1984), p. 31.

4. Bergthold, *Purchasing Power in Health*, p. 2; Jill Quadagno, David MacPherson, and Jennifer Reid Keene, "The Effect of a Job Loss on the Employment Experience, Health Insurance, and Retirement Benefits of Workers in the Banking Industry," in *Ensuring Health and Income Security for an Aging Workforce*, edited by Peter P. Budetti, Richard V. Burkhauser, Janice Gregory, and Allan Hunt (Ann Arbor, Mich.: W. E. Upjohn Institute for Employment Research, 2001), p. 219.

5. Jonathan Oberlander, *The Political Life of Medicare* (Chicago: University of Chicago Press, 2003), p. 55.

6. Carolyn Tuohy, *Accidental Logics: The Dynamics of Change in the Health Care Arena in the United States, Britain, and Canada* (New York: Oxford University Press, 1999), p. 130.

7. Testimony of the Blue Cross and Blue Shield Association on Health Coverage for the Uninsured before the before the U.S. Bipartisan Commission on Comprehensive Health Care (Pepper Commission), p. 3, October 24, 1989, Pepper Library, Florida State University, Tallahassee, Series 302, Box 63, File 8.

8. Letter from Richard Ludwig to Senator John Heinz, October 11, 1989, Pepper Library, Series 302, Box 63, File 8.

9. Jacob S. Hacker, *Blurring the Boundaries: The Battle over Public and Private Social Benefits in the United States* (Cambridge: Cambridge University Press, 2002), p. 256.

10. Testimony of John Motley, Director of Federal Governmental Relations, National Federation of Independent Business, before the Pepper Commission, pp. 3–6, October 24, 1989, Pepper Library, Series 302, Box 63, File 8.

11. Letter from Muriel Mathis, Account Executive, Blue Cross and Blue Shield, September 20, 1989, Pepper Library, Series 302, Box 63, File 8.

12. Thomas Bodenheimer, "Should We Abolish the Private Health Insurance Industry?" *International Journal of Health Services* 20, 2 (1990): 206.

13. Karen Titlow and Ezekiel Emanuel, "Employer Decisions and the Seeds of Backlash," *Health Affairs* 24, 5 (1999): 943.

14. Daniel Fox and Daniel Schaffer, "Health Policy and ERISA: Interest Groups and Semipreemption," *Journal of Health Politics, Policy and Law* 14, 2 (1989): 245, 252; Arnold Birenbaum, *Managed Care: Made in America* (Westport, Conn.: Praeger, 1997), p. 39; Timothy Stoltzfus Jost, *Disentitlement: The Threats Facing Our Public Health-Care Programs and a Rights-Based Response* (New York: Oxford University Press, 2003), p. 185. Corporations also often purchased reinsurance against large, unpredictable claims that they might not be able to pay through their reserve funds.

15. Leyerle, *The Private Regulation of American Health Care*, p. 28. The shift toward self-insurance was not only a response to the failure of many insurers to develop and use effective cost containment data, but also was motivated by a desire to provide equal coverage of employees in different states and avoid state premium taxes.

16. Jeff Goldsmith, "Death of a Paradigm: The Challenge of Competition," *Health Affairs* 3, 3 (1984): 9.
17. Birenbaum, *Managed Care: Made in America*, p. 39; Bodenheimer, "Should We Abolish the Private Health Insurance Industry," p. 205.
18. Birenbaum, *Managed Care: Made in America*, p. 39.
19. Marie Gottschalk, *The Shadow Welfare State: Labor, Business, and the Politics of Health Care in the United States* (Ithaca, N.Y.: Cornell University Press, 2000), p. 121.
20. Robert Blendon, Jennifer Edwards, and Ulrike Szalay, "Managed Care: Key to Health Insurance Reform?" *Health Affairs*, winter 1991.
21. Califano, *America's Health Care Revolution*, p. 11.
22. Lee Iacocca with William Novak, *Iacocca: An Autobiography* (New York: Bantam Books, 1984), pp. 92, 114, 126, 144.
23. Ibid., p. 152.
24. Ibid., p. 192.
25. Ibid., p. 306.
26. Califano, *America's Health Care Revolution*, p. 11.
27. Gottschalk, *The Shadow Welfare State*, p. 100.
28. Califano, *America's Health Care Revolution*, p. 23.
29. Iacocca, *Iacocca*, p. 308.
30. Califano, *America's Health Care Revolution*, p. 29; Melissa Hardy, Lawrence Hazelrigg, and Jill Quadagno, *Ending a Career in the Auto Industry: 30 and Out* (New York: Plenum Press, 1996), p. 87.
31. Iacocca, *Iacocca*, p. 307.
32. Donald Light, "The Practice and Ethics of Risk-Related Health Insurance," *Journal of the American Medical Association* 267, 18 (1992): 2505.
33. Blendon, Edwards, and Szalay, "Managed Care: Key to Health Insurance Reform?"
34. Betty Leyerle, *The Private Regulation of American Health Care* (Armonk, N.Y.: M.E. Sharpe, 1994), pp. 109–10; Titlow and Emanuel, "Employer Decisions and the Seeds of Backlash," p. 943.
35. Leyerle, *The Private Regulation of American Health Care*, pp. 105–6; Tuohy, *Accidental Logics*, p. 137.
36. Quoted in Bergthold, *Purchasing Power in Health*, p. 55.
37. Susan Goldberger, "The Politics of Universal Access: The Massachusetts Health Security Act of 1988," *Journal of Health Politics, Policy and Law* 15, 4 (1990): 857; Bergthold, *Purchasing Power in Health*, pp. 5, 107; Richard Kronick, "The Slippery Slope of Health Care Finance: Business Interests and Hospital Reimbursement in Massachusetts," *Journal of Health Politics, Policy and Law* 15, 4 (1990): 888.
38. Quoted in Bergthold, *Purchasing Power in Health*, p. 54.
39. Testimony of Bruce Miller, Vice President, Motorola, Inc. on behalf of the National Association of Manufacturers before the U.S. Bipartisan Commission on Comprehensive Health Care (Pepper Commission), October 24, 1989, p. 173, Pepper Library; Linda Demkovich, "On Health Issues, This Business Group Is a Leader, But Is Anyone Following?" *National Journal*, June 18, 1983, p. 1278–80.
40. Bergthold, *Purchasing Power in Health*, p. 43.
41. Lawrence D. Brown, "Dogmatic Slumbers: American Business and Health Policy," *Journal of Health Politics, Policy and Law* 18, 2 (1993): 349.

42. Jennifer Klein, *For All These Rights: Business, Labor, and the Shaping of America's Public-Private Welfare State* (Princeton, N.J.: Princeton University Press, 2003), p. 255.

43. Califano, *America's Health Care Revolution*, pp. 13–15.

44. Gottschalk, *The Shadow Welfare State*, p. 110.

45. Oberlander, *The Political Life of Medicare*, p. 49.

46. Robert Clark, Linda Shumaker Ghent, and Alvin Headen, "Retiree Health Insurance and Pension Coverage: Variations and Firm Characteristics," *Journal of Gerontology* 49, 2 (1994): S53; Hardy, Quadagno, and Hazelrigg, *Ending a Career in the Auto Industry*, p. 44.

47. Jill Quadagno and Melissa Hardy, "Private Pensions, State Regulation and Income Security for Older Workers: The U.S. Auto Industry," in *The Privatization of Social Policy? Occupational Welfare and the Welfare State in America, Scandinavia, and Japan*, edited by Michael Shalev (London: Macmillan, 1996), p. 141.

48. Gottschalk, *The Shadow Welfare State*, p. 127.

49. John Neilsen, "Sick Retirees Could Kill Your Company," *Fortune*, March 2, 1987, p. 98.

50. Quoted in Carolyn Rinkus Thompson, "The Political Evolution of the Medicare Catastrophic Health Care Act of 1988," doctoral dissertation, Johns Hopkins University, 1990, p. 131.

51. Neilsen, "Sick Retirees Could Kill Your Company," pp. 98–99.

52. Oberlander, *The Political Life of Medicare*, pp. 53–54; Thompson, "The Political Evolution of the Medicare Catastrophic Health Care Act," p. 132.

53. Richard Himelfarb, *Catastrophic Politics: The Rise and Fall of the Medicare Catastrophic Coverage Act of 1988* (University Park: Pennsylvania State University Press, 1995), p. 19; Paul Charles Light, *Artful Work: The Politics of Social Security Reform* (New York: Random House, 1985), p. 122.

54. Himelfarb, *Catastrophic Politics*, pp. 12–14.

55. Martha Holstein and Meredith Minkler, "The Short Life and Painful Death of the Medicare Catastrophic Coverage Act," *International Journal of Health Services* 21 (1991): 1016; Fernando M. Torres-Gil, "The Politics of Catastrophic and Long-Term Care Coverage," *Journal of Aging and Social Policy* 1 (1989): 65; Steven Rathgeb Smith, "The Role of Institutions and Ideas in Health Care Policy," *Journal of Health Politics, Policy and Law* 20, 2 (1995): 386.

56. "Reagan Tries to Silence Reports of Iran Arms Deal," *Los Angeles Times*, November 6, 1986, Part 1, p. 1.

57. "U.S. Looks for Sign in Captors' Move," *New York Times*, November 4, 1986, p. A11.

58. Quoted in Thompson, *The Political Evolution of the Medicare Catastrophic Health Care Act*, p. 76.

59. Hobart Rowen, *Self-Inflicted Wounds: From LBJ's Guns and Butter to Reagan's Voodoo Economics* (New York: Random House, 1994), p. 211; Robert Pear, "Lawmakers Assail Reagan over Plan for Major Illness," *New York Times*, January 29, 1987, p. A2.

60. Quoted in Himelfarb, *Catastrophic Politics*, p. 22; Julie Rovner, "Reagan Sides with Bowen on Medicare Plan," *Congressional Quarterly*, February 14, 1987, p. 297.

61. Robert Englund, "The Catastrophic Health Care Blunder," *American Spectator*, November 1988, p. 28.

62. Himelfarb, *Catastrophic Politics*, p. 19.
63. Steven Prokesch, "Medicare Expansion Under Fire," *New York Times*, February 12, 1987, p. 1A.
64. Quoted in Debra Street, "Maintaining the Status Quo: The Impact of the Old-Age Interest Groups on the Medicare Catastrophic Coverage Act of 1988," *Social Problems* 40 (1993): 437.
65. Englund, "Catastrophic Blunder," p. 28.
66. Cited in Thompson, "Political Evolution of the Medicare Catastrophic Health Care Act," p. 199.
67. Street, "Maintaining the Status Quo," 435.
68. "The Hospital Lobby Is Suffering from Self-Inflicted Wounds," *National Journal*, October 1, 1977, p. 1526. See also Hospital Costs Containment, Background Report by Office of Media Liaison, The White House Press Office, March 5, 1979, Carter Library, Atlanta, Records of Chief of Staff Butler, Box 101, File: Hospital Cost Containment, 2/24/79–10/29/79.
69. Street, "Maintaining the Status Quo," p. 436.
70. Statement of William S. Hoffman, Director, Social Security Department, UAW, on the subject of Medicare Catastrophic Health Insurance before the Subcommittee on Health, Committee on Ways and Means, U.S. House of Representatives, Washington, D.C., March 10, 1987, Pepper Library, Series 309A, Box 155A, File 1.
71. Himelfarb, *Catastrophic Politics*, pp. 38–39.
72. Englund, "Catastrophic Blunder," p. 30.
73. Julie Rovner, "Catastrophic Costs Conferees Irked by Lobbying Assaults," *Congressional Quarterly*, March 26, 1988, pp. 777–78.
74. Ibid.
75. Spencer Rich, "Drug Makers Fight New Outpatient Benefit," *Washington Post*, September 14, 1987, p. A4.
76. Julie Rovner, "House OKs Medicare Expansion," *Congressional Quarterly*, July 25, 1987, p. 1639.
77. Cited in Thompson, *Political Evolution of the Medicare Catastrophic Health Care Act*, p. 172.
78. Michelle Murphy, "Elderly Lobby Continues to Thrive," *Congressional Quarterly*, March 26, 1988, pp. 778–79.
79. Quoted in Himelfarb, *Catastrophic Politics*, p. 52.
80. Peter J. Ferrera, "The Hidden Costs of Health Coverage for the Elderly," *Wall Street Journal*, April 26, 1988, Pepper Library, Series 302A, File 42, Box 7.
81. Mike Causey, "Spreading the Burden," *Washington Post*, January 5, 1989.
82. Marilyn Moon, *Medicare Now and in the Future*, 2nd ed. (Washington, D.C.: Urban Institute, 1993), p. 108.
83. Englund, "The Catastrophic Health Care Blunder," p. 26; Oberlander, *The Political Life of Medicare*, p. 68
84. Himelfarb, *Catastrophic Politics*, pp. 12–14; Henry J. Pratt, *Gray Agendas: Interest Groups and Public Pensions in Canada, Britain, and the United States* (Ann Arbor: University of Michigan Press, 1993), p. 194; E. M. Abramson, "Planning Ahead for the New Medicare Catastrophic Coverage Act," *Washington Post*, November 7, 1988; "Tax-Snatchers," *Washington Post*, May 2, 1988, Pepper Library, Series 302A, File 42, Box 7.
85. Statement of William S. Hoffman, Director, Social Security Department, UAW, on the subject of Medicare Catastrophic Health Insurance before

the Subcommittee on Health, Committee on Ways and Means, U.S. House of Representatives, Washington, D.C., March 10, 1987, Pepper Library, Series 309A, Box 155A, File 1.

86. Ibid.

87. *Statement of Alan Reuther, Associate General Counsel, UAW, Before the Senate Finance Committee Hearings on Medicare Catastrophic Coverage, July 11, 1989, First Session* (Washington, D.C.: Government Printing Office, 1989), p. 39.

88. Letter from Robert L. Landon to Claude Pepper, October 10, 1988, Pepper Library, Series 309A, Box 155A, File 1; Street, "Maintaining the Status Quo," p. 437; Mike Causey, "A System Gone Haywire," *Washington Post*, January 23, 1989; letter to the editor from Lloyd Unsell, *Washington Post*, October 31, 1989, p. A22; Susan A. MacManus with Patricia A. Turner, *Young v. Old: Generational Combat in the 21st Century* (Boulder, Colo.: Westview Press, 1996), p. 176.

89. Letter from Robert L. Landon to Claude Pepper, October10, 1988, Pepper Library, Series 309A, Box 155A, File 1.

90. Street, "Maintaining the Status Quo," p. 437.

91. Mike Causey, "A System Gone Haywire," *Washington Post*, January 23, 1989.

92. Letter to the editor from Lloyd Unsell.

93. MacManus and Turner, *Young v. Old*, p. 176.

94. Himelfarb, *Catastrophic Politics*, p. 74.

95. Quoted in Pratt, *Gray Agendas*, p. 195.

96. Julie Rovner, "Surtax Reduction a Possibility But Critics Demand Repeal," *Congressional Quarterly*, April 22, 1988, p. 902.

97. Julie Rovner, "Catastrophic Coverage Law Narrowly Survives Test," *Congressional Quarterly*, June 10, 1989, p. 1402.

98. Julie Rovner, "Both Chambers in Retreat," *Congressional Quarterly*, October 7, 1989, p. 2635.

99. Stephen Crystal, "Health Economic, Old-Age Policies and the Catastrophic Medicare Debate," *Journal of Gerontological Social Work* 15 (1990): 21–31; Christine Day, "Older American Attitudes Toward the Medicare Catastrophic Coverage Act of 1988," *Journal of Politics* 55 (1993): 167–77.

100. Julie Rovner, "The Catastrophic Costs Law: A Massive Miscalculation," *Congressional Quarterly*, October 4, 1989, p. 2715.

101. Julie Rovner, "Catastrophic Insurance Law: Costs vs. Benefits," *Congressional Quarterly*, December 3, 1988, p. 3452.

102. Gottschalk, *The Shadow Welfare State*, p. 128; *Retiree Health Benefits: Employer-Sponsored Benefits May Be Vulnerable to Further Erosion*, Report to the Chairman, Committee on Health, Education, Labor and Pensions, U.S. Senate (Washington, D.C.: General Accounting Office, 2001), p. 2.

103. *Retiree Health Trends and Implications of Possible Medicare Reforms* (Washington, D.C.: Kaiser Family Foundation, 2001), p. 1; *Retiree Health Benefits*, p. 10.

104. James Causey, "Pabst to Cut Retiree Benefits," *Milwaukee Journal Sentinel*, August 6, 1996, p. 1.

105. *Retiree Health Benefits*, p. 6; Titlow and Emanuel, "Employer Decisions and the Seeds of Backlash," p. 942

106. Causey, "Pabst to Cut Retiree Benefits," p. 1.

107. *Retiree Health Benefits: Employer-Sponsored Benefits May Be Vulnerable to Further Erosion*, pp. 16–17.

108. George Anders, *Health Against Wealth: HMOs and the Breakdown of Medical Trust* (Boston: Houghton Mifflin, 1996), p. 24.
109. Califano, *America's Health Care Revolution*, pp. 33–34.
110. Leyerle, *The Private Regulation of American Health Care*, p. 21.
111. Anders, *Health Against Wealth*, p. 16.
112. Ibid., p. 30.
113. Ibid., p. 32.
114. Ibid., p. 36.
115. Leyerle, *The Private Regulation of American Health Care*, p. 6.
116. Tuohy, *Accidental Logics*, p. 147; Bodenheimer, "Should We Abolish the Private Health Insurance Industry," p. 208.
117. Statement of Steven P. Kang, M.D., President-Elect, Greater Albuquerque Medical Association, at the Hearings of the Human Resources and Intergovernmental Relations Subcommittee of the Committee on Government Operations, U.S. House of Representatives, 103rd Congress, 1st Session, September 26, 1993, pp. 16–17.
118. Statement of Carol Merovka, M.D., Past President, Greater Albuquerque Medical Association, at the Hearings of the Human Resources and Intergovernmental Relations Subcommittee of the Committee on Government Operations, U.S. House of Representatives, 103rd Congress, 1st Session, September 26, 1993, pp. 28–29.
119. Ibid., p. 30.
120. Ibid., p. 29.
121. Peter Jacobson, "Who Killed Managed Care? A Policy Whodunit," *Saint Louis University Law Journal* 47 (2003): 365–96.
122. Testimony by Cornelia Lange at the Hearings of the Human Resources and Intergovernmental Relations Subcommittee of the Committee on Government Operations, U.S. House of Representatives, 103rd Congress, 1st Session, October 5, 1993, pp. 52–53.
123. Jamie Court and Francis Smith, *Making a Killing: HMOs and the Threat to Your Health* (New York: Common Courage Press, 1999), p. 6.
124. "Prez Rips Health Biz Insurers," *Daily News* (New York), July 8, 1998, p. 26.
125. Birenbaum, *Managed Care*, p. 128.
126. Ibid., p. 135.
127. Court and Smith, *Making a Killing*, p. 8.
128. Anders, *Health Against Wealth*, p. 210; see Chapter 7.
129. Birenbaum, *Managed Care*, p. 121; Clark C. Havighurst, "How the Health Care Revolution Fell Short," *Law and Contemporary Problems* 65, 4 (2002): 61–62.
130. Birenbaum, *Managed Care*, pp. 137, 139.
131. Ibid., p. 139.
132. Gillian Fairfield, David Hunter, David Mechanic, and Flemming Rosleff, "Managed Care: Implications of Managed Care for Health Systems, Clinicians and Patients," *British Medical Journal* 314 (June 1997): 1895.
133. Jerry Geisel, "HMOs See Glory Days Under Clinton," *Business Insurance*, December 18, 1992, p. 6.
134. Anders, *Health Against Wealth*, p. 19.
135. Schwartz, "How Law and Regulation Shape Managed Care," p. 31.
136. Anders, *Health Against Wealth*, p. 216; Birenbaum, *Managed Care*, p. 140.

137. Quoted in Leyerle, *The Private Regulation of American Health Care*, p. 115; Clark C. Havighurst, "Consumers Versus Managed Care: The New Class Actions," *Health Affairs*, 20, 4 (2001): 12.

138. Miriam Laugesen and Thomas Rice, "Is the Doctor In? The Evolving Role of Organized Medicine in Health Policy," *Journal of Health Politics, Policy and Law* 28, 2–3 (2003): 291.

139. Catherine Wilson, "Mediation to Continue in Cigna's Racketeering Suit," *Miami Herald*, April 29, 2003, p. 8B.

140. "Court, 5–4, Upholds Authority of States to Protect Patients," *New York Times*, June 20, 2002, p. 1A.

141. Tom Daschle and Edward Kennedy, "For Patients, a Better Bill of Rights," *Washington Post*, July 13, 1999, p. A19.

142. Donald Baker, "Insurance Proposals Bring Out Lobbyists," *Washington Post*, February 21, 1999, p. C1.

143. Ibid.

144. Fred Barnes, "Patients' Bill of Goods," *Weekly Standard*, August 6, 2001, p. 11.

145. Dan Morgan, "Health Care Lobby Targets GOP Senators on Air," *Washington Post*, July 5, 1999, p. A3.

146. Bennett Roth, "Congress Will Contend Again over Health Issues," *Houston Chronicle*, December 13, 1997, p. A1.

147. Amy Goldstein, "House Approves GOP's Health Insurance Tax Breaks," *Washington Post*, October 7, 1999, p. A12.

148. "AMA Calls on Congress to Vote on Patients' Rights Before August Recess," PR Newswire, www.prnewswire.com, July 19, 2001.

149. Barnes, "Patients' Bill of Goods," p. 11.

150. Robert Pear, "Measure Defining Patients' Rights Passes in House," *New York Times*, August 3, 2001, p. A1; "House Approves Patients' Bill of Rights," United Press International, August 2, 2001.

151. Melanie Eversley, "Georgia Congressman Revives Patients' Rights Bill," *Atlanta Journal and Constitution*, March 9, 2003, p. A1.

152. Robert Hurley, Joy Grossman, Timothy Lake, and Lawrence Casalino, "A Longitudinal Perspective on Health Plan-Provider Risk Contracting," *Health Affairs* 21 (2002): 144–53; Debra Draper, Robert Hurley, Cara Lesser, and Bradley Strunk, "The Changing Face of Managed Care," *Health Affairs* 21, 1 (2003): 14; Suzanne Felt-Lisk and Glen Mays, "From the Field: Back to the Drawing Board: New Directions in Health Plan Care Management Strategies," *Health Affairs* 21, 5 (2003): 216.

153. Birenbaum, *Managed Care*, p. 144.

154. David Mechanic, "The Rise and Fall of Managed Care," *Journal of Health and Social Behavior* 45 (Extra Issue) (2004): 76–86.

Chapter Seven

1. Jeff Goldsmith, "Death of a Paradigm: The Challenge of Competition," *Health Affairs* 3, 3 (1984): 10.

2. U.S. House of Representatives, Committee on Energy and Commerce, Subcommittee on Oversight and Investigations, Hearings on Insurance Company Failures, 101st Congress, 1st Session, August 3, 1989, p. 587.

3. Nursing Home Insurance: Exploiting Fear for Profit? Joint Hearing before the Subcommittee on Health and Long-Term Care and the Subcommittee

on Housing and Consumer Interests, Select Committee on Aging, U.S. House of Representatives, 100th Congress, 1st Session, August 6, 1987, p. 42.

4. Claude Pepper, "Long-Term Care Insurance: The First Step Toward Comprehensive Health Insurance," *Journal of Aging and Social Policy* 1 (1989): 10–11.
5. Jill Quadagno, Madonna Harrington Meyer, and Blake Turner, "Falling Through the Medicaid Gap: The Hidden Long Term Care Dilemma," *Gerontologist* 31 (1991): 521–26.
6. Madonna Harrington Meyer, "Universalism vs. Targeting as the Basis of Social Distribution: Gender, Race and Long Term Care in the U.S.," doctoral dissertation, Florida State University, Tallahassee, 1991, p. 105.
7. Madonna Harrington Meyer and Michelle Kesterke Storbakken, "Shifting the Burden Back to Families?" in *Care Work: Gender, Labor and the Welfare State*, edited by Madonna Harrington Meyer (New York: Routledge, 2000), p. 219.
8. Ibid., p. 221.
9. Joseph Angelelli, Vincent Mor, Orna Intrator, Zhanlian Feng, and Jacqueline Zinn, "Oversight of Nursing Homes: Pruning the Tree or Just Spotting Bad Apples?" *Gerontologist* 43 (2003): 74.
10. Martha Holstein and Meredith Minkler, "The Short Life and Painful Death of the Medicare Catastrophic Coverage Act," *International Journal of Health Services* 21 (1991): 1016; Fernando M. Torres-Gil, "The Politics of Catastrophic and Long-Term Care Coverage," *Journal of Aging and Social Policy* 1 (1989): 68; Steven Rathgeb Smith, "The Role of Institutions and Ideas in Health Care Policy," *Journal of Health Politics, Policy and Law* 20, 2 (1995): 386.
11. Charlene Harrington, "Social Security and Medicare: Policy Shifts in the 1980s," in *Fiscal Austerity and Aging: Shifting Government Responsibility for the Elderly*, edited by Carroll L. Estes, Robert Newcomer, et al. (Beverly Hills, Calif.: Sage, 1983), p. 93; Torres-Gil, "The Politics of Catastrophic and Long-Term Care Coverage," p. 74.
12. Harrington, Meyer, and Storbakken, "Shifting the Burden Back to Families?" p. 219.
13. Ibid., p. 225.
14. Ibid., p. 224.
15. Jeff Goldsmith, "Death of a Paradigm: The Challenge of Competition," *Health Affairs* 3, 3 (1984): 9–10; Thomas Bodenheimer, "Should We Abolish the Private Health Insurance Industry?" *International Journal of Health Services* 20, 2 (1990): 205.
16. Jon Gabel and Alan Monheit, "Will Competition Plans Change Insurer-Provider Relationships?" *Milbank Memorial Fund Quarterly* 61 (1983): 610–40.
17. Laurence F. Lane, "The Potential of Private Long Term Care Insurance," p. 17, Pepper Library, Florida State University, Tallahassee, Series 302A, File 60, Box 5.
18. *Abuses in the Sale of Health Insurance to the Elderly in Supplementation of Medicare*, House of Representatives, Select Committee on Aging (Washington, D.C.: U.S. Government Printing Office, 1977), pp. 102–3.
19. Nursing Home Insurance: Exploiting Fear for Profit, p. 38.
20. Richard Himelfarb, *Catastrophic Politics: The Rise and Fall of the Medicare Catastrophic Coverage Act of 1988* (University Park: Pennsylvania State University Press, 1995), p. 13.

21. Bodenheimer, "Should We Abolish the Private Health Insurance Industry," p. 214.
22. Private Long-Term Care Insurance: Unfit for Sale? Report by the Chairman of the Subcommittee on Health and Long-Term Care of the Select Committee on Aging, U.S. House of Representatives, 101st Congress, 1st Session, May 1989, p. 1.
23. Donald Light, "The Practice and Ethics of Risk-Related Health Insurance," *Journal of the American Medical Association* 267, 18 (1992): 2506.
24. *Retiree Health Benefits: Employer-Sponsored Benefits May Be Vulnerable to Further Erosion*, Report to the Chairman, Committee on Health, Education, Labor and Pensions, U.S. Senate (Washington, D.C.: General Accounting Office, 2001), p. 24.
25. Lane, "The Potential of Private Long Term Care Insurance," pp. 18–19.
26. Nancy Benac, "Lies, Abuses Cited in Long-Term Health Policy Sales," Associated Press, n.d., Pepper Library, Series 302A, File 42, Box 7.
27. Letter from Roger Singer, Commissioner of Insurance, Commonwealth of Massachusetts, to Claude Pepper, August 4, 1987, Pepper Library, Series S302A, Box 60, File 1.
28. Statement of Bonnie Burns, Medicare Specialist and Consumer Advocate, Before the Subcommittee on Health and Long-Term Care, House of Representatives, August 6, 1987, Pepper Library, Series 507A, Box 100, File 3.
29. "Insurance for Elderly Increasing," *Washington Post*, March 18, 1987, Pepper Library, Series S302A, Box 60, File 5.
30. "Catastrophic Health Insurance: Filling the Long-Term Care Gap," Statement of the American Association of Retired Persons Before the House Select Committee on Aging, Subcommittee on Health and Long Term Care, July 2, 1987.
31. Private Long-Term Care Insurance: Unfit for Sale, pp. 2–4.
32. Robert Pear, "Wide Abuse Cited in Nursing Home Insurance," *New York Times*, June 26, 1991, p. A1.
33. "Long Term Care Insurance," Statement of Michael Zimmerman, Human Resource Division of GAO, Before the Subcommittee on Health and Long-Term Care, House of Representatives, August 6, 1987, Pepper Library, Series S307A, Box 100, File 3.
34. Letter from Robert T. Matteson to Hon. Claude Pepper, May 25, 1988. Pepper Library, Series S302A, Box 60, File 1.
35. Letter from Janet Dimaya Ramos to Senate Commission on Aging, September 28, 1985. Pepper Library, Series S302A, Box 27, File 7.
36. The bill would also establish a home care quality assurance program that would create peer review organizations. The PROs would be responsible for monitoring the quality of home care services, conduct unannounced inspections of home care agencies, and impose penalties on noncomplying organizations.
37. Letter from Claude Pepper and Edward Roybal to House of Representatives, May 31, 1988, Pepper Library, Series 302A, File 42, Box 3.
38. "Catastrophic Health Insurance: The Long-Term Care Gap," statement of Claude Pepper, chairman of the Subcommittee on Health and Long-Term Care of the House Committee on Aging, July 2, 1987, Pepper Library, Series 307A, Box 100, File 1.
39. Health Insurance Association of America Comments on H.R. 3436, April 26, 1988, p. 1, Pepper Library, Series 302A, File 42, Box 7.

40. Ibid., pp. 2–4.

41. Ibid., p. 17.

42. Letter to Claude Pepper from Coordinating Committee for Long Term Care, April 22, 1988, Pepper Library, Series 302A, File 42, Box 7.

43. Letter from Albert Bourland, vice president for Congressional relations, Chamber of Commerce, May 23, 1988, Pepper Library, Series 302A, File 42, Box 7.

44. Letter from John Motley, director, Federal Government Relations, National Federation of Independent Business, June 2, 1988, Pepper Library, Series 302A, File 42, Box 7.

45. Letter from Jerry Jasinowski, executive vice president, National Association of Manufacturers, May 17, 1988, Pepper Library, Series 302A, File 42, Box 7.

46. "Elderly Lobby Peppers the House on Health Bill," *Wall Street Journal*, May 6, 1988, Pepper Library, Series 302A, File 42, Box 7.

47. Letter from Otis R. Bowen, Secretary of Health and Human Services, June 8, 1988, Pepper Library, Series 302A, File 42, Box 7.

48. Letter from Linda Kenckes, vice president, federal affairs, Health Insurance Association of America, Pepper Library, Series 302A, File 42, Box 7; "Long-Term Care Bill Derailed—For Now," *Congressional Quarterly*, June 11, 1988, p. 1604.

49. "Faces of Medicaid," Kaiser Commission on Medicaid and the Uninsured, Kaiser Family Foundation, Washington, D.C., April 2004, p. 7.

50. Colleen Grogan and Eric Patashnik, "Universalism Within Targeting: Nursing Home Care, the Middle Class, and the Politics of the Medicaid Program," *Social Service Review* 77, 1 (2003): 61.

51. Testimony of Gail Shearer, Consumers Union, before the Subcommittee on Health and Environment, Energy and Commerce Committee and the Subcommittee on Health and Long-Term Care, Select Committee on Aging, U.S. House of Representatives, Hearings on Abuses in the Sale of Long Term Care Insurance to the Elderly, n.d., Pepper Library, Series 302A, Box 28, File 7.

52. Private Long Term Care Insurance: Unfit for Sale, p. 2.

53. Ibid., p. 3.

54. Testimony of John Gilmore before the Subcommittee on Health and Long Term Care, Select Committee on Aging, U.S. House of Representatives, 101st Congress, 1st Session, May 1989, mimeograph, Pepper Library, Series 309A, Box 100, File 3.

55. Justin Keen, Donald Light, and Nicholas May, *Public-Private Relations in Health Care* (London: King's Fund Publishing, 2001), p. 120.

56. Hans Riedel, "Private Compulsory Long Term Care Insurance in Germany," *Geneva Papers on Risk and Insurance* 28, 2 (2003): 275–93.

57. Linda Bergthold, *Purchasing Power in Health: Business, the State, and Health Care Politics* (New Brunswick, N.J.: Rutgers University Press, 1990), p. 41; Mark A. Peterson, "Clinton's Plan Goes to Congress—Now What," *Journal of Health Politics, Policy and Law* 14, 2 (1994): 265.

58. Karen Pollitz, "Extending Health Insurance Coverage for Older Workers and Early Retirees," in *Ensuring Health and Income Security for an Aging Workforce*, edited by Peter B. Budetti, Richard V. Burkhauser, Janice M. Gregory, and H. Allan Hunt (Kalamazoo, Mich.: Upjohn Institute for Employment Research, 2001), p. 239.

59. Cindy Mann, Diane Rowland, and Rachel Garfield, "Historical Overview of Children's Health Care Coverage," *The Future of Children* 13, 1 (2003): 35.
60. Ibid., p. 36.
61. Linda Bilheimer and David Colby, "Expanding Coverage: Reflections on Recent Efforts," *Health Affairs*, January/February 2001, p. 84.
62. Marsha Gold, Jessica Mittler, Anna Aizer, Barbara Lyons, and Cathy Schoen, "Health Insurance Expansion Through States in a Pluralistic System," *Journal of Health Politics, Policy and Law* 26, 3 (2001): 593.
63. Leighton Ku and Bowen Garrett, "How Welfare Reform and Economic Factors Affected Medicaid Participation: 1984–1996," Discussion Paper, Urban Institute, Washington, D.C., 2000, p. 11.
64. H. E. Freeman, L. H. Aiken, R. J. Blendon, and C. R Corey, "Uninsured Working-Age Adults: Characteristics and Consequences," *Health Services Research* 24 (1990): 812–23.
65. Keen, Light, and May, *Public-Private Relations in Health Care*, pp. 115–16; Light, "The Practice and Ethics of Risk-Related Health Insurance," pp. 2503–4.
66. Statement of the American Medical Association Before the Bipartisan Commission on Comprehensive Health Care, Re: Providing Adequate Health Insurance Coverage to the Uninsured and Underinsured, October 24, 1989, p. 73, Pepper Library, Series 302, Box 63, File 8; Light, "The Practice and Ethics of Risk-Related Health Insurance," p. 2507; see also Bodenheimer, "Should We Abolish the Private Health Insurance Industry?" p. 213.
67. Mark Schlesinger, "Reprivatizing the Public Household? Medical Care in the Context of American Public Values," *Journal of Health Politics, Policy and Law* 29, 4–5 (2004): 969–2004.
68. "Catastrophic Health Insurance: The Long-Term Care Gap," Statement of Claude Pepper, Chairman of the Subcommittee on Health and Long-Term Care, of the House Committee on Aging, July 2, 1987, Pepper Library, Series 307A, Box 100, File 1.
69. Pepper Commission, Health Legislation and Regulation, F&G, vol. 16, no. 9, March 7, 1990, Pepper Library, Series 302A, Box 63, File 1.
70. Statement of the American Medical Association Before the Bipartisan Commission on Comprehensive Health Care, p. 73.
71. Statement of Paul Rettig Before the Bipartisan Commission on Comprehensive Health Care, October 24, 1989, Pepper Library, Series 302, Box 63, File 8.
72. Marie Gottschalk, *The Shadow Welfare State: Labor, Business and the Politics of Health Care in the United States* (Ithaca, N.Y.: ILR Press, 2000), p. 106.
73. Lee Iacocca with Sonny Kleinfield, *Talking Straight* (New York: Bantam Books, 1988), p. 260.
74. "GM Weighs National Health Care," *Detroit News*, March 16, 1988, pp. 1–2C.
75. Cited in Cathie Jo Martin, "Together Again: Business, Government and the Quest for Cost Control," *Journal of Health Politics, Policy and Law* 18, 2 (1993): 369.
76. Peter Swenson and Scott Greer, "Foul Weather Friends: Big Business and Health Care Reform in the 1990s in Historical Perspective," *Journal of Health Politics, Policy and Law* 27, 4 (2002): 605.

77. Statement of John Motley III, National Federation of Independent Business, Before the Bipartisan Commission on Comprehensive Health Care, October 24, 1989, Pepper Library, Series 302, Box 63, File 8.

78. Testimony of Charles Kahn, Executive Vice President of the Health Insurance Association of America, Before the House Subcommittee on Health and the Environment, Hearings on H.R. 1200, American Health Security Act of 1993, U.S. House of Representatives, Washington, D.C., February 1, 1994.

79. Testimony of Carl Schramm, President of the Health Insurance Association of America, before the Bipartisan Commission on Comprehensive Health Care, October 24, 1989, pp. 3–11, Pepper Library, Series 302, Box 63, File 8.

80. Jerry Geisel, "HMOs See Glory Days Under Clinton," *Business Insurance*, December 18, 1992, p. 6.

81. Alain Enthoven, *Health Plan: The Only Practical Solution to the Soaring Cost of Medical Care* (Reading, Mass.: Addison-Wesley, 1980); "Clinton Plan Rewards Big Insurers," letter to the editor, *New York Times*, November, 7, 1993.

82. Statement by Samuel Havens, Group Health Association of America, before the Bipartisan Commission on Comprehensive Health Care, October 24, 1989, Pepper Library, Series 302, Box 63, File 8.

83. Haynes Johnson and David Broder, *The System: American Politics at the Breaking Point* (Boston: Little, Brown, 1997), p. 60.

84. Jacob S. Hacker, *The Road to Nowhere: The Genesis of President Clinton's Plan for Health Security* (Princeton, N.J.: Princeton University Press, 1997), pp. 27–28.

85. Cited in ibid., p. 105.

86. Rowen, *Self-Inflicted Wounds*, p. 214.

87. Bob Woodward, *The Agenda: Inside the Clinton White House* (New York: Simon and Schuster, 1994), p. 164.

88. Johnson and Broder, *The System*, p. 96.

89. Hillary Rodham Clinton, *Living History* (New York: Simon and Schuster, 2003), p. 154.

90. Theda Skocpol, *Boomerang: Health Care Reform and the Turn Against Government in U.S. Politics* (New York: W. W. Norton, 1996), p. 78.

91. Clinton, *Living History*, pp. 115–16.

92. Woodward, *The Agenda*, p. 169.

93. Clinton, *Living History*, p. 190.

94. Johnson and Broder, *The System*, p. 188.

95. Clinton, *Living History*, p. 189.

96. Ibid., p. 193.

97. Hacker, *The Road to Nowhere*, p. 53.

98. Ibid., p. 56; Carolyn Tuohy, *Accidental Logics: The Dynamics of Change in the Health Care Arena in the United States, Britain and Canada* (New York: Oxford University Press, 1999), p. 75.

99. Jim Duffett, "Private Health Insurers Cost Too Much," *Chicago Sun-Times*, December 18, 1993, p. 16.

100. Darrell M. West, Diane Heith, and Chris Goodwin, "Harry and Louise Go to Washington: Political Advertising and Health Care Reform," *Journal of Health Politics, Policy and Law* 21, 1 (1996): 41.

101. "Insurance File: Diagnosis for a Reformed Health System," *Lloyd's List International*, November 2, 1993, p. 4.
102. Darrell M. West and Burdette Loomis, *The Sound of Money: How Political Interests Get What They Want* (New York: W. W. Norton, 1999), p. 79.
103. Raymond Goldsteen, Karen Goldsteen, James Swan, and Wendy Clemena, "Harry and Louise and Health Care Reform: Romancing Public Opinion," *Journal of Health Politics, Policy and Law* 26, 4 (2001): 1329; Johnson and Broder, *The System*, pp. 90–92.
104. Skocpol, *Boomerang*.
105. Dana Priest, "First Lady Lambasts Health Insurers," *Washington Post*, November 2, 1993, p. A1.
106. Goldsteen, Goldsteen, Swan, and Clemena, "Harry and Louise and Health Care Reform," p. 1332.
107. West and Loomis, *The Sound of Money*, p. 100.
108. West, Heith, and Goodwin, "Harry and Louise Go to Washington," p. 61.
109. Center for Public Integrity, "Well-Heeled: Inside Lobbying for Health Care Reform: Part II," *International Journal of Health Services* 25 (1995): 613.
110. Christopher Connell, "Health Insurers Mount Attack on Clinton Plan," Associated Press, October 18, 1993.
111. Center for Public Integrity, "Well-Heeled," p. 609.
112. Martin, "Together Again," 383.
113. Tuohy, *Accidental Logics*, p. 81.
114. Gottschalk, *The Shadow Welfare State*, p. 130.
115. Johnson and Broder, *The System*, p. 317.
116. Swenson and Greer, "Foul Weather Friends," p. 610.
117. Johnson and Broder, *The System*, p. 221.
118. Clinton, *Living History*, p. 246.
119. Miriam Laugesen and Thomas Rice, "Is the Doctor In? The Evolving Role of Organized Medicine in Health Policy," *Journal of Health Politics, Policy and Law* 28, 2–3 (2003): 296.
120. Tuohy, *Accidental Logics*, pp. 153–54.
121. Johnson and Broder, *The System*; Skocpol, *Boomerang*; Hacker, *The Road to Nowhere*, p. 28.
122. Quoted in Clinton, *Living History*, p. 230.
123. Johnson and Broder, *The System*, p. 195.
124. Center for Public Integrity, "Well-Heeled," p. 607.
125. Ibid., p. 608.
126. Gottschalk, *The Shadow Welfare State*, p. 153; Center for Public Integrity, "Well-Heeled," pp. 594–95.
127. Clinton, *Living History*, p. 233.
128. Ibid., p. 230.
129. West and Loomis, *The Sound of Money*, p. 93.
130. Clinton, *Living History*, p. 247.
131. Skocpol, *Boomerang*, p. 171.
132. TANF did allow states some flexibility in instituting these new regulations. John Holahan and Niall Brennan, "Who Are the Adult Uninsured?" National Survey of America's Families, Series B, No. B-14, Urban Institute, Washington, D.C., March 2000, p. 2.
133. Ku and Garrett, "How Welfare Reform and Economic Factors Affected Medicaid Participation," p. 12; Leighton Ku and Brian Bruen, "The Continuing

Decline in Medicaid Coverage," Assessing the New Federalism, Series A, No. A-37, Urban Institute, Washington, D.C., 1999, p. 3.

134. Bowen Garrett and John Holahan, "Welfare Leavers, Medicaid Coverage and Private Health Insurance," National Survey of America's Families, Series B, No. B-13, Urban Institute, Washington, D.C., 2000, p. 1.

135. Marilyn Ellwood and Carol Irvin, "Welfare Leavers and Medicaid Dynamics: Five States in 1995," Mathematica Policy Research, Cambridge, Mass., April 14, 2000, p. 2; Garrett and Holahan, "Welfare Leavers," p. 1.

136. Ku and Bruen, "The Continuing Decline in Medicaid Coverage, " p. 2; Ruth Almedia and Genevieve Kenney, "Gaps in Insurance Coverage for Children: A Pre-CHIP Baseline," Assessing the New Federalism, Series B, No. B-19, Urban Institute, Washington, D.C., 2000, p. 2. After 2002 states were required to provide Medicaid coverage to all children under age 19 whose family income fell below the federal poverty level. See Mann, Rowland, and Garfield, "Historical Overview of Children's Health Care Coverage," p. 36; Gabrielle Lessard and Leighton Ku, "Gaps in Coverage for Children in Immigrant Families," The Future of Children 13, 1 (2003): 101.

137. B. C. Strunk and J. D. Reschovsky, "Trends in U.S. Health Insurance Coverage, 2001–2003: Results from the Community Tracking Survey," Robert Wood Johnson Foundation Tracking Report No. 9, August 2004.

138. P. J. Cunningham, "SCHIP Making Progress: Increased Take-Up Contributes to Coverage Gains," Health Affairs 22, 4 (2003): 163–72; Holahan and Brennan, "Who Are the Adult Uninsured?" p. 1.

139. Gulnur Scott and Hanyu Ni, "Access to Health Care Among Hispanic/Latino Children: United States, 1998–2001," Advance Data from Vital and Health Statistics 344 (2004): 3.

140. Mann, Rowland, and Garfield, "Historical Overview of Children's Health Care Coverage," p. 36.

141. Ibid., p. 36; Lessard and Ku, "Gaps in Coverage for Children in Immigrant Families," p. 101.

142. Gold, Mittler, Aizer, Lyons, and Schoen, "Health Insurance Expansion Through States in a Pluralistic System," pp. 598, 600.

143. Mann, Rowland, and Garfield, "Historical Overview of Children's Health Care Coverage," p. 42.

144. Testimony of Charles Kahn, Executive Vice President of the Health Insurance Association of America, Before the House Subcommittee on Commerce, Consumer Protection and Competitiveness, U.S. House of Representatives, November 16, 1993.

145. Robert Pear, "Insurers Fighting a Bipartisan Bill for Health Care," New York Times, February 2, 1996, p. A1.

146. David G. Smith, Entitlement Politics: Medicare and Medicaid, 1995–2001 (New York: Aldine de Gruyter, 2002), p. 159.

147. Katherine Swartz and Betsey Stevenson, "Health Insurance Coverage of People in the Ten Years Before Medicare Eligibility," in Ensuring Health and Income Security for an Aging Workforce, edited by Peter B. Budetti, Richard V. Burkhauser, Janice M. Gregory, and H. Allan Hunt (Kalamazoo, Mich.: Upjohn Institute for Employment Research, 2001), pp. 13–40; Timothy Stoltzfus Jost, Disentitlement? The Threats Facing Our Public Health-Care Programs and a Rights-Based Response (New York: Oxford University Press, 2003), pp. 188–89.

148. "Pulling Back on Health Care," editorial, *Washington Post*, April 13, 1998, p. A22.
149. Jody Miller and Matt Miller, "Singled Out," *New York Times Magazine*, April 18, 2004, p. 48, 50.
150. Jennifer Mellor, "Filling in the Gaps in Long Term Care Insurance," in *Care Work: Gender, Labor and the Welfare State*, edited by Madonna Harrington Meyer (New York: Routledge, 2000), p. 205.
151. Ibid., p. 208.
152. Joshua Weiner, "Financing Reform for Long Term Care: Strategies for Public and Private Long Term Care Insurance," in *From Nursing Homes to Home Care*, edited by Marie Cowart and Jill Quadagno (New York: Haworth Press, 1996), p. 116.
153. Testimony by Bertram Scott, Executive Vice President, TIAA-CREF, before the Senate Special Committee on Aging Hearing on Offering Retirement Security to the Federal Family: A New Long Term Care Initiative, April 10, 2002.
154. Sally Roberts, "More Employers Offering Long Term Care Programs," *Business Insurance*, September 29, 2003, p. T4.
155. "For More Insurers, It's LTC Ya Later," Crain Communications, *Investment News*, September 1, 2003, p. 1.
156. William D. Spector, Joel W. Cohen, and Irena Pesis-Katz, "Home Care Before and After the Balanced Budget Act of 1997," *Gerontologist* 44, 1 (2004): 40.
157. Gail Wilensky, "The Balanced Budget Act of 1997: A Current Look at its Impact on Patients and Providers," Statement before the Subcommittee on Health and Environment, Committee on Commerce, U.S. House of Representatives, Washington, D.C., July 19, 2000, p. 2.
158. "The Future of Retiree Health Benefits: Challenges and Options," Testimony of Patricia Neuman, Henry J. Kaiser Foundation, Before the Subcommittee on Employer-Employee Relations, U.S. House of Representatives, November 1, 2001, p. 4; Marsha Gold and Timothy Lake, *Medicare+Choice in California: Lessons and Insights*, Henry J. Kaiser Family Foundation, Washington, D.C., September 2002, p. 1.
159. Jacob Hacker and Theodore Marmor, "Medicare Reform: Fact, Fiction and Foolishness," *Public Policy and Aging Report* 13, 4 (2004): 1.
160. Jonathan Oberlander, "The Politics of Medicare Reform," *Washington and Lee Law Review* 60, 4 (2003): 1135.
161. Quoted in William Weissert, "Medicare Rx: Just a Few of the Reasons Why It Was So Difficult to Pass," *Public Policy and Aging Report* 13, 4 (2004): 3–4.
162. I owe this insight to William Weissert.
163. Skocpol, *Boomerang*, pp. 163–64, 71; Gottschalk, *The Shadow Welfare State*, pp. 157–58; Marie Gottschalk, "It's the Health-Care Costs, Stupid: Ideas, Institutions and the Politics of Organized Labor and Health Policy in the United States," *Studies in American Political Development* 14, 2 (2000): 234; Lawrence R. Jacobs and Robert Shapiro, "Don't Blame the Public for Failed Health Care Reform," *Journal of Health Politics, Policy and Law* 20, 2 (1995): 413; James Morone, "Nativism, Hollow Corporations and Managed Competition: Why the Clinton Health Care Reform Failed," *Journal of Health Politics, Policy and Law* 20, 2 (1995): 392–93; Sven Steinmo and Jon Watts,

"It's the Institutions, Stupid! Why Comprehensive National Health In-surance Always Fails in America," *Journal of Health Politics, Policy and Law* 20, 2 (1995): 330; Vincente Navarro, "Why Congress Did Not Enact Health Care Reform," *Journal of Health Politics, Policy and Law* 20, 2 (1995): 458.

Chapter Eight

1. Strunk and Reschovsky, "Trends in U.S. Health Insurance Coverage," p. 1. This figure actually overstates the amount of employment-based cov-erage, because it includes Medicare beneficiaries who have supplemen-tal medigap benefits from a former employer, employees who purchase a group health insurance package through an employer but pay all of the costs themselves, and government employees whose insurance is paid with tax dollars. Once these groups are excluded from estimates, only 43 percent of the population is insured through a private employer. See Olveen Carrasquillo, David Himmelstein, Steffie Woolhandler, and David Bor, "A Reappraisal of Private Employers' Role in Providing Health In-surance," *New England Journal of Medicine* 340, 2 (1999): 111.
2. *Retiree Health Benefits: Employer-Sponsored Benefits May Be Vulnerable to Further Erosion*, Report to the Chairman, Committee on Health, Educa-tion, Labor and Pensions, U.S. Senate (Washington, D.C.: General Account-ing Office, 2001), p. 6.
3. Holly J. McCammon, Karen E. Campbell, Ellen M. Granberg, and Chris-tine Mowery, "How Movements Win: Gendered Opportunity Structures and U.S. Women's Suffrage Movements, 1866 to 1919," *American Socio-logical Review* 66 (2001): 51.
4. Margaret R. Somers, "What's Political or Cultural About Political Cul-ture and the Public Sphere? Toward an Historical Sociology of Concept Formation," *Sociological Theory* 13, 2 (1995): 123.
5. Murray Edelman, *Constructing the Political Spectacle* (Chicago: University of Chicago Press, 1995); Anne E. Kane, "Theorizing Meaning Construc-tion in Social Movements: Symbolic Structures and Interpretation Dur-ing the Irish Land War, 1879–1882," *Sociological Theory* 15, 3 (1997): 249–76; Deborah Stone, *Policy Paradox: The Art of Political Decision Making* (New York: W. W. Norton, 1997), p. 11; Nicholas Pedriana and Robin Stryker, "Political Culture Wars 1960s Style: Equal Employment Opportunity— Affirmative Action Law and the Philadelphia Plan," *American Journal of Sociology* 103 (1997): 634–91.
6. Jan E. Mutchler and Jeffrey A. Burr, "Racial Differences in Health and Health Care Service Utilization in Later Life: The Effect of Socioeconomic Status," *Journal of Health and Social Behavior* 32, 4 (1991): 351.
7. Gwendolyn Mink, *Welfare's End* (Ithaca, NY: Cornell University Press, 1998), p. 23; James Morone, "Nativism, Hollow Corporations, and Man-aged Competition: Why the Clinton Health Care Reform Failed," *Journal of Health Politics, Policy and Law* 20, 2 (1995): 393.
8. Paul Pierson, "Increasing Returns: Path Dependence and the Study of Politics," *American Political Science Review* 94, 2 (2000): 252.
9. Volker Amelung, Sherry Glied, and Angelina Topan, "Health Care and the Labor Market: Learning from the German Experience," *Journal of Health Politics, Policy and Law*, 28, 4 (2003): 693–94.

10. Justin Keen, Donald Light, and Nicholas May, *Public-Private Relations in Health Care* (London: King's Fund Publishing, 2001), pp. 116–17.

11. "Findings from 17 State Survey," America's Health Insurance Plans, April 12, 2004.

12. Timothy Stoltzfus Jost, *Disentitlement? The Threats Facing Our Public Health Care Programs and a Rights-Based Response* (New York: Oxford University Press, 2003), p. 272.

13. "Bush Administration Medicaid/SCHIP Proposal," May, 2003, Kaiser Commission on Medicaid and the Uninsured, Henry J. Kaiser Family Foundation, Washington, D.C., 2003, p. 4

14. Kathleen Stoll and Kim Jones, "One in Three: Non-Elderly Americans Without Health Insurance 2002–2003," Families USA Foundation, Washington, D.C., 2004, p. 10.

15. "Challenges and Tradeoffs in Low-Income Family Budgets: Implications for Health Coverage," Kaiser Commission on Medicaid and the Uninsured, Henry J. Kaiser Family Foundation, Washington, D.C., 2004, p. 3.

16. Judith Feder, Larry Levitt, Ellen O'Brien, and Diane Rowland, "Covering the Low-Income Uninsured: The Case for Expanding Public Programs," *Health Affairs* 20, 1 (2001): 28.

17. Kenneth E. Thorpe, "Federal Costs and Savings Associated with Senator Kerry's Health Care Plan," Rollins School of Public Health, Emory University, Atlanta, Georgia, August 2, 2004.

18. "Job Loss, Rising Premiums Take Toll on Employer Health Coverage in 2003," Robert Wood Johnson Foundation news release, August 20, 2004.

19. "Bush Administration Medicaid/SCHIP Proposal," p. 2.

20. "Challenges and Tradeoffs in Low-Income Family Budgets," p. 4.

21. "The State of Retiree Health Benefits: Historical Trends and Future Uncertainties," Testimony of Patricia Neuman to the Special Committee on Aging, U.S. Senate, Washington, D.C., May 17, 2004, p. 2.

22. Quoted in Gail Sheehy, *New Passages: Mapping Your Life Across Time* (New York: Random House), p. 261.

23. "The State of Retiree Health Benefits," p. 1.

24. Stoll and Jones, "One in Three," p. 6.

25. Carrasquillo, Himmelstein, Woolhandler, and Bor, "A Reappraisal of Private Employers' Role," p. 112.

26. Kenneth E. Thorpe, "The Impact of Sen. John Kerry's Health Care Proposal on Health Care Costs," Rollins School of Public Health, Emory University, Atlanta, Georgia, June 2004, p. 1.

27. Ibid., p. 3.

28. Keen, Light, and May, *Public-Private Relations in Health Care*, p. 132.

29. "Employer Health Benefits: 2004 Summary of Findings," Kaiser Commission on Medicaid and the Uninsured, Kaiser Family Foundation, Washington, D.C., 2004, p. 1.

30. Thorpe, "The Impact of Sen. John Kerry's Health Care Proposal on Health Care Costs," p. 3.

31. Linda Bilheimer and David Colby, "Expanding Coverage: Reflections on Recent Efforts," *Health Affairs*, January/February 2001, p. 86.

32. John Holahan and Niall Brennan, "Who Are the Adult Uninsured?" National Survey of America's Families, series B, no. B-14, Urban Institute, Washington, D.C., March 2000, p. 2.

33. Colin Gordon, *Dead on Arrival: The Politics of Health Care in Twentieth-Century America* (Princeton, N.J.: Princeton University Press, 2003), p. 11.
34. Doug McAdam and Yang Su, "The War at Home: Antiwar Protests and Congressional Voting, 1965–1973," *American Sociological Review* 67, 5 (2002): 696–721.
35. Constance Nathanson, "The Skeptic's Guide to a Movement for Universal Health Insurance," *Journal of Health Politics, Policy and Law* 28, 2–3 (2003): 443–72; Paul Pierson, *Dismantling the Welfare State: Reagan, Thatcher and the Politics of Retrenchment* (Cambridge: Cambridge University Press, 1994), p. 22.
36. Theda Skocpol, Marshall Ganz, and Ziad Munson, "A Nation of Organizers: The Institutional Origins of Civic Volunteerism in the United States," *American Political Science Review* 94, 3 (2000): 528.

Index

Ackerman, Carl, 106
Addams, Jane, 18–19
Advisory Council on Social Security, 54
Aetna: and Bettercare, 73; and Blue Shield,
  100; and Jackson Hole group, 190; on
  patients' rights, 165; political
  contributions, 193; and retirees, 175, 210
African-Americans, 210
aged. *See* senior citizens
Age Discrimination in Employment Act, 159
AIDS (Acquired Immune Deficiency
  Syndrome), 145
Aid to Dependent Children, 14
Aid to Families with Dependent Children
  (AFDC), 74, 103, 110, 181, 194, 204
Alabama, 79, 81, 82, 90, 91, 92
Alliance for Labor Action, 112
Alliance for Managed Competition, 190, 193
Allied Signal, 160
Alzheimer's disease, 152, 174, 175, 197
Amerasia (journal), 28
American Academy of Family Physicians, 192
American Academy of Pediatrics, 192
American Association for Labor Legislation
  (AALL), 18–19, 201, 202
American Association of Health Plans, 166,
  199
American Association of Retired Persons
  (AARP): and insuring retirees, 61; and
  long-term care, 172, 175; and Medicare
  Catastrophic Coverage Act (1988), 155,
  156–57; and prescription drug coverage,
  153; and Reagan administration, 134
American College of Physicians, 192
American College of Surgeons, 192
American Communist Party, 18, 28
American Federation of Labor (AFL): AFL-
  CIO merger, 53; on compulsory health
  insurance, 8; and disability insurance,
  53; and health benefits, 49; investigation
  of, 31; and labor party, 203; members
  insured, 51
American Federation of Labor–Congress of
  Industrial Organizations (AFL-CIO):
  and AMA, 67, 203; and Carter, 124; on
  compulsory health insurance, 21; and
  disability insurance, 54, 203, 206; and

health care cost containment, 128; on
  Kennedy-Mills plan, 121; leadership,
  110–12; and Medicare, 9, 203; merger of
  AFL and CIO, 53; and national health
  insurance, 117; and retirees, 55–69, 71,
  74–75, 156. *See also individual entries for*
  AFL *and* CIO
American Hospital Association (AHA): and
  AMA, 38, 41, 72, 75; and Blue Cross, 23–
  24, 97; and Carter, 10; and cost of health
  care, 125, 147; and DRGs, 136; and group
  plans, 22; and Medicare, 114, 153; and
  retirees, 72; and Title VI, 89; and Truman
  plan, 38; on uninsured Americans, 183;
  and Washington Business Group on
  Health, 147
American Medical Association (AMA): and
  AFL-CIO, 67, 203; and AHA, 38, 41, 72,
  75; and Blue Cross, 7, 75; and Blue
  Shield, 7, 25; and Clinton's Health
  Security plan, 192; and disability
  coverage, 54, 55, 106; and Eisenhower,
  46; and Ewing, 29; and fee schedules,
  137–38; and Hill-Burton Hospital Survey
  and Construction Act, 78; and HMOs,
  163; influence of, 7–8, 36, 38, 206; on
  Kennedy-Mills plan, 121; and Medicare,
  8–9, 94–95, 99, 153, 176; and Medicredit
  program, 116, 123; and National Council
  of Senior Citizens, 66–67; on national
  health insurance, 113; and Nixon, 60,
  116, 118, 119; opposition to health care
  reform, 22, 23; organizational strength,
  212; and professional standards review
  organizations (PSROs), 107; public
  support for, 39, 40; and Reagan
  administration, 133; and "reinsurance"
  plans, 45; and senior citizens, 56, 58, 59,
  62, 68, 69, 72–73, 202, 206; and Social
  Security, 7, 25–26; and Title VI, 89; and
  Truman, 34–43, 202; on uninsured
  Americans, 183; and Washington
  Business Group on Health, 147;
  women's auxiliaries, 35, 41–42, 68
American Medical International, 125
American Medical Political Action
  Committee (AMPAC), 68

265

Long, Russell, 98, 114, 122, 211
long-term care, 11, 170–81, 197–98, 201, 205
Long Term Care Insurance Model Act and Regulation, 175
low-wage workers, 4
LTV, 149
Lucent, 210
Ludwig, Richard, 141
Lynchburg General Hospital, Virginia, 83

MacPherson, Diane, 3
Magaziner, Ira, 185–86, 190
Makarewicz, Roman, 158–59
malpractice, 164–66
managed care, 10–11, 159–66, 167, 184, 199
managed competition, 187, 190
mandates from the state, 141
Martin Marietta, 160
Massachusetts, 146, 174
Matteson, Robert, 175–76
McCarthy, Joseph, 41, 43
McCarthyism, x
McCord, James, 120
McGovern, George, 109, 119
McIntyre, Ross, 23
McNerney, Walter, 59
McNutt, Paul, 29
Meany, George, 49, 53, 111–12, 116–17, 203
media, 35
Medicaid: and Aid to Families with Dependent Children (AFDC), 181; and DRGs, 136; eligibility for, 168, 170, 178, 181–82, 208–9; and Entitlement Commission, ix; future of, 207–9; and HealthCare plan, 131; implementation of, 102–4; and long-term care, 170–71; origins of, 74; and private insurers, 6; and Reagan administration, 133; and TANF, 194–95
Medical Economics (trade publication), 43
medical societies, 25. *See also* American Medical Association (AMA)
Medicare, 94–108; and AFL-CIO, 9, 203; and AMA, 8–9; and antistatist values, 12, 202; and Balanced Budget Act (1997), 198; and catastrophic health care, 148, 149–59; and civil rights issues, 86–92, 204; and cost containment, 129, 205; and Democrats, 206; and DRGs, 136; eligibility for, 188, 191; and Entitlement Commission, ix; fraud and abuses, 101, 106; and HMOs, 118; and home care services, 176, 177; implementation, 95–102, 106; and long-term care, 170; Medicare+Choice, 198–99; and medigap policies, 201; payment system, 10, 135, 136, 137; and prescription drug benefits, 199–200; and private insurers, 6; professional standards review organizations (PSROs), 106–7; and prospective payment systems, 140, 147; and Reagan administration, 133; and retirees, 62–69, 70–76; and senior citizens' movement, 205; and Social Security, 134, 135; and the state

structure, 15; support for, 114; and unions, 8–9, 76, 111
Medicare Advantage, 199
Medicare Catastrophic Coverage Act (1988), 114, 168, 177, 207
Medicare+Choice, 198–99
Medicare Modernization Act (2003), 199
Medicore Company, 125
Medicredit program, 113–14, 116, 123
medigap market, 152, 173, 174
Meese, Edwin, 152
mental health services, 141
Meredith organization, 146
Merovka, Carol, 161
MetLife, 188, 190, 193
Metropolitan, 20, 21
Meyer, Bernard, 40
Michigan, 65
Michigan Medical Service Plan, 36
middle class, 18
military service, 26, 49
Miller, Jody and Matt, 196–97
Mills, Wilbur, 67, 72, 118–19, 121, 122–23
miners, 48–49
Minneapolis, 146
Mississippi, 91, 92
Mississippi Medical Society, 100
Mobile Infirmary, Alabama, 90
Morgan, Ray, 140
Morse, Wayne, 97
Moses Cone Hospital, Greensboro, 83
Motley, John, 137
Mulliner, Maureen, 32
Murphy, Ray, 37
Murray, James, 91
Mutual of Omaha, 61–62, 100, 152
Myers, Robert, 60, 71–72, 97–98, 99
Mylans, Brendan, 101

Nash, Robert, 86, 91
National Academy of Elder Law Attorneys, 178
National Association for the Advancement of Colored People (NAACP), 80–81, 82, 83, 91
National Association of Insurance Commissioners, 45, 175, 181
National Association of Manufacturers (NAM): and Clinton, 192; and Goldbeck, 147; and long-term care, 177; on mandatory price controls, 126; and patients' bill of rights, 165; and physicians, 8, 10; on prospective payment regulations, 137; and unions, 51
National Child Labor Committee, 18
National Civic Federation, 8, 21
National Commission on Social Security Reform, 134
National Committee to Preserve Social Security and Medicare, 155, 156
National Consumers League, 18
National Council of Senior Citizens, 64–67, 70, 75, 116, 134, 202
National Education Campaign, 34